Transfer Pricing Developments Around the World 2021

Transfer Pricing Developments Around the World 2021

Edited by

Michael Lang
Raffaele Petruzzi

Wolters Kluwer

Published by:
Kluwer Law International B.V.
PO Box 316
2400 AH Alphen aan den Rijn
The Netherlands
E-mail: international-sales@wolterskluwer.com
Website: lrus.wolterskluwer.com

Sold and distributed by:
Wolters Kluwer Legal & Regulatory U.S.
7201 McKinney Circle
Frederick, MD 21704
United States of America
E-mail: customer.service@wolterskluwer.com

ISBN 978-94-035-3525-8

e-Book: ISBN 978-94-035-3531-9
web-PDF: ISBN 978-94-035-3533-3

Editors

Prof. Dr DDr h.c. Michael Lang is Head of the Institute for Austrian and International Tax Law of WU (Vienna University of Economics and Business) and academic director of both the LLM Program in International Tax Law and the Doctoral Program in International Business Taxation (DIBT) of this university. He is President of the Austrian branch of the International Fiscal Association (IFA) and has been a visiting professor at Georgetown University, New York University, Sorbonne, Bocconi, Peking University (PKU), University of New South Wales (Sydney), and at other universities.

Dr Raffaele Petruzzi, LLM, is Managing Director of the WU Transfer Pricing Center at the Institute for Austrian and International Tax Law at WU (Vienna University of Economics and Business) and an international tax advisor specializing in international corporate taxation and transfer pricing. Since 2007, Raffaele has gained relevant experience in international tax and transfer pricing by working in different countries within advisory companies and in the tax department of a multinational. Raffaele is a frequent speaker in international conferences, lecturer of numerous courses, and author of publications on international tax and transfer pricing topics. Among others, Raffaele is a member of the United Nations (UN) Subcommittee on Article 9 (Associated enterprises: Transfer Pricing), of the IFA, and of Transfer Pricing Economists for Development (TPED). Raffaele holds a Master of Science in Business Administration and Law (major: Corporate Taxation) from Bocconi University (Italy), a Master of Laws (LLM) in International Tax Law at WU, and a PhD in International Business Taxation at WU.

Contributors

Mary C. Bennett is a Senior Counsel in Baker McKenzie's Washington DC office, where she advises multinational companies on tax policy, international tax planning, and tax controversy matters. She has previously served as head of the Tax Treaty, Transfer Pricing & Financial Transactions Division of the Organisation for Economic Co-operation and Development's (OECD's) Centre for Tax Policy & Administration in Paris and as deputy international tax counsel of the US Treasury Department. A graduate of Radcliffe College, Columbia Law School, and Boston University's Tax LLM program, Mary has written over seventy articles and spoken worldwide on international tax issues.

Thomas D. Bettge is a manager with KPMG LLP's Washington National Tax – Economic and Valuation Services practice, where he specializes in transfer pricing and international tax dispute resolution and planning. He is a co-author of the Warren Gorham & Lamont treatise *Transfer Pricing Strategies*, as well as an ongoing monthly column in *International Tax Review* and numerous other articles on transfer pricing and other tax topics. Prior to joining KPMG, Thomas began his career with the tax practice of a leading law firm. He obtained his JD from the Pennsylvania State University Dickinson School of Law, where he graduated first in his class.

Mukesh Butani is the founder and managing partner of BMR Legal Advocates. With specialization in domestic corporate international tax and transfer pricing, he has over three decades of experience in advising multinationals and Indian conglomerates on a wide range of matters relating to FDI policy, business re-organizations, cross-border tax structuring, tax controversy, and regulatory policy across a range of sectors. He has led the international tax and transfer pricing practice for two of the Big 4 firms and was co-founder and tax practice leader of BMR Advisors before enrolling at the Bar. He is an acknowledged expert in the area of international tax policy, controversy and advocacy. He has several judicial pronouncements to his credit, laying down landmark principles of law, bilateral Advance Pricing Agreements (APAs) and MAPs in this area. He has deposed as an expert witness on contentious cross-border tax treaty and TP matters in foreign jurisdictions. Mukesh has participated in many committees of the Indian Government and deposed before them on a host of tax issues pertaining to e-commerce, APAs, safe harbours, the GAAR, indirect transfers tax and, in particular, the Kelkar Task Force Tax Reforms (2002) & Tax Administrative Reforms Commission (2013). He was a member of Tax Bureau of OECD – BIAC, PSC member of IFA (2012-2016), and is presently Chairman of IFA India branch, Vice-Chairman of the Taxation Commission of ICC Paris and a non-resident senior associate at Wadhwani Chair In US-India Policy Studies at Centre of Strategic and International Studies, Washington DC. He is a founder member (2015) of ITRAF, a think tank to carry out research and analysis in international taxation to ensure superior tax policy and effective tax administration in India and is presently Chairman of the IFA India branch. Mukesh is also a trustee at the Foundation of International Tax and Joint Conference Director with IBFD for the annual conference. Mukesh is a Commerce graduate from the University of Mumbai, holds a Bachelor's in Law and practices as an advocate. He qualified as a Chartered Accountant in 1985 and enrolled as an advocate in 2010. He is a member of the Bar Council of Delhi and practices in various tribunals, high courts, and the Supreme Court of India.

Stefaan De Baets has been a Senior Counsel in the transfer pricing team of PwC Belgium since 1 January 2016, where he is responsible for avoiding and settlement of transfer pricing controversy, further development of the transfer pricing market, and promoting the key presence of PwC on that market as well as delivering contributions to the development of transfer pricing policies. From 1 April 2011 to 31 December 2015, he was a transfer pricing advisor at the OECD in Paris, France. Until he joined the OECD, Stefaan worked for the Federal Public Service of Finances in Belgium, mostly on transfer pricing and international tax, for more than twenty years. He was a delegate for Belgium to OECD Working Party 6 (transfer pricing) from March 1996 to March 2011 and to the Joint Transfer Pricing Forum from March 2003 to March 2011. Stefaan is a guest lecturer on international taxation at the University of Lausanne (Switzerland) and the Catholic University of Leuven (Belgium). He is a regular guest speaker or panellist at international tax events.

Gianni De Robertis is the chief economist, head of transfer pricing and economic consulting services of Studio Associato (a KPMG international affiliate in Italy), and GTPS Leader for the KPMG EMA Region. Gianni has provided assistance for more than twenty years to multinational companies operating in Europe, America, and the Asia Pacific regions. His main areas of expertise include the economics of international taxation, intra-firm trade (economic, fiscal, and management aspects), value chain and IP analyses, pricing analyses, and management.

Sean F. Foley is a principal with KPMG's Washington National Tax Practice and the head of KPMG's Global Transfer Pricing Dispute Resolution Services. He is based in Santa Clara, California, in Silicon Valley. Sean has over twenty-five years of experience in analysing intercompany transactions for major multinational corporations. Sean's primary areas of focus include APAs, competent authority matters, and transfer pricing risk management. Before joining KPMG, Sean was the director of the IRS APA Program. Sean is a past chair of the American Bar Association Transfer Pricing Committee. He was an associate professor teaching in the University of Florida LLM program in 2011 and at the Georgetown University Law Center LLM program from 2005-2007. Sean clerked for Justice Ruth Bader Ginsburg when she served on the DC Circuit; he also served as legislative director to Congressman Sander M. Levin, the former chair and ranking member of the House Ways and Means Committee.

Dr Raphael Holzinger has studied Business Administration (BSc and MSc) and Business Law (LLB and LLM) at Vienna University of Economics and Business. Besides that, he also received an LLM in Tax Law and Accounting from the University of Vienna. Moreover, he holds a PhD in Business Law from Vienna University of Economics and Business. From an academic perspective, he is a post-doctoral research and teaching fellow at the Institute for Austrian and International Tax Law at Vienna University of Economics and Business and constantly conducts research in the areas of transfer pricing, business tax law, and international tax law and is a frequent speaker on those topics in professional and academic courses, workshops and conferences. He also frequently publishes articles in national and international journals and books. From a professional perspective, he is a Certified Tax Advisor and a Certified Transfer Pricing Manager and works for Deloitte Vienna, Austria. His practical focus lies in consultancy in the areas of transfer pricing, business tax law, and international tax law. In that regard, Dr Holzinger manages client engagements, designs, prepares, and defends transfer pricing settings, advises in cross-border tax planning situations, supports clients with different documentation tasks, and has extensive experience in the area of transfer pricing dispute prevention and resolution (transfer pricing audits, unilateral and bilateral APAs, and MAPs).

Seema Kejriwal is an experienced Chartered Accountant with two decades of experience in transfer pricing and tax litigation, advisory, and documentation. She has worked with leading firms in India. She has also worked in the United States with one of the Big4 firms and handled US litigation, advisory, and documentation. She has worked with Fortune 500 companies and clients across industries. She has hands-on experience in addressing transfer pricing matters and complex transfer pricing advisory matters, and dispute resolution.

Kevin D. Kramer, is a Senior Associate with KPMG LLP's Washington National Tax – Economic and Valuation Services group. Kevin has experience with a wide range of transfer pricing issues, including global and domestic compliance and planning, global transfer pricing documentation, APAs, cost allocation and management services, and operational transfer pricing. He has worked with clients across various industries, including consumer products, retail, technology, and financial services. Prior to joining KPMG, Kevin graduated from the Villanova School of Business with a double major in Finance and International Business.

Josh D. McConkey is a senior manager with KPMG LLP's Washington National Tax – Economic and Valuation Services group. He focuses his practice on developing, implementing, and documenting tax-efficient transfer pricing structures for North American, European, and Asian markets. In addition, Josh advises clients on US tax controversy matters and international dispute resolution procedures, including APAs and mutual agreement procedure cases. Prior to law school, Josh served in the speechwriting office at the White House and later as an executive director of a national political organization in Washington DC. Josh obtained his JD from Georgetown University Law Center and his LLM in Taxation from New York University School of Law.

Emily Muyaa is the managing principal for Sub-Saharan Africa in the IBFD Africa and Middle East Department. In this capacity, she oversees IBFD's product offering in the region. Ms Muyaa regularly works in an advisory capacity for African Governments on international tax (including transfer pricing) and lectures at IBFD international tax training courses. She is a member of the UN Transfer Pricing Subcommittee. Ms Muyaa is the manager for the IBFD Centre of Studies in African Taxation (CSAT), a think tank devoted to the study and development of African taxation. She is a founding member of the Transfer Pricing Economists for Development (TPED – www.tped.eu), a Paris-based think tank that aims to promote business economics knowledge sharing in transfer pricing for emerging economies. Ms Muyaa is a visiting lecturer at the University of Cape Town, South Africa, and the University of Amsterdam in the Netherlands. Before joining IBFD in 2014, she worked in the transfer pricing division of the Large Taxpayers Office at the Kenya Revenue Authority. She holds a certificate in Tax Administration from the Kenya Revenue Authority Training Institute (now Kenya School of Revenue Administration), an undergraduate degree in Law from the University of Nairobi, a postgraduate diploma in Law from the Kenya School of Law, and an LLM (Adv.) in international taxation from the International Tax Center at Leiden University, the Netherlands. During her LLM studies, Ms Muyaa also worked at the Transfer Pricing Division of EY Amsterdam. Ms Muyaa is an Association of Chartered Certified Accountants (ACCA) member and a member of the Law Society of Kenya.

Erika Scuderi is a Teaching and Research Associate at the Institute for Austrian and International Tax Law and a Doctoral Candidate in Business Law at WU (Vienna University of Economics and Business). She graduated in Law from the University of Milano-Bicocca after spending the last academic year deepening her knowledge and conducting research in International and Comparative Tax Law at the Université Catholique de Louvain-la-Neuve. In 2018, she gained a Master's in Tax Law from Bocconi University. After an internship within the Transfer Pricing Team of PwC – Tax and Legal Services (Milan), she also gained practical experience in domestic tax law, tax litigation, and consultancy to private and corporate clients working in a leading Italian law firm.

Lillie M. Sullivan is a manager with KPMG LLP's Washington National Tax – Economic and Valuation Services practice. She specializes in resolving transfer pricing disputes and international tax controversy matters on behalf of multinational enterprises. Her work in transfer pricing dispute resolution has focused on working on APAs and competent authority cases. She also prepares transfer pricing documentation, advises on intercompany agreements, and assists with international tax planning and controversy. Prior to joining KPMG, Lillie worked as an associate with the tax practice of a leading law firm. Lillie obtained her JD from the University of Texas School of Law.

Prof. Dr Jean-Philippe Van West is a Senior Counsel in international tax with PwC Belgium and a guest professor at the Vrije Universiteit Brussel, as well as the author of various publications on international and European Union (EU) tax law.

Isabel Verlinden leads PwC's Global Transfer Pricing practice with over 3,000 full-time transfer pricing experts. In that capacity, she is a member of PwC's Global Tax Leadership team. She gathered first-hand knowledge of the TP challenges faced by companies operating across the globe based on over thirty years of experience working for PwC (and its legacy firms) in Brussels and Washington DC. Isabel helps to navigate leading global companies in a vast array of industries through the pitfalls stemming from cross-border transacting as multilateralism is under pressure, and domestic rules may hence lack coherence and consistency. Her work is often accompanied by ensuring upfront certainty through APAs. In the absence of upfront assurance, seeking effective means to alleviate double taxation is part of her day-to-day practice as well. This is particularly relevant as anti-avoidance (GAAR) rules increasingly risk to be opted for rather than a robust TP analysis. She is actively involved in PwC's input vis-à-vis the OECD in all transfer pricing related matters. She is an active writer for international tax and business periodicals. She has (co-) authored over 125 articles and books to date. She is often solicited by academia and event organizers. Isabel has a degree in Applied Economics (University of Louvain) – major in International Business Affairs, a degree in Financial Economics (Brussels University) – major in Accountancy, and a degree in commercial and Financial Sciences (Brussels University) – major in Fiscal Sciences.

Summary of Contents

Table of Contents

Preface

Transfer pricing is currently one of the most relevant and challenging topics in the international tax environment. It is under constant development around the globe, and the years 2020-2021 have certainly been no different in this regard. The intense work of international organizations has provided new guidance on transfer pricing topics with several projects.

The global legislative framework on transfer pricing has undergone several relevant changes during the past year in the wake of international guidelines. The year 2020 has witnessed uncertainty spreading from several directions: the need to find an agreement on Brexit, political tensions, trade frictions, and international discussions on digital services taxes. In this context, the spread of COVID-19 had devastating effects on human health, political stability, and global economy. Therefore, international organizations mostly focused on addressing the pandemic's significant challenges while providing additional guidance on the implementation of significant reforms introduced in the past years.

The OECD and the Inclusive Framework on Base Erosion and Profit Shifting (BEPS) continued to provide several guidelines on specific transfer pricing issues that could be viewed as a follow-up for ensuring effective implementation of the BEPS Action Plan. In early 2020, the OECD issued its Transfer Pricing Guidance on financial transactions while, in December 2020, it provided guidelines on the transfer pricing implications of the COVID-19 pandemic.

In the transfer pricing realm, the UN has updated the Practical Manual on Transfer Pricing for Developing Countries. Meanwhile, the UN has also proposed a new Article 12B in its model convention related to income from automated digital services to deal with the tax treatment of digital services payments.

The EU continued to undertake several measures for ensuring tax transparency. Further, the EU's presence in international transfer pricing developments was significant during 2020. The EU Commission continued its efforts into investigations to assess whether the Member States granted MNEs selective advantages by means of transfer pricing rulings that might have resulted in illegal state aid according to Article 107 TFEU. In one of the landmark cases, the Apple case, the European General Court decided in favour of Apple. However, on 25 September 2020, the EU Commission stated that it would appeal the decision before the Court of Justice of the European Union. Moreover, on 15 July 2020, the EU Commission published an action plan included in the tax package for fair and simple taxation, announcing the willingness to establish an Expert Group on Transfer Pricing that will elaborate solutions to practical problems posed by transfer pricing practices relevant for the EU. The group is intended to increase tax certainty and reduce double taxation risks.

The above guidance and reports aim to complement the guidelines that have come into force as part of the legislative changes in several countries. The work of international organizations and the EU (concerning the EU Member States) also provided further clarity and support to tax administrations and multinational enterprises to understand the evolution of transfer pricing provisions at the local and global levels. The proposals of the OECD, the UN, and the EU will significantly affect the future understanding of the international tax environment. Consequently, an in-depth understanding of the proposed concepts and their implications for multinationals, governments, advisors, and academia is crucial.

The WU Transfer Pricing Center at the Institute for Austrian and International Tax Law is conducting research projects to analyse the transfer pricing topics mentioned above and their global impacts. The current research is based on seven topic-based papers that have been drafted by well renowned international experts on transfer pricing. The results of this work were presented and discussed at the fourth 'Global Transfer Pricing Conference: Transfer Pricing Developments around the World' in February 2021, organized by the Transfer Pricing Center at WU Vienna University of Economics and Business. This book is aimed at academics, practitioners (including the business community and advisory firms), international organizations, and government officials who are tax and transfer pricing experts, as well as CEOs and CFOs who are interested in this topic. The book provides an in-depth analysis of the topics described above and the global impacts and suggestions for future solutions to any issues that are raised.

The editors would like to express their sincere thanks to the authors who made it possible to provide this ambitious work. Many thanks are forwarded to Kluwer Law International B.V. for supporting and cooperating with this publication project. Last but not least, the editors would like to thank Raphael Holzinger and Erika Scuderi for their precious support and Jenny Hill for providing linguistic support to the authors during the publishing process.

Prof. Dr DDr h.c. Michael Lang
Dr Raffaele Petruzzi, LLM

CHAPTER 1

Global Transfer Pricing Developments*

*Erika Scuderi & Raphael Holzinger***

* This Chapter has been drafted in February 2021 and, therefore, the subsequent legislative developments and political evolutions are not here reported. For more information, *see* E. Scuderi & R. Holzinger, 2021 WU Global Transfer Pricing Conference: "Transfer Pricing Developments around the World", 28 Intl. Transfer Pricing J. 4 (2021), Journals IBFD (https://research.ibfd.org/#/doc?url=/document/itpj_2021_04_int_4).

** The authors wish to thank Dr Raffaele Petruzzi, Managing Director of the WU Transfer Pricing Center, for its valuable feedback. The views expressed here are solely the views of the authors.

1 INTRODUCTION

The global legislative framework on transfer pricing has undergone several relevant changes during the past year in the wake of international guidelines. The year 2020 has witnessed uncertainty spreading in several directions: the need to find an agreement on Brexit, political tensions, trade frictions, and international discussions on digital services taxes (DSTs). In this context, the spread of COVID-19 has had devastating effects on human health, political stability, and the global economy.[1] Therefore, international organizations mostly focused on addressing the pandemic's enormous challenges while providing additional guidance on the implementation of significant reforms introduced in the past years. The Organisation for Economic Co-operation and Development (OECD) and the Inclusive Framework on Base Erosion and Profit Shifting (BEPS and the IF)[2] continued to provide several guidelines on specific transfer pricing issues that could be viewed as a follow-up for ensuring effective implementation of the BEPS Action Plan.[3] In early 2020, the OECD issued its Transfer Pricing Guidelines for Financial Transactions[4] (TPGFT) while, in December 2020, it provided guidelines on the transfer pricing implications of the COVID-19 pandemic (COVID-19 Guidance).[5]

---

1. https://www.internationaltaxreview.com/article/b1ptfdvf9wd0z1/2020-the-best-of-transfer-pricing, accessed 17 January 2021.
2. The Inclusive Framework on BEPS consists of 137 countries and jurisdictions committed to collaborating on implementing the OECD/ G20 Base Erosion and Profit Shifting (BEPS) Project. For a full list of Inclusive Framework Membership as of December 2019, *see* https://www.oecd.org/tax/beps/inclusive-framework-on-beps-composition.pdf.
3. OECD, *Aligning Transfer Pricing Outcomes with Value Creation, Actions 8-10 – 2015 Final Reports*, OECD/G20 Base Erosion and Profit Shifting Project (Paris: OECD Publishing, 2015).
4. OECD, *Transfer Pricing Guidance on Financial Transactions, Inclusive Framework on BEPS: Actions 4, 8-10*, OECD/G20 Base Erosion and Profit Shifting Project (Paris: OECD Publishing, 2020). *See* www.oecd.org/tax/beps/transfer-pricing-guidance-on-financial-transactions-inclusive-framework-on-beps-actions-4-8-10.htm.
5. OECD, *Guidance on the Transfer Pricing Implications of the COVID-19 Pandemic*, OECD Policy Responses to Coronavirus (COVID-19) (Paris: OECD Publishing 2020) https://doi.org/10.1787/731a59b0-en.

In the transfer pricing realm, the United Nations (UN) has updated the Practical Manual on Transfer Pricing for Developing Countries.[6] Meanwhile, the UN has also proposed a new Article 12B in its model convention that is related to income from automated digital services (ADS) to deal with the tax treatment of digital services payments.[7]

The European Union (EU) continued to undertake several measures for ensuring tax transparency. Further, the EU's presence in international transfer pricing developments was significant during 2020. The EU Commission continued its efforts into investigations to assess whether the Member States granted multinational enterprises (MNEs) selective advantages by means of transfer pricing rulings that might have resulted in illegal state aid according to Article 107 TFEU. In one of the landmark cases, the Apple case, the European General Court decided in favour of Apple. However, on 25 September 2020, the EU Commission stated that it would appeal the Decision before the Court of Justice of the European Union (CJEU). Moreover, on 15 July 2020, the EU Commission published an Action Plan included in the tax package for fair and simple taxation, announcing the willingness to establish an Expert Group on Transfer Pricing, which will elaborate solutions to practical problems posed by transfer pricing practices relevant for the EU. The group is intended to increase tax certainty and reduce double taxation risks.

The above guidance and reports aim to complement the guidelines that have come into force as part of the legislative changes in several countries. The work of international organizations and the EU (concerning the EU Member States) also provided further clarity and support to tax administrations and MNEs to understand the evolution of transfer pricing provisions at the local and global levels. The proposals of the OECD, the UN, and the EU will significantly affect the future understanding of the international tax environment. Consequently, in-depth comprehension of the proposed concepts and their implications for multinationals, governments, advisors, and academia is crucial.

This chapter will examine the above developments in detail. *Section I* will describe the developments under the work of the international organizations and the EU, and *section II* will look into the influence of these developments on country-specific transfer pricing legislation and jurisprudence.

6. United Nations, *Practical Manual on Transfer Pricing for Developing Countries* (updated in October 2020). *See* https://www.un.org/development/desa/financing/sites/www.un.org.development.desa.financing/files/2020-10/CRP40%20Transfer%20Pricing%20Manual%20Combined%20compressed.pdf.
7. Committee of Experts on International Cooperation in Tax Matters – Twentieth session – 20-23 and 26-29 October 2020, *Tax consequences of the digitalized economy – issues of relevance for developing countries*. *See* https://www.un.org/development/desa/financing/sites/www.un.org.development.desa.financing/files/2020-10/CITCM%2021%20CRP.41_Digitalization%2010102020%20Final%20A.pdf.

2 RECENT DEVELOPMENTS ON THE WORK OF INTERNATIONAL ORGANIZATIONS

2.1 Transfer Pricing Developments at the OECD

2.1.1 OECD Guidance on the Transfer Pricing Implications of the COVID-19 Pandemic (COVID Guidance)

As a result of the unique circumstances faced during the COVID-19 pandemic in combination with governments' measures that were put in place, taxpayers applying transfer pricing rules for the financial years impacted by the coronavirus and tax administrations that will investigate their correct implementation may face several challenges for the application of the arm's length principle (ALP).

The COVID Guidance addresses crucial transfer pricing topics about which the need to provide clarifications emerged and provided guidelines on how the ALP and the OECD Transfer Pricing Guidelines (OECD TPG) apply to issues that may arise or be exacerbated in the context of the COVID-19 crisis. In particular, the COVID Guidance addresses the following issues:

- Comparability Analysis
- Losses and Allocation of COVID-19 Specific Costs
- Government Assistance Programmes
- Advance Pricing Arrangements

Comparability Analysis

The first chapter of the COVID Guidance addresses the comparability analysis issues by answering nine pivotal questions.[8]

1. What sources of contemporaneous information may be used to support the performance of a comparability analysis applicable for FY 2020?

In this respect, the COVID Guidance[9] states that, in general, any publicly available information regarding the effects of the pandemic on business, industry, and controlled transactions may be considered relevant in ascertaining the arm's length nature of an enterprise's transfer pricing policy implemented for 2020. A list of possible sources of information is provided, including an analysis of how sales volumes have changed during COVID-19, an analysis of the effects on profitability or on third party behaviour observed in previous recessionary periods or using any data available in the current year, and details regarding government interventions that have affected the pricing and performance of controlled transactions.

8. https://home.kpmg/us/en/home/insights/2020/12/tnf-oecd-guidance-transfer-pricing-implications-covid-19-pandemic.html, accessed 6 January 2021.
9. Paragraph 11 of the COVID Guidance.

The additional guidance provided by the OECD regarding this general question is nothing completely new but can already be properly derived from the OECD TPG 2017. However, in fact, some of the clarifications on possible approaches that could be chosen in order to ensure a proper comparability analysis in times of the pandemic (e.g., explicit mentioning of macroeconomic information, statistical methods like regression analysis, etc.) are to be seen as useful as such clarification usually enhances the acceptance of such approaches during the course of TP audits thus increasing legal certainty.

2. Can budgeted financial information be used to support the setting of arm's length prices?

Comparing budgeted (or forecast) financial results to those actually achieved during the coronavirus times is another possible approach that can be used in setting transfer prices as part of a more general set of the methodology used to evaluate the context and the factors that may impact the arm's length nature of prices. The COVID Guidance[10] states that '*financial outcomes that taxpayers within a controlled transaction would have achieved "but for" the impact of COVID-19 may provide useful information*', especially when assessing the financial impacts from the coronavirus (such as reduced sales volume or increased operating expenses) and determining, in light of contractual terms and risk assumption of the parties, any appropriate resulting impact on inter-company prices.

Even though the OECD tried to clarify how budgeted and actual numbers may be applied during the course of a transfer pricing analysis, the respective paragraphs of the COVID Guidance eventually appear to be written rather superficially, thus not strongly enhancing the guidance, which could already have been derived from the OECD TPG 2017 in that regard.

3. Under what circumstances are timing issues most pronounced?

According to the COVID Guidance,[11] information concerning contemporaneous uncontrolled transactions is the most reliable when performing a comparability analysis. The OECD notes that, while in some instances, a comparability analysis can be performed using contemporaneous (or near contemporaneous) uncontrolled transactions, in other circumstances, timing issues may result in challenging the application of the transactional net margin method (TNMM) as 2020 information will typically not be available until mid-2021 at the earliest. However, not every application of the TNMM will, in principle, require contemporaneous information for the fiscal year 2020.

In fact, the OECD also addressed that the obvious lack of contemporaneous external database information regarding the fiscal year 2020 '*suggests that in these circumstances taxpayers will need to perform a comparability analysis based on available prior year financial information and, depending on the facts and circumstances of the case, utilising whatever current year information is available to support their transfer*

10. Paragraphs 12-13 of the COVID Guidance.
11. Paragraphs 14-17 of the COVID Guidance.

prices'.[12] Reading this statement of the OECD together with the previously addressed questions, it becomes evident that, for a TNMM analysis, not just the mere use of databases but also the combination with other external and internal information (e.g., budgeted versus actual numbers or Gross Domestic Product information) or approaches (e.g., statistical measures) eventually increases the reliability from an arm's length perspective.

4. What practical approaches may be available to address information deficiencies?

The significant time lag between the occurrence of controlled transactions and the availability of information relating to contemporaneous uncontrolled transactions may give rise to difficulties for the taxpayer in determining arm's length conditions. The COVID Guidance,[13] noting these information deficiencies, invites tax administrations to consider practical approaches to reduce disputes when taxpayers make reasonable efforts to determine the arm's length pricing. These practical approaches may include:

- allowing for the use of reasonable commercial judgment supplemented by contemporaneous information to set a reasonable estimate of the arm's length price;
- when feasible, allowing for an arm's length 'outcome-testing approach' – instead of an ex ante approach (so-called 'price-setting') – which may incorporate information available after the close of the taxable year to determine arm's length conditions and report results on the tax return; and
- allowing for the use of more than one transfer pricing method in order to support the arm's length price.

From a practical perspective – even though the OECD TPG 2017 generally allows for both price-setting and price-testing approaches – plenty of countries either favour one or the other of them, which eventually often results in legal uncertainty and TP disputes. By again clarifying that price-testing approaches might be a proper approach in order to account for the complexities during COVID-19 from a TP perspective, the OECD again highlighted its legitimacy.

5. Can data from other crises be used to support price-setting?

The COVID Guidance[14] discourages performing a comparability analysis based only on financial information from the global financial crisis of 2008/2009. The OECD explains that – given the coronavirus pandemic's unprecedented nature and its effect on economic conditions – such a comparability analysis would raise significant concerns. Therefore, it suggests that a comparability analysis should be performed by reference to the specific delineation of the controlled transaction, including its actual economic circumstances.

12. Paragraphs 16 of the COVID Guidance.
13. Paragraphs 18-24 of the COVID Guidance.
14. Paragraph 25 of the COVID Guidance.

6. How might the period of data used to evaluate arm's length pricing be established to support a comparability analysis?

According to the COVID Guidance,[15] the principles concerning the use of multiple year data and averages outlined in the OECD TPG[16] remain applicable. To improve reliability, a pragmatic approach of dealing with divergent economic conditions between different phases of the pandemic may consist of having separate testing periods (and periods considered for price-setting) for the duration of the crisis or the periods most impacted by it as long as the data from independent comparables can be consistently measured over a similar period. However, in other fact patterns, reliability may be improved by using years that are and are not impacted by the pandemic. Under this approach, the financial results of FY 2020, which may be exceptional, would be aggregated with the more 'standard' results of the previous FYs to test the arm's length nature of the transfer pricing policy applied in FY 2020.

7. Would price adjustment mechanisms be appropriate?

The COVID Guidance[17] considers that when admissible by domestic law, price adjustment mechanisms that allow the adjustment of prices relevant for 2020 in a later period when more accurate information to establish the arm's length transfer price becomes available would be able to give flexibility to taxpayers and tax administrations while also ensuring ultimate compliance with the ALP. The OECD warns that, given the scope of the potential adjustments, care needs to be taken with their appropriate characterization, any effects that the payment may have on the comparability analysis for 2021, and their potential resultant Value Added Tax (VAT)/Goods and Services Tax (GST) and customs duty implications.

What is more, besides the tax (e.g., VAT/GST) and customs implications raised by the OECD, also accounting (company law) aspects are to be considered. Whereas different countries have a rather simple system to correct transfer prices in the tax returns only, other countries rather have a strong link between accounting records and tax records, meaning that a retroactive adjustment of transfer prices might also require an adjustment of accounting records (either retroactively in the financials of 2020 or – under certain circumstances – in the financial records of a later period).

8. What actions may be taken to evaluate the set of comparable companies or transactions used?

The year 2020 has been characterized by unprecedented economic conditions, which, of course, lead to the necessity to review the suitability of existing comparables. The COVID Guidance[18] notes that, in some cases, it may be useful to revise the set based on updated search criteria.

15. Paragraphs 26-29 of the COVID Guidance.
16. Section B.5 of Chapter III of the OECD TPG.
17. Paragraph 30 of the COVID Guidance.
18. Paragraphs 31-32 of the COVID Guidance.

9. Can loss-making comparables be used?

In the OECD TPG,[19] there is no overriding rule on the inclusion or exclusion of loss-making comparables. Therefore, the COVID Guidance[20] affirms that, when performing a comparability analysis for FY 2020, loss-making comparables should not be rejected on the sole basis that they suffer losses in periods affected by the COVID-19 pandemic if they satisfy comparability criteria. In other words, it would be appropriate to include them when the accurate delineation of the transaction indicates that they are reliable (e.g., they assume similar levels of risk and have been comparably impacted by the pandemic).

Some countries generally tend to refuse (or at least hardly argue against) the inclusion of (constant) loss-making comparables in the final set of comparables in the case that a routine entity is tested based on a benchmarking study. However, given the economic shock in the financial year 2020, it will likely turn out that comparables will face a significant loss in 2020 that could bring them to an overall loss-making situation in a specific period under review (e.g., 2018-2020). In such a situation, it seems to be questionable whether such a comparable should be excluded from the final set in the case that the comparability factors (from a holistic perspective) suggest that it was reasonably comparable in the case at hand. In light of the general guidance laid down in the OECD TPG 2017 in that regard, care has to be taken on a case-by-case basis.[21] Given the likelihood of TP disputes in this area, the clarification by the OECD regarding the potential inclusion of loss-making comparables tends to be welcomed by taxpayers.

Losses and Allocation of COVID-19 Specific Costs

Chapter 2 of the COVID Guidance deals with the losses that MNE groups may have suffered due to COVID-19. Paragraphs 34-37 state that, when considering the issue of losses and the allocation of COVID-19 specific costs, three issues warrant specific discussion:

(1) First, it should be noted that the analysis of risks in commercial or financial relations will be particularly relevant for determining how losses are allocated between associated parties as it affects how profits or losses resulting from the

19. *See* paras 3.64 and 3.65 of Chapter III of the OECD TPG.
20. Paragraph 33 of the COVID Guidance.
21. *See* para. 3.63 of Chapter III of the OECD TPG, where it says: 'Extreme results might consist of losses or unusually high profits. Extreme results can affect the financial indicators that are looked at in the chosen method (e.g. the gross margin when applying a resale price, or a net profit indicator when applying a transactional net margin method). They can also affect other items, e.g. exceptional items which are below the line but nonetheless may reflect exceptional circumstances. Where one or more of the potential comparables have extreme results, further examination would be needed to understand the reasons for such extreme results. The reason might be a defect in comparability, or exceptional conditions met by an otherwise comparable third party. An extreme result may be excluded on the basis that a previously overlooked significant comparability defect has been brought to light, not on the sole basis that the results arising from the proposed "comparable" merely appear to be very different from the results observed in other proposed "comparables".'

transaction are allocated at arm's length through the pricing of the transaction.

(2) Second, it is necessary to consider how exceptional, non-recurring operating costs arising from the coronavirus should be allocated between associated parties based on an assessment of how independent enterprises under comparable circumstances operate.

(3) Finally, as a result of COVID-19, associated parties may consider whether they have the option to apply force majeure clauses, revoke, or otherwise revise their intercompany agreements.

In order to provide guidance on losses and the allocation of COVID-19 specific costs, the OECD answers five crucial questions.

1. Can entities operating under limited-risk arrangements incur losses?

The COVID Guidance[22] states that, when determining if a limited-risk entity could incur losses at arm's length, it is necessary to consider the specific facts and circumstances. As noted in the COVID Guidance,[23] by virtue of *a contrario* reading of paragraph 3.64 of Chapter III of the OECD TPG,[24] routine or low-risk functions may incur losses in the short run. In particular, in determining whether a limited-risk entity may incur losses, it is essential to evaluate the risks assumed by the entity because, at arm's length, the allocation of risks between the parties of an arrangement affects how profits or losses resulting from the transaction are allocated. For example, it is possible that a limited-risk distributor, which assumes some market risk at arm's length, incurs a loss associated with the materialization of this risk because of a significant decline in demand due to the COVID-19 crisis. On the contrary, the COVID Guidance[25] reminds that it would not be appropriate for a limited-risk distributor that *does not* assume any market risk or another specific risk to bear a portion of the loss associated with the materialization of that risk. Finally, according to the COVID Guidance,[26] when considering the risks assumed by a party to a controlled transaction, tax administrations should evaluate the commercial rationale for any purported change in the risks assumed by a party before and after the outbreak of COVID-19 and analyse whether a taxpayer's position is consistent with the accurate delineation of the transaction.

Based on that, it becomes evident that the OECD points out that 'low risk' does not mean 'no risk'. Depending on the actual risks assumed by a low-risk business unit within an MNE (based on the OECD risk framework),[27] there might be cases in which a (certain) loss attribution during times of crisis is perfectly in line with the ALP. However, there might also be cases in which the risk allocation between the parties to

22. Paragraphs 38-41 of the COVID Guidance.
23. Paragraph 39 of the COVID Guidance.
24. Paragraph 3.64 of Chapter III of the OECD TPG states that 'simple or low risk functions in particular are not expected to generate losses for a long period of time'.
25. Paragraph 40 of the COVID Guidance.
26. Paragraph 41 of the COVID Guidance.
27. *See* paras 1.60 et seq. of Chapter I of the OECD TPG.

the transaction suggests that a low-risk business unit within an MNE should still receive small and stable profits.

2. Under what circumstances may arrangements be modified to address the consequences of COVID-19?

As a consequence of the COVID-19 pandemic, associated parties may consider revising their intercompany agreements or the conduct in their commercial relationships. To determine whether renegotiations are at arm's length, tax administrations should review the agreements and the conduct of associated enterprises in light of the guidance in section D of Chapter I of the OECD TPG, together with observations of relevant behaviour of independent parties and this guidance. In determining whether a renegotiation represents the parties' best interests to a transaction, it would be necessary to consider the options that are realistically available, the long-run effects on the profit potential of the parties, and whether the economic impact resulting from the renegotiation may require indemnification. Finally, the OECD concludes that, in the absence of clear evidence that independent parties in comparable circumstances would have revised their existing agreements, the modification of existing intercompany arrangements should be treated with caution and well-supported by documentation outlining how the modification is in line with the ALP.

3. How should operational or exceptional costs arising from COVID-19 be allocated between related parties?

In 2020, many enterprises incurred exceptional, non-recurring operating costs such as expenditures on personal protective equipment, reconfiguration of workspaces to enable physical distancing, and IT infrastructure expenses. In order to determine which associated enterprise should bear these exceptional costs, it is essential to consider how these costs would be allocated between independent parties operating in comparable circumstances and to understand: (a) who has the responsibility for performing activities related to the relevant costs, and (b) who assumes risks related to these activities.

4. How should exceptional costs arising from COVID-19 be taken into account in a comparability analysis?

To answer this question, the COVID Guidance states the following three principles:

(1) exceptional costs should generally be excluded, at the level of the tested party and the comparables, from the net profit indicator except when those costs relate to the accurately delineated controlled transaction;
(2) when determining a cost basis, it is crucial to consider whether exceptional costs that are deemed to relate to the controlled transactions are included or excluded from the cost basis and, if included, whether such costs should be treated as pass-through elements;
(3) accounting consistency adjustments may be required to improve comparability when exceptional costs arising from COVID-19 may be accounted for as

either operating or non-operating items by different taxpayers for different transactions.

5. How may force majeure affect the allocation of losses derived from the COVID-19 pandemic?

A party may invoke a force majeure clause and assert that the extreme circumstances justify the non-performance of a contract because of the COVID-19 pandemic. The OECD affirms that when an intercompany contract contains a force majeure clause, it cannot be automatically assumed that the COVID-19 pandemic is sufficient for a party to that contract to invoke force majeure[28] Additionally when it is not contained within the relevant intercompany agreement, it cannot be automatically assumed that renegotiation with a potentially similar outcome at arm's length would be inappropriate.[29] Therefore, in order to ascertain whether revision or renegotiation should be respected under the OECD TPG and transfer pricing outcomes are appropriate in light of the accurate delineation of the transaction, tax administrations should review the agreements and the conduct of associated enterprises in light of the guidance in section D of Chapter I of the OECD TPG together with observations of relevant behaviour of independent parties.

Government Assistance Programmes

During the pandemic, governments provided financial and liquidity supports to ensure enterprises can continue to operate despite the reduction in business activity through loan guarantees, direct financing to business on preferential terms, loan deferrals, tax reliefs, and specific grants. According to the COVID Guidance,[30] when determining the potential impact of these programmes on controlled transactions and comparing their effects with those of other pre-existing assistance programmes, the terms and conditions of such government assistance programs on the accurately delineated transaction need to be considered. The COVID Guidance specifically addresses a series of five questions on government assistance programs. Furthermore, because of the differences between the various support programmes and the practical issues in obtaining detailed and timely information, it may be challenging to identify the nature of government assistance received by potential comparables.

In order to address specific government assistance programmes' issues, the COVID Guidance answers five questions.

1. Is the receipt of government assistance an economically relevant characteristic?

First, according to the OECD TPG,[31] economically relevant characteristics that pertain to a controlled transaction should be evaluated when accurately delineating the

28. Paragraph 57 of the COVID Guidance.
29. Paragraph 59 of the COVID Guidance.
30. Paragraphs 64-66 of the COVID Guidance.
31. Paragraph 1.33 of Chapter I of the OECD TPG.

controlled transaction and facilitating the comparison between the accurately delineated controlled transaction and comparable uncontrolled transactions to price the controlled transaction. The COVID Guidance notes that the extent to which the receipt of government assistance is an economically relevant characteristic may vary on the basis of the circumstances[32] but, if the government assistance is an economically relevant characteristic, this information should be included as a part of the documentation to support the transfer pricing analysis.

Prima vista, the additional guidance provided by the OECD, seems to be definitely undecided in terms of 'strong' statements. However, giving the general complexity of the relevance of government assistance, the approach chosen by the OECD seems to be understandable. However, in fact, the OECD even provided some guidance on specific government subsidies (i.e., wage subsidy, a government debt guarantee or short-term liquidity support) that they consider to be rather an economically relevant characteristic. Other types of government assistance like the provision of local infrastructure might only be indirectly linked to a controlled transaction, thus not having to be seen as an economically relevant characteristic in an arm's length analysis. However, the borderline between being directly or only indirectly linked to a controlled transaction was not further specified by the OECD in the COVID Guidance.

2. Is guidance on other local market features relevant when analysing the transfer pricing implications of government assistance?

As a general rule, according to the OECD TPG,[33] government interventions should be treated as conditions of the market in the particular country; therefore, the receipt of government assistance may be part of the parties' economic circumstances and a feature of the market in which the parties operate. Furthermore, the COVID Guidance also refers to the OECD TPG when explaining that the analysis of the implications of the receipt of government support would need to consider several factors, namely: the existence of a *market advantage* as a result of the government assistance; the amount of any *increased revenues/decreased costs* compared to reliable comparables; how the subsidies are or are not passed on to *independent customers and suppliers*; and, when they are not fully passed on, how *independent enterprises* operating under similar circumstances would allocate such benefits between them. In conclusion, since, under certain circumstances, the particular nature of the government assistance may not be a general feature of the market and it may not generate benefits for either party, it should always be reviewed in the transfer pricing analysis.

---

32. In some cases, such as the provision of a wage subsidy, a government debt guarantee, or short-term liquidity support, the receipt of government assistance may have a direct impact on the controlled transaction and comparable transactions between independent parties. In other circumstances, such as the provision of local infrastructure by a government that might be only indirectly linked to the controlled transaction and the compensation, it may be less economically relevant. Furthermore, when the parties to a controlled transaction do not receive government assistance but another party does, this may influence the economically relevant characteristics of the transaction. *See* para. 68 of the COVID Guidance.
33. Section D.4 of Chapter I of the OECD TPG.

3. Does the receipt of government assistance affect the price of controlled transactions?

According to the COVID Guidance,[34] the potential effect of the receipt of government assistance on the pricing of a controlled transaction depends on the economically relevant characteristics of the transaction following an accurate delineation of the controlled transaction and the performance of a comparability analysis. Indeed, it would be contrary to the ALP to assume that the mere receipt of government assistance would affect the price of the accurately delineated controlled transaction without performing a careful comparability analysis.

When analysing the impact of government assistance on the price of controlled transactions, several aspects should be taken into account:

- the availability, purpose, and duration of the government assistance;[35]
- conditions imposed by the government in granting the assistance, such as (a) legal conditions that limit or prevent the capacity of the party receiving the assistance from modifying the pricing of its transactions with other parties across the value chain, (b) eligibility criteria that require the recipients to demonstrate a significant downturn in revenue or could be intended to preserve the viability of businesses during the pandemic, and (c) uncertainty around the amounts involved;[36]
- economic circumstances on the market that could influence the pricing of the accurately delineated controlled transaction such as the level of competition, the elasticity of the demand within the relevant markets, and the availability of benefits to competitors in the market;[37] and
- the allocation of the economically significant risks under the accurate delineation of the controlled transaction, the impact of the pandemic on the outcome of the economically significant risks, and the linkage between the type of government assistance and those risks.[38]

In light of the additional guidance provided by the OECD, it seems to be reasonable to conclude that the OECD rather holistically based its clarification on the general understanding of the ALP. Accordingly, the analysis should be based on the question of how an independent third party (e.g., under consideration of competition, the elasticity of demand, etc.) would have considered government assistance in its pricing (e.g., lowering the prices or not).

4. Does the receipt of government assistance modify the allocation of risk in a controlled transaction?

The COVID Guidance underlines that government assistance may reduce the quantitative negative impact of a risk. However, this aspect must be distinguished from the

34. Paragraph 73 of the COVID Guidance.
35. Paragraph 74 of the COVID Guidance.
36. Paragraph 75 of the COVID Guidance.
37. Paragraph 76 of the COVID Guidance.
38. Paragraph 77 of the COVID Guidance.

allocation of risks under the OECD TPG. In this respect, indeed, the provision of government assistance to an associated party will not change the allocation of risk in a controlled transaction for transfer pricing purposes.[39]

5. Does the receipt of government assistance affect the comparability analysis?

The OECD answers this question in the affirmative and underlines that the receipt of government assistance may affect both (i) how the parties establish their commercial or financial relations and (ii) how they price their transactions. The suggested approach in identifying reliable comparables involves referring to data regarding comparable uncontrolled transactions in the same/similar geographic market between independent enterprises performing similar functions, assuming similar risks and using similar assets. Further, when applying a one-sided method such as the TNMM, the Resale Price Method, or the Cost-Plus Method, the accounting treatment of the government assistance in both the tested party and any comparable may need to be specifically identified, especially when the tested party and the comparables apply different accounting standards.[40]

Advance Pricing Arrangements

The COVID-19 pandemic may also affect the application of existing Advance Pricing Agreements (APAs) and affect those under negotiation. While encouraging taxpayers and tax administrations to adopt a constructive and collaborative approach, the COVID Guidance analyses specific issues related to this topic. However, the OECD's indications do not seem to be incredibly innovative compared to what could already be derived from the applicable rules on APAs, but they offer a few critical considerations by answering five questions.

1. Are taxpayers and tax administrations still bound by existing APAs in light of the changes in economic conditions?

First, the OECD reassures that existing APAs should be respected and upheld by both taxpayers and tax administrations, and their terms cannot be disregarded as a consequence of the mere change of economic circumstances unless a condition that leads to the cancellation of revision of the APA occurs.

2. Does the change in economic conditions constitute a breach of a critical assumption?

In general, unless expressly stated in the APA, a mere change in business results during the period affected by the pandemic would not result in a breach of a critical assumption. However, since the COVID-19 crisis did not have the same impact on all enterprises, any breach in a critical assumption should be assessed on a case-by-case basis and should consider the individual circumstances of the taxpayer and commercial environment.

39. Chapter I of the OECD TPG.
40. Paragraph 88 of the COVID Guidance.

3. How should tax administrations respond to the failure to meet critical assumptions?

In the case of a failure to meet critical assumptions, tax administrations and taxpayers should consider the APA's terms, any agreement between relevant tax administrations as to how to deal with the failure, and any applicable domestic law or procedural provisions. The OECD TPG provides detailed guidance on this issue. When the guidance in Chapter IV of the OECD TPG applies, a breach of critical assumption with the APA could have three potential outcomes.[41]

Table 1.1 Tax Administrations' Response to the Failure to Meet Critical Assumptions

Response	*When Appropriate*	*Consequences*
Revision	Material change in conditions noted in a critical assumption in the APA and the tax administration and the taxpayer agrees on how to revise the APA	The taxpayer and tax administrations still benefit from the APA for the whole of the proposed period, albeit those different terms apply before and after the revision date
Cancellation	In the context of the COVID-19 pandemic, two situations must be considered: (i) material breach in an APA's critical assumption as a result of a change in economic circumstances; or (ii) the taxpayer failed to materially comply with any term or condition of the APA.	The APA is treated as being effective and in force but only up to the cancellation date and not for the whole of the proposed period
Revocation	(i) there is a misrepresentation, mistake, or omission that was attributable to the neglect, carelessness, or wilful default of a taxpayer when filing an APA request and submission, the annual reports, or other	The taxpayer is treated as if the APA had never been concluded

41. Section E.3 Annex II to Chapter IV of OECD TPG.

Response	When Appropriate	Consequences
	supporting documentation or in supplying any related information; or (ii) the taxpayer fails to materially comply with a fundamental term or condition of the APA.	

4. When should taxpayers notify tax administrations of the failure to meet critical assumptions?

In line with the general cooperative and collaborative approach suggested by the OECD, taxpayers should notify the relevant tax administrations as soon as the change occurs or when the taxpayer becomes aware of the change. Furthermore, early notification is encouraged to give the affected parties more time to reach an agreement on revising the APA, thereby reducing the likelihood of cancellation.

5. How should taxpayers document the failure to meet critical assumptions?

The COVID Guidance[42] also provides for a (non-exhaustive) list of supporting documentation that the taxpayer should prepare in order to demonstrate the failure to meet critical assumptions.

6. How should tax administrations respond to non-compliance with an existing APA?

The OECD affirms that when tax administrations deal with non-compliance with terms and conditions of an existing APA, they should adopt an approach similar to situations when there is a failure to meet critical assumptions. Therefore, they should consider the terms of the agreement, any agreement between relevant tax administrations as to how to deal with non-compliance, and any applicable domestic law or procedural provisions.

7. What impact does COVID-19 have on APAs under negotiation?

The COVID-19 pandemic caused an unprecedented level of economic uncertainty and would probably make taxpayers less inclined to start or continue APA applications. However, APAs, the purpose of which is securing tax certainty for taxpayers and tax administrations and preventing future tax disputes, would also play an essential role under the current circumstances.

In this respect, the COVID Guidance emphasizes the pivotal value of achieving advanced certainty and effective dispute prevention through APAs and encourages taxpayers and tax administrations to adopt innovative and flexible approaches to ensure collaborative working, such as virtual meetings, virtual functional interviews

42. Paragraph 104 of the COVID Guidance.

with taxpayers' employees, electronic documentation sharing, etc., in order to minimize delays in concluding APAs under negotiation. Furthermore, in line with the cooperative and flexible approach suggested, the COVID Guidance[43] provides a list of possible solutions that can be adapted to face the COVID-19 crisis:

(1) short period APA covering the period affected by the COVID-19 crisis and a separate APA covering the post-COVID period;
(2) APA for the whole period with the condition that the relevant impacts of the COVID-19 pandemic will be analysed and reported each year once they are known and retrospective amendments made accordingly when needed;
(3) extend the period of the APA to mitigate the short-term effect of the pandemic, depending on the magnitude and the length of such an effect;
(4) the use of a cumulative or term test throughout the APA period could be given consideration.

In conclusion, the COVID Guidance emphasizes that solutions to transfer pricing issues related to COVID-19 should be found among the OECD TPG's existing framework and principles. The OECD stresses that the pandemic's impact needs to be assessed and thoroughly documented and that taxpayers and tax administrations should accurately identify the economically significant risks, the impact on local governments and how other parties would address it while taking into account their contractual relationships and options realistically available.

For more information on Recent Developments on the Transfer Pricing and COVID-19, please refer to Chapter 6 of this volume.

2.1.2 Digitalization of the Economy

Digitalization has already posed significant challenges to the current tax landscape and will continue to do so for national and international tax systems that rely on physical presence and physical production factors. Within this framework, disputes and uncertainty have increased due to unilateral (and uncoordinated) actions taken by several countries and the even more rapid acceleration of the digitalization of the economy during the COVID-19 pandemic.

For these reasons, addressing the digitalized economy's tax challenges remained a priority on the OECD's agenda in 2020.

In this respect, in 2019, the IF agreed, on a without prejudice basis, to undertake work on the following two pillars:[44]

43. Paragraph 109 of the COVID Guidance.
44. OECD, *Addressing the Tax Challenges of the Digitalisation of the Economy – Policy Note*, approved by the Inclusive Framework on BEPS on 23 January 2019 OECD/G20 Base Erosion and Profit Shifting Project, available at https://www.oecd.org/tax/beps/policy-note-beps-inclusive-framework-addressing-tax-challenges-digitalisation.pdf. For a detailed description of Pillar One and Pillar Two, please refer to Lang, M., Petruzzi, R. *Transfer Pricing Development Around the World*, 2020. Kluwer Law International BV, The Netherlands.

- Pillar One addresses the allocation of taxing rights between jurisdictions and describes proposals for new profit allocation and nexus rules based on the concepts of 'significant economic presence' as well as the exploitation of 'user participation' and 'marketing intangibles' in a jurisdiction.
- Pillar Two (also referred to as the GloBE proposal) calls for the development of a coordinated set of rules to address ongoing risks from structures that allow MNEs to shift profit to jurisdictions where they are subject to no or very low taxation.

Although countries had initially targeted the end of 2020 for political consensus on the two-pillar approach, political disagreements over crucial issues and difficulties stemming from the COVID-19 pandemic made the timeline untenable. Therefore, the G20 and the IF members suggested extending the deadline until mid-2021.

A programme of work to be conducted on Pillar One and Pillar Two was adopted in May 2019 and later endorsed by the G20 in June 2019. As part of the work programme, the OECD Secretariat was mandated to carry out an economic analysis and impact assessment of the Pillar One and Pillar Two proposals. In July 2020, the G20 mandated the IF to produce reports on the Blueprints of Pillar One and Pillar Two by the G20 Finance Ministers meeting in October 2020. Indeed, on 8-9 October 2020, the IF approved a package consisting of reports on Pillar One[45] and Pillar Two[46] Blueprints that explore alternatives in relation to the design of a global minimum tax that tackles the remaining BEPS issues.

In particular, the Report on the Pillar One Blueprint was conceived to provide a sustainable tax framework that reflects today's digitized economy aiming to achieve a more efficient and fair allocation of taxing rights. The Report on the Pillar Two Blueprint, on the other hand, aims at providing a basis for a comprehensive solution to address the remaining BEPS challenges.

2.1.2.1 *Report on the Pillar One Blueprint*

The OECD report on the Pillar One Blueprint focuses on new nexus and profit allocation rules in the digital age to separate the allocation of taxing rights concerning business profits from physical presence.

In particular, Pillar One expands the taxing rights of market jurisdictions (which, for some business models, are the jurisdictions where the users/consumers are located) where there is active and sustained participation of a business in the economy of that jurisdiction through activities in or remotely directed at that jurisdiction. It also aims to significantly improve tax certainty by introducing innovative dispute prevention and resolution mechanisms.

45. OECD, *Tax Challenges Arising from Digitalisation – Report on Pillar One Blueprint: Inclusive Framework on BEPS*, OECD/G20 Base Erosion and Profit Shifting Project (Paris: OECD Publishing, 2020) https://doi.org/10.1787/beba0634-en.
46. OECD, *Tax Challenges Arising from Digitalisation – Report on Pillar Two Blueprint: Inclusive Framework on BEPS*, OECD/G20 Base Erosion and Profit Shifting Project (Paris: OECD Publishing, 2020) https://doi.org/10.1787/abb4c3d1-en.

In order to achieve this, key elements of Pillar One can be grouped into three components:

(1) *Amount A*: a new taxing right for market jurisdictions over a share of residual profit calculated at an MNE group (or segment) level;
(2) *Amount B*: a fixed return for certain baseline marketing and distribution activities taking place physically in a market jurisdiction in line with the ALP; and
(3) processes to improve tax certainty through effective dispute prevention and resolution mechanisms.

Eleven building blocks have been identified as essential to the construction of Pillar One and constitute the bedrock of this Blueprint.

Table 1.2 Pillar One Overview

Amount A			*Amount B*	*Tax Certainty*
Scope	Nexus	Tax base determination	Scope	Dispute prevention and resolution for Amount A
Revenue sourcing	Profit allocation	Elimination of double taxation	Quantum	Dispute prevention and resolution beyond Amount A
Implementation and administration				

While the technical work on the Pillar One building blocks is very advanced, political decisions are required on a number of issues in order to complete the package.

Amount A

The new taxing right under Amount A would be an overlay to the existing nexus and profit allocation rules, would apply broadly, and would not be limited to a small number of MNEs in a particular industry. However, IF members – considering its innovative characteristics – will consider the possibility of introducing thresholds and/or other features that would help maintain the targeted approach, minimize compliance costs, and be mindful of capacity considerations for tax administrations. The key design features of the new taxing right would include:

- A revenue threshold based on annual consolidated group revenue coupled with a *de minimis* foreign in-scope revenue carve-out.
- Scoping rules covering ADS and, more broadly, Consumer-Facing Business (CFB).
- The nexus rules are supported by detailed sourcing rules that are reflective of the particularities of digital services and CFBs and balance the need for accuracy with the ability of in-scope MNEs to comply and the cost of doing so.

- An administrable approach for reallocating residual profit.
- A loss carry-forward regime to ensure that there is no Amount A allocation when the relevant business is not profitable over time.
- In addition to the proposed mechanism to eliminate double taxation, different options are being considered to adjust the allocation of Amount A to market jurisdictions when an MNE already leaves residual profits under the existing ALP-based profit allocation rules (so-called double-counting issues), including a marketing and distribution profits safe harbour.
- The mechanism to eliminate double taxation will have two components: (a) identification of the paying entities and (b) the methods to eliminate double taxation.
- When an MNE is subject to the new taxing right, a simplified administrative process will be developed to minimize the complexity, burden, and cost of filing and payment, which is aimed at benefitting tax administrations and taxpayers alike.
- The new Amount A taxing right would be implemented through changes to domestic law and by way of public international law instruments; in particular, a multilateral convention (MLI) would be required.

Eventually, Amount A is to be seen as the 'key game changer' under Pillar One in the currently applicable international tax landscape. Regarding the questions of the jurisdiction to tax, this is mainly caused by the foreseen nexus rules as they would allow for taxing rights of market jurisdictions that are not interlinked with a physical presence there. Eventually, the taxing rights of market jurisdictions would be increased (a corresponding decrease of the taxing rights of the residence states would widely avoid double taxation). However, Pillar One also leads to novelties in terms of quantifications of taxing rights in international tax law since Amount A – on its merits – is in no way based upon the ALP (besides the consideration of already existing taxing rights of market jurisdictions on residual profits (i.e., double-counting issues)) but rather aims to estimate a new taxing right for market jurisdictions. On the one hand, there are concerns that moving away from the ALP could create uncertainties and increase disputes as there is no possibility to refer back to the overarching principle and try to figure out what independent parties would have agreed to and what the rule is supposed to achieve. On the other hand, there is no evidence that using an apportionment method is going to result in more disputes than what there would be under the ALP, so the crucial point is to wait for the OECD's final solution and hope it will be comprehensive enough to avoid a 'numbers game'.

Amount B

The purpose of Amount B is two-fold:

(1) First, it aims at simplifying the administration of transfer pricing rules for tax administrations and lowering compliance costs for taxpayers.
(2) Second, it is intended to enhance tax certainty and reduce controversy between tax administrations and taxpayers.

Amount B will standardize the remuneration of related-party distributors that perform 'baseline marketing and distribution activities' in the market jurisdiction.[47] The activities in scope are defined by a positive list of typical functions performed, risks assumed, and assets owned at arm's length by routine distributors. A negative list of typical functions that *should not* be performed, risks that *should not* be assumed, and assets that *should not* be owned at arm's length by routine distributors is used to (qualitatively) measure the additional factors that would deem a distributor as being outside the scope of Amount B.

The OECD, in its Report on Pillar One, underlined that Amount B aims at approximating results determined under the ALP. Therefore, it would be based on comparable company benchmarking analyses under the TNMM with the quantum potentially varying by industry and region, provided that the relevant benchmarking analysis supports any such variation. Consequently, Amount B could result in several potentially appropriate fixed returns, each of which is intended to deliver a result that approximates results determined under the ALP.

The Report on Pillar One assumes that distributors within scope should be determined based on a narrow scope of core activities. However, some IF members (in particular developing countries) believe that the rule will be only useful in its policy objective if it has a broad scope and wish to explore broadening Amount B's scope. There is also interest in investigating the implementation of Amount B through an initial pilot program to measure how simplification benefits may be achieved.

Tax certainty

Tax certainty is a critical component of Pillar One. The criticality of this topic is, of course, strongly driven by the fact that Pillar One - especially through nexus rules and Amount A calculations - aims to reshuffle the profit attribution rationale in international tax law in parallel to the still existing traditional rules. This will of, course, result in complex interpretational issues regarding overlays of new rules and traditional rules as well as simple interpretational issues regarding the new rules on their own. Accordingly, the criticality of tax certainty goes hand in hand with a necessity for respective dispute prevention and resolution approaches.

In particular, as far as dispute prevention is concerned, the new taxing right will be ex ante determined by applying a formula to a newly defined tax base.[48] The Blueprint provides a mechanism that aims to ensure that the application of the new taxing right to a particular MNE group is agreed upon among all interested countries. A panel mechanism would be put in place for tax administrations working with the relevant MNEs to agree on:

- the tax base, in particular when there is business line segmentation;
- the result of the implementation of the formula; and

47. The definition of baseline marketing and distribution activities covers distributors that (i) buy from related parties and resell to unrelated parties; and (ii) have a routine distributor functionality profile.
48. Corresponding to a portion of the residual profit of large MNEs' in-scope activities.

- any other feature of the new taxing right, including the paying entities and elimination of double taxation.

The Blueprint also includes innovative dispute resolution mechanisms. Members of the IF agreed that in the event a dispute related to Amount A might arise that is not dealt with by the Amount A dispute prevention process, appropriate mandatory binding dispute resolution mechanisms will be developed. They also agreed to study mandatory binding timely dispute resolution mechanisms for disputes not related to the application of the new taxing right. These mechanisms should be respectful of jurisdictions' sovereignty with consideration paid to the case of certain developing economies with no or fewer numbers of Mutual Agreement Procedure (MAP) cases.

2.1.2.2 Report on the Pillar Two Blueprint

The Report on Pillar Two focuses on remaining BEPS challenges and proposes specific solutions designed to ensure that large, internationally operating businesses pay a minimum tax regardless of where they are headquartered or where they operate.[49]

In other to achieve this goal, some interlocking rules seek to:

(1) ensure minimum taxation while avoiding double taxation or taxation when there is no economic profit;
(2) deal with different tax system designs by jurisdictions as well as different operating models by businesses;
(3) ensure transparency and a level playing field; and
(4) minimize administrative and compliance costs.

There are still outstanding political and technical questions about the design of these pillars. As part of the ongoing work to develop a common solution, the OECD/G20 IF invited public comments on the Reports on the Pillar One and Pillar Two Blueprints. This public consultation meeting held on 14 and 15 January 2021 focused on the key questions identified in the consultation document and raised in the written submissions received as part of the consultation process. During the meeting, it was highlighted that, while it is true that these reports constitute the synthesis of convergent views on many of the critical principles, on the other hand, they try to identify policy issues when there is no consensus among IF members and focus on the remaining technical and administrative issues.[50]

The public consultation showed a common concern among contributors arising from the complexity of solutions provided in the reports. Consequently, the OECD must

49. Johnston, S.S. *OECD Now Aiming for Global Corporate Tax Reform Deal by Mid-2021*. 100 Tax Notes Int'l 344 (19 October 2020); OECD (2020), *infra* n. 51.
50. Orlandi, A., Iervolino R., Rizzo, A. *The Interplay Between FAR Analysis and AOA in a Digitalized Economy*. 32 Intl. Transfer Pricing J. 1 (2021), Journal Articles & Papers, accessed 5 January 2021.

further work to make the final product as simple as possible. The main criticalities that emerged from public consultation are the following:

(1) continued strong support for an international consensus-based solution with the removal of unilateral measures;
(2) uncertainty about policy objectives and principles;
(3) calls for greater simplifications;
(4) convergence on the technical parts on a number of the Amount A building blocks;
(5) NGOs consider the reform too narrow, in particular the amount of profit to be redistributed.

When considering the link between Pillar One and Pillar Two, a couple of considerations are worth mentioning. First, keeping the discussions on these projects linked to each other is complicating negotiations. Indeed, a solution could be to separately deal with, on the one hand, the digital economy-related issues and, on the other hand, whether there should be a minimum tax. Secondly, it could be affirmed that these projects are not actually facing digital companies. In this respect, it is crucial to find an accurate definition of what constitutes a digital company. According to the Economic Impact Assessment Report,[51] CFBs are now a major part of the pillars. Indeed, looking at the Economic Impact Assessment Report released by the OECD in October 2020 and assuming a 10% profitability threshold, it is easy to see that the total global residual profit in scope would amount to USD 493 billion, out of which only 16% is from ADSs, and 84% is from CFBs.[52] If a 20% profitability threshold is considered, the total global residual profit in scope will amount to USD 174 billion, out of which 22% is from ADSs, and 78% is from CFBs. Based on this data, it could be assumed that these projects are not about digitalization or tax avoidance but are really about the political willingness of allocating more profits to market jurisdictions, which is a policy decision.

For more information on Recent Developments on the Tax Challenges of the Digitalization of the Economy, please refer to Chapter 5 of this volume.

2.1.3 OECD Transfer Pricing Guidelines for Financial Transactions

In July 2018, the OECD released a Public Discussion Draft on BEPS Actions 8-10 on Financial Transactions (henceforth, Discussion Draft).[53] During 2019, Working Party 6

51. OECD, *Tax Challenges Arising from Digitalisation – Economic Impact Assessment: Inclusive Framework on BEPS*, OECD/G20 Base Erosion and Profit Shifting Project (Paris: OECD Publishing, 2020) https://doi.org/10.1787/0e3cc2d4-en.
52. OECD (2020), *supra* n. 51, p. 35, Table 2.3.
53. OECD, *Public Discussion Draft, BEPS Actions 8-10, Financial Transactions* (3 July-7 September 2018), available at https://www.oecd.org/tax/transfer-pricing/BEPS-actions-8-10-transfer-pricing-financial-transactions-discussion-draft-2018.pdf.

on the Taxation of MNE held several meetings to resolve the twenty-five areas of disagreements identified in the non-consensus Discussion Draft.[54]

On 12 February 2020, the OECD/G20 finally published a long-awaited TPGFT.[55] This document marks a significant development of the TPG that previously did not include any specific guidance on determining the arm's length nature of intra-group financial transactions. The TPGFT aims to help eliminate, to a certain extent, the transfer pricing disputes, inconsistencies, and unclarities around the pricing of financial arrangements. More specifically, the TPGFT clarifies the accurate delineation of the actual financial transaction concerning the characterization of the financing instruments as debt or loan, treasury functions, financial guarantees, captive insurance, and determining risk-free and risk-adjusted rates of return. The TPGFT's most likely significant changes on the pricing of intra-group loans compared to the Discussion Draft are the more elaborated clarifications on the use of credit ratings and the impact of a group membership.[56]

For a detailed analysis of the TPGFT, please refer to Chapter 1 of the Volume 'Transfer Pricing Development around the World 2020'.[57]

2.2 Transfer Pricing Developments at the EU

2.2.1 Digitalization of the Economy

On the one hand, the EU Commission welcomes the OECD's Blueprints for Pillar One and Pillar Two proposals for rebuilding corporate tax rules for an increasingly digital and globalized economy. On the other hand, it remains ready to take action if international talks fail.

In the speech of the Executive Vice-President Dombrovskis at the informal Economic and Financial Affairs Council of the European Union (ECOFIN) press conference of 12 October 2020, it was highlighted how 'large digital companies may emerge more profitable from the COVID-19 crisis and with a larger market share, while traditional businesses are bearing the brunt of the recession'. Moreover, the need was also expressed for global minimum taxation to secure much-needed tax revenues and ensure that everyone contributes their fair share.[58]

Finally, it was ensured that the commission would follow up on the work to the reform of the international corporate tax framework that is currently ongoing in the OECD and confirmed that, if consensus is not reached at the global level, the EU will

---

54. Martin, J. Agreement Reached on OECD Transfer Pricing Guidelines for Financial Transactions, Official Says MNE Tax, 8 June 2019, available at https://mnetax.com/final-financial-transaction-transfer-pricing-guidelines-expected-by-year-end-oecd-official-says-34225.
55. Transfer Pricing Guidance on Financial Transactions: Inclusive Framework on BEPS: Actions 4, 8-10.
56. van Herksen, M. et al. INSIGHT: New OECD Guidance on Transfer Pricing Aspects of Financial Transactions – Part 1 https://news.bloombergtax.com/transfer-pricing/insight-36.
57. Lang, M., Petruzzi, R. *Transfer Pricing Development Around the World*, Chapter 1. 2020. Kluwer Law International BV, The Netherlands.
58. https://ec.europa.eu/commission/presscorner/detail/en/speech_20_1636, accessed 17 January 2021.

move ahead with a digital tax proposal in the first half of 2021.[59] From a political perspective, of course, it is an understandable chess move by the EU to announce their own digital tax proposal in order to put pressure on the OECD to come up with a proper solution on a more global level. However, bearing in mind the international arena and the different economic players around the world, a 'unilateral' act by the EU might certainly also result in certain countermeasures by other states or trade blocks which naturally – legitimately – aim to secure their own tax revenues.

2.2.2 *Administrative Cooperation in the Field of Taxation*

2.2.2.1 *Council Directive (EU) 2018/822: DAC 6*

As part of new initiatives in the field of tax transparency at the level of the EU, Council Directive 2011/16/EU[60] has been subject to a series of amendments over the last few years. In this context, on 25 May 2018, Council Directive 2018/822/EU on mandatory automatic exchange of information (EOI) in the field of taxation in relation to reportable cross-border arrangements (DAC 6)[61] was adopted. DAC 6 aims to improve the functioning of the internal market by discouraging the use of aggressive cross-border tax planning arrangements and creating an environment of fair taxation in the European internal market by enhancing the automatic EOI regarding those potentially aggressive arrangements among the Member States.

DAC 6 became effective on 1 July 2020 with a specific reporting date of 31 August 2020 for arrangements between 25 June 2018 and 30 June 2020. However, due to COVID-19, on 24 June 2020, the European Council reached an agreement on an optional six-month deferral to the reporting deadlines for intermediaries or relevant taxpayers and a deferral to exchanging information until the beginning of 2021. Austria and Germany did not opt for the deferral.[62]

As far as transfer pricing is concerned, according to hallmark E, three kinds of transfer pricing arrangements fall under the scope of the new reporting obligations, namely, (i) arrangements that involve the use of unilateral safe harbour rules,[63]

59. Johnston, S.S. *EU Will Respect New OECD Deadline for Reaching Global Tax Deal.* 100 Tax Notes Int'l 427 (19 October 2020).
60. Council Directive 2011/16/EU of 15 February 2011 on administrative cooperation in the field of taxation and repealing Directive 77/799/EEC (OJ L 64, 11.3.2011, p. 1).
61. Council Directive (EU) 2018/822 of 25 May 2018 amending Directive 2011/16/EU regarding mandatory automatic exchange of information in the field of taxation in relation to reportable cross-border arrangements https://eur-lex.europa.eu/legal-content/EN/TXT/?uri=CELEX%3A32018L0822.
62. https://research.ibfd.org/#/hdoc?url=/home/content/dac6.
63. Hallmark E.1. of Directive 2018/822/EU states: 'An arrangement which involves the use of unilateral safe harbour rules.'

(ii) arrangements involving the transfer of hard-to-value-intangibles,[64] and (iii) arrangements involving an intra-group transfer of functions and/or risks and/or assets.[65]

All of the transfer pricing hallmarks laid down in DAC 6 are subject to various interpretational issues. First of all, regarding transfer pricing, DAC 6 seems to widely refer to wording laid down in the OECD TPG 2017 (e.g., regarding the notion of hard-to-value-intangibles). However, from a legal dogmatic perspective, it is questionable to what extent interpretational material of the OECD can be used to interpret an EU directive. Based on that, many EU Member States – when implementing DAC 6 into their domestic law – made explicit reference to the OECD TPG 2017 in order to ensure a common understanding of the transfer pricing terms used in DAC 6.

Besides the said general interpretational issue regarding the relevance of the OECD TPG 2017 for the interpretation of DAC 6, also numerous smaller interpretational issues arise. Regarding the safe harbour hallmark, it is a very legitimate question in which situations a safe harbour is even actually 'used'. What is more, the term 'safe' in safe harbour might underpin the interpretational position that a safe harbour is to be based on law and not just on any kind of administrative guidance by the tax authorities since it might otherwise not be 'safe'. Regarding the HTVI hallmark, plenty of interpretational difficulties of the OECD TPG 2017 automatically transfer themselves to the interpretation of DAC 6 and the respective domestic implementation laws; the 'business restructuring hallmark' is also subject to various qualitative (e.g., how to define the EBIT) and quantitative (e.g., how to calculate the 50% decrease in EBIT) interpretational difficulties.

In order to overcome some of the interpretational issues, plenty of the EU Member States made additional explanations (e.g., in the explanatory notes to the domestic implementation laws). For example, regarding the safe harbour hallmark, specific implementing laws or administrative explanations (e.g., Austria, Portugal, and the United Kingdom) state that only those safe harbours that are not included in the OECD TPG (e.g., the simplified approach) are to be considered as safe harbour rules in light of the reporting obligations.

2.2.2.2 DAC 7 Proposal

In November 2020, the EU reached a consensus on a proposal for another Council Directive amending Directive 2011/16/EU on administrative cooperation in the field of

64. Hallmark E.2. of Directive 2018/822/EU states: 'An arrangement involving the transfer of hard-to-value intangibles. The term "hard-to-value intangibles" covers intangibles or rights in intangibles for which, at the time of their transfer between associated enterprises: (a) no reliable comparables exist; and (b) at the time the transaction was entered into, the projections of future cash flows or income expected to be derived from the transferred intangible, or the assumptions used in valuing the intangible are highly uncertain, making it difficult to predict the level of ultimate success of the intangible at the time of the transfer.'
65. Hallmark E.3. of Directive 2018/822/EU states: 'An arrangement involving an intragroup cross-border transfer of functions and/or risks and/or assets, if the projected annual earnings before interest and taxes (EBIT), during the three-year period after the transfer, of the transferor or transferors, are less than 50 % of the projected annual EBIT of such transferor or transferors if the transfer had not been made.'

taxation requiring an automatic EOI on revenues generated by sellers on digital platforms (DAC 7). On 1 December 2020, the ECOFIN agreed to the EU Commission proposal's technical level and showed its support to DAC 7.[66] The provisions of the Directive are supposed to be effective starting 1 January 2023.

The purpose of the proposed Directive is two-fold:

(1) first, to ensure the effectiveness of the EOI and the cooperation between the Member States, amending certain existing provisions of Directive 2011/16/EU related to the EOI on request and including provisions to further clarify the framework for conducting joint audits; and
(2) extending the scope of application of the automatic EOI among the Member States to digital platform operators that will have to provide information to the competent tax authorities on income earned by sellers of goods and providers of services carrying out a reportable activity through the digital platform.

It is expected that once the EU Parliament and the EU Economic and Social Committee have submitted their opinions, the EU Council will adopt DAC 7.[67]

Meanwhile, the EU Commission is expected to publish a roadmap on DAC 8, which would focus on alternative means of payment and investment such as crypto assets.

2.2.3 Fiscal State Aid and Transfer Pricing

In 2020, the General Court of the European Union (GCEU) issued a landmark decision in the *Apple* case[68] for which it held that the EU Commission failed to show that Apple got a selective advantage from Ireland. This profit attribution case stemmed from the EU Commission's decision of 30 August 2016. In its decision, the EU Commission claimed that the tax rulings issued by the Irish tax authorities in 1991 and 2007[69] '*entailed a reduction in the amount of ASI and AOE's tax liability*' and, therefore, '*Ireland had renounced tax revenue, which had given rise to a loss of State resources.*'[70] Second, the contested tax rulings were liable to affect trade within the EU.[71] Thirdly, the contested tax rulings led to a reduction in Apple's Irish branches' tax bases, and, as

66. Rodriguez, B. *ECOFIN Agrees on DAC7 and Exchanges Views on International Tax Issues*. Report, 7 December 2020, IBFD available at https://research.ibfd.org/#/doc?url=/data/tns/docs/html/tns_2020-12-07_e2_1.html.
67. Lamer., E. *EU Hopes for Quick Agreement on DAC7, Prepares DAC8*. 100 Tax Notes Int'l 426 (9 October 2020).
68. General Court of the European Union, Judgment in Joined Cases T-778/16 and T-892/16 *Apple Sales International and Apple Operations Europe v. Commission*.
69. In favour of Apple Sales International (ASI) and Apple Operations Europe (AOE).
70. General Court of the European Union, Judgment in Joined Cases T-778/16 and T-892/16 *Apple Sales International and Apple Operations Europe v. Commission*, para. 27.
71. General Court of the European Union, Judgment in Joined Cases T-778/16 and T-892/16 *Apple Sales International and Apple Operations Europe v. Commission*, para. 28.

they were granted only to ASIs and AOEs, they constituted unlawful state aid in light of Article 107 TFEU.[72]

In conclusion, the EU Commission considered the APAs' methods of allocation of assets, functions, and risks to non-resident head offices as discretionary,[73] not compliant with the ALP principle, and lacking any factual or economic justification.[74] The GCEU annulled the EU Commission's decision because it failed to show to the requisite legal standard that there was a selective advantage for the purposes of Article 107(1) TFEU.[75] The decision of the GCEU was not just based on the interpretation of the ALP in light of the European state aid rules but also on applicable Irish (case) law regarding profit attribution to branches.

On 25 September 2020, Executive Vice-President, Margrethe Vestager, stated:

> The Commission has decided to appeal before the European Court of Justice the General Court's judgment of July 2020 on the Apple State aid case in Ireland, which annulled the Commission's Decision of August 2016 finding that Ireland granted illegal State aid to Apple through selective tax breaks. The General Court judgment raises important legal issues that are of relevance to the Commission in its application of State aid rules to tax planning cases. The Commission also respectfully considers that in its judgment the General Court has made a number of errors of law. For this reason, the Commission is bringing this matter before the European Court of Justice.[76]

On 8 October 2020, the CJEU issued its judgment following the request for a preliminary ruling on the interpretation of Articles 49 and 63 TFEU. The request was made in proceedings between *Impresa Pizzarotti & C SPA Italia Sucursala Cluj* and Romanian National Tax Administration Office regarding the annulment of a fiscal, administrative act issued by that office and the tax assessment based on that act.[77] In its decision, the CJEU affirmed:

> Article 49 TFEU must be interpreted as not precluding, in principle, legislation of a Member State under which a transfer of money from a resident branch to its parent company established in another Member State may be reclassified as a 'revenue-generating transaction', with the consequent obligation to apply the rules on transfer pricing, whereas, if the same transaction had been effected between a company branch and a parent company, both of which were established in the

72. General Court of the European Union, Judgment in Joined Cases T-778/16 and T-892/16 *Apple Sales International and Apple Operations Europe v. Commission*, para. 29.
73. *See* Sheppard, L. *EU Year in Review-National Sovereignty and Dividend Withholding Refunds*. 100 Tax Notes Int'l 1574 (21 December 2020).
74. *See* Morales, T. *Report: Apple Wins State Aid Case*. 15 July 2020, IBFD.
75. General Court of the European Union, Judgment in Joined Cases T-778/16 and T-892/16 *Apple Sales International and Apple Operations Europe v. Commission*, para. 507.
76. Statement by Executive Vice-President, Margrethe Vestager, on the Commission's Decision to appeal the General Court's judgment on the Apple tax State aid case in Ireland, 25 September 2020, Brussels https://ec.europa.eu/commission/presscorner/detail/en/STATEMENT_20_1746. Case before the European Court of Justice: C-465/20 P – *Commission v. Ireland and Others*.
77. Court of Justice of the European Union, Judgment in Case C-558/19, *Impresa Pizzarotti & C SPA Italia Sucursala Cluj v. Agenţia Naţionala de Administrare Fiscala – Direcţia Generala de Administrare a Marilor Contribuabili*, 8 October 2020.

same Member State, that transaction would not have been classified in the same way and the rules on transfer pricing would not have been applied.

On 3 December 2020, the Advocate General (AG) Kokott delivered her opinion on the EU Commission's 'aid scheme' case against *Belgium and Magnetrol International.* Two questions were at the heart of the appeal brought by the EU Commission against the judgment of the General Court:

(1) First, can the concept of an aid scheme within the meaning of Article 1(d) of Regulation 2015/1589/EU laying down detailed rules for the application of Article 108 TFEU also encompass a consistent administrative practice of authorities in a Member State?
(2) If so, what requirements are to be set in relation to the European Commission's task of demonstrating such a consistent administrative practice?

After a careful analysis of the legal framework and the facts of the case, AG Kokott affirmed that the CJEU should set aside the 2019 judgment of the General Court on the grounds that '*the Commission sufficiently demonstrated that the Belgian practice of making downward adjustments of the profits of undertakings forming part of a multinational group constitutes an aid scheme*'.[78]

Meanwhile, in 2020, the EU Commission continued to feature its activity around investigations into specific countries' TP practices and their compatibility under EU law in relation to the prohibition of state aid. It is worth noting that, in 2019, the EU Commission opened in-depth investigations to examine whether tax rulings granted by the Netherlands to Nike[79] and by Luxembourg to Huhtamaki[80] may have given those companies unfair advantages over their competitors, which is in breach of EU state aid rules. Furthermore, in September 2019, thirty-nine Belgian MNEs became a target of the EU Commission in a major investigation of the 'excess profits' tax rulings granted to these companies by Belgian tax authorities.[81] This investigation was followed by the General Court's Decision from February 2019[82] that annulled the Commission's earlier Decision concluding that the Belgian 'Excess Profit' tax scheme is not illegal.[83]

78. https://eur-lex.europa.eu/legal-content/EN/ALL/?uri=CELEX:62019CC0337.
79. EC: *State aid: Commission opens in-depth investigation into tax treatment of Nike in the Netherlands,* Press release, 10 January 2019 https://ec.europa.eu/commission/presscorner/detail/en/IP_19_322.
80. EC: *State aid: Commission opens in-depth investigation into tax treatment of Huhtamäki in Luxembourg,* Press release, 7 March 2019 https://ec.europa.eu/commission/presscorner/detail/en/IP_19_1591.
81. EC: *State aid: Commission opens in-depth investigations into individual 'excess profit' tax rulings granted by Belgium to 39 multinational companies,* 16 September 2019 https://ec.europa.eu/commission/presscorner/detail/en/IP_19_5578.
82. EC: *State aid: Commission concludes Belgian 'Excess Profit' tax scheme illegal; around €700 million to be recovered from 35 multinational companies,* Press release 11 January 2016 https://ec.europa.eu/commission/presscorner/detail/en/ip_16_42. Commission Decision (EU) 2016/1699 of 11 January 2016 on the excess profit exemption State aid scheme SA.37667 (2015/C) (ex 2015/N.N.) implemented by Belgium (OJ 2016 L 260, p. 61).
83. General Court of the European Union, Judgment in Joined Cases T-131/16 *Belgium v. Commission* and T-263/16 *Magnetrol International v. Commission.*

2.2.4 *EU 'Blacklist'*

On 6 October 2020, the Council of the EU (Council) adopted a revised list of non-cooperative jurisdictions, including Anguilla and Barbados, while the Cayman Islands and Oman were removed from the list after having passed the necessary reforms to improve their tax policy framework.[84] As a consequence, the current EU blacklist is composed of:[85]

- American Samoa;
- Anguilla;
- Barbados;
- Fiji;
- Guam;
- Palau;
- Panama;
- Samoa;
- Seychelles;
- Trinidad and Tobago;
- The US Virgin Islands; and
- Vanuatu.

Due to the COVID-19 pandemic, the Council decided to extend several deadlines for the relevant commitments. It also decided to remove Mongolia as well as Bosnia and Herzegovina from the so-called grey list after those countries deposited the instruments of ratification of the OECD Convention on Mutual Administrative Assistance in Tax Matters, as amended. The next revision is due in February 2021.

Chapter 2 of this volume will take a closer look at each transfer pricing case related to the EU Commission's investigation and the Court's Decision delivered in 2020, as well as practical transfer pricing aspects.

2.3 Transfer Pricing Developments at the UN

2.3.1 *The UN Practical Manual on Transfer Pricing for Developing Countries: Update*

In 2017, during the fifteenth session of the UN Committee of Experts on International Cooperation in Tax Matters, a new Subcommittee on Article 9 (Associated Enterprises)

84. https://www.consilium.europa.eu/en/press/press-releases/2020/10/06/eu-list-of-non-cooperative-jurisdictions-for-tax-purposes-anguilla-and-barbados-added-cayman-islands-and-oman-removed/.
85. https://eur-lex.europa.eu/legal-content/en/TXT/PDF/?uri=uriserv:OJ.C_.2020.331.01.0003.01.ENG.

Transfer Pricing was formed with the mandate to review and update the UN Practical Manual on Transfer Pricing for Developing Countries.[86]

The Subcommittee reports on its progress at the Committee's sessions and is expected to provide its final updated draft manual for discussion and adoption no later than the twenty-second session of the UN Committee meeting in 2021.

For detailed information about the work of the UN on the Practical Manual on Transfer Pricing for Developing Countries, please refer to Chapter 4.

2.3.2 *Update on Work on Taxation Issues Related to the Digitalization of the Economy*

In 2020, the UN also kept tackling the digital economy's challenges.

In October 2020, the UN proposed a new Article 12B in the UN Model Double Taxation Convention between Developed and Developing Countries on 'income from automated digital services'. According to the proposal, this type of income arising in a contracting state and paid to a resident of the other contracting state may be taxed in that other state (i.e., General Rule according to Article 12B(1) UN Model). However, in Article 12B(2), the provision states:

> income from automated digital services arising in a Contracting State may also be taxed in the Contracting State in which it arises and according to the laws of that State, but if the beneficial owner of the income is a resident of the other Contracting State, the tax so charged shall not exceed _ percent (the percentage is to be established through bilateral negotiations) of the gross amount of the income.

Based on that, a new source of taxation (market taxation) would be established based on the UN Model. The approach chosen by the UN can be seen as an alternative proposal vis-à-vis the OECD's Pillar One suggestions that more strongly focus on instruments that tend to be aligned with the currently applicable international tax landscape and might therefore also be easier to manage and to deal with by both taxpayers and tax administrations. Whereas the Pillar One suggestions introduce a complex system of allocating additional taxing rights and tax revenue to market jurisdictions based on scope, nexus, Amount A, and Amount B, the UN approach simply introduces a new 'source tax' for a specific type of income (i.e., ADS); the quantity of this source tax (i.e., the percentage of gross income) is to be bilaterally agreed between the contracting states.

For detailed information about the UN's work on taxation issues related to the digitalization of the economy, please refer to Chapter 4.

86. https://www.un.org/development/desa/financing/sites/www.un.org.development.desa.financing/files/2020-10/CRP40%20Transfer%20Pricing%20Manual%20Combined%20compressed.pdf.

2.4 Other Organizations

The year 2020 was not a groundbreaking year when it comes to TP developments, among other international organizations.

In September 2019, the Platform for Collaboration on Tax published a draft version of its Practical Toolkit to Support the Successful Implementation by Developing Countries of Effective Transfer Pricing Documentation Requirements.[87] The toolkit was designed to support the successful implementation of effective transfer pricing documentation requirements by developing countries. It was supposed to take into account measures concerning the documentation of all of the stages of a taxpayer's transfer pricing analysis that governments could put in place. On 19 January 2021, the final version of the 'Practical Toolkit to Support the Successful Implementation by Developing Countries of Effective Transfer Pricing Documentation Requirements' was released and serves as guidance on implementing transfer pricing documentation requirements for developing countries.

As declared in the *PCT Progress Report 2020*,[88] the OECD has incorporated the toolkits into its global relations program of multilateral training, and the approaches discussed in the Toolkit on Difficulties in Accessing Comparables Data for Transfer Pricing Analyses have been considered in the revision of the UN Practical Manual on Transfer Pricing for Developing Countries.

3 RECENT DEVELOPMENTS IN COUNTRIES SPECIFIC TRANSFER PRICING LEGISLATION, GUIDELINES, AND JURISPRUDENCE

In 2020, despite the COVID-19 pandemic, many countries intensified their efforts to frame implementation rules to align them with the OECD TPG.

This section summarizes critical recent developments in country-specific transfer pricing legislation, administrative guidelines, and case law. These developments have been broadly identified in relation to the following topics:

- ALP and transfer pricing methods.
- Digitalization of the economy.
- Intangibles.
- Transfer pricing.
- Documentation.
- Country-by-Country (CbC) reporting.
- Dispute resolution.
- Other developments.
- Significant domestic case law.

87. http://documents.worldbank.org/curated/en/505481569449944639/Practical-Toolkit-to-Support-the-Successful-Implementation-by-Developing-Countries-of-Effective-Transfer-Pricing-Documentation-Requirements, accessed 19 December 2019.
88. Platform for Collaboration on Tax. PCT Progress Report 2020, p. 19 https://www.tax-platform.org/sites/pct/files/publications/Platform-for-Collaboration-on-Tax-PCT-Progress-Report-2020.pdf, accessed 6 January 2021.

3.1 ALP and Transfer Pricing Methods

In 2020, again, several countries worked on the application of the ALP (or, more specifically, on the application of transfer pricing methods) in their jurisdictions. Perhaps most importantly, three countries can be mentioned as those that introduced the most significant amendments – Vietnam, Germany, and Mongolia.

In particular, Vietnam revised its transfer pricing rules and replaced its earlier guidance, publishing Decree No. 132/2020/NĐ-CP (5 November 2020). The decree introduced a new arm's length range and defined the standard arm's length range to be the 35th to 75th percentile value derived from at least five independent comparables.[89]

On 3 December 2020, the German Ministry of Finance issued the Administrative Principles 2020 and reinterpreted the ALP following the revision of the OECD TPG. In particular, German tax authorities are allowed to select the most appropriate transfer pricing method to test the arm's length nature of transfer prices and perform the arm's length test based on data that becomes known later (price-testing dimension). On the other hand, taxpayers are allowed to perform the arm's length test based on data available at the time of agreeing (price-setting dimension) and on the basis of data that becomes known at a later point in time (price-testing dimension). As noticed by some practitioners,[90] this aspect could raise the concern that German tax authorities may argue for a transfer pricing adjustment even when the taxpayer prepares contemporaneous transfer pricing documentation.[91]

Mongolia revised its rules on corporate taxation, which also includes the introduction of dealing at arm's length between related parties.[92] Tax authorities were given the power to adjust the transaction to a fair market value should the parties have failed to deal at arm's length.

On 6 November 2020, Thailand's Minister of Finance published Ministerial Regulation No. 369. This regulation prescribes certain rules, conditions, and methods for tax officers to assess or adjust the income and expenses of taxpayers who engage in related-party transactions but do not comply with the ALP.[93]

On 14 December 2020, Rwanda introduced new general rules on transfer pricing aiming to be in line with the OECD TPG.[94]

89. https://home.kpmg/us/en/home/insights/2020/12/tnf-vietnam-transfer-pricing-rules-are-updated.html, accessed 13 January 2021.
90. https://globaltaxnews.ey.com/news/2020-6588-german-ministry-of-finance-issues-new-administrative-principles-regarding-examination-of-income-allocation-between-internationally-associated-enterprises, accessed 17 January 2021.
91. https://home.kpmg/us/en/home/insights/2020/02/tnf-germany-arms-length-principle-rules-proposed-amendments.html, accessed 17 January 2021.
92. https://www.ey.com/gl/en/services/tax/international-tax/alert--mongolia-amends-its-transfer-pricing-regulations, accessed 7 January 2020.
93. https://home.kpmg/us/en/home/insights/2020/11/tnf-thailand-new-transfer-pricing-regulation.html, accessed 17 January 2021.
94. https://www.lexology.com/library/detail.aspx?g = 5915ee23-b1eb-4354-b47c-7d2fe339a8d0, accessed 17 January 2021.

3.2 Taxation of the Digital Economy

Taxation of the digital economy continues to be a hot topic at both international and domestic levels and has resulted in numerous countries initiating or approving relevant works in this field. European countries have been heavily involved in the introduction of relevant regimes[95] and, in general, prefer to introduce their solutions unilaterally rather than waiting for a multilateral compromise at the OECD or EU level so far. In case a solution to cope with the challenges of the digital economy on an OECD or EU level can be found, unilateral rules might again be abolished.

At the time of the preparation of this chapter (i.e., February 2021), the following countries have implemented a DST: Austria, France, Hungary, Italy. Poland, Spain, Turkey, and the United Kingdom.

At the time of the preparation of this chapter (i.e., February 2021), the following countries have published proposals to enact a DST: Belgium, the Czech Republic, and Slovakia.

At the time of the preparation of this chapter (i.e., February 2021), the following countries have either officially announced or shown intentions to implement such a tax: Latvia, Norway, and Slovenia.

The following table shows the recent developments on DSTs and other direct and indirect taxes in the EU.

95. Asen, E. Announced, Proposed, and Implemented Digital Services Taxes in European OECD Countries, as of 14 October 2020 https://taxfoundation.org/digital-tax-europe-2020/, accessed 17 January 2021.

Table 1.3 Recent Developments on DSTs and Other Direct and Indirect Taxes in the EU

Country	*Tax Rate*	*Scope*	*Global Revenue Threshold*	*Domestic Revenue Threshold*	*Status*
Austria[96]	5%	Revenues from advertising services on digital interfaces or any type of software or websites rendered in Austria	EUR 750 million (USD 840 million)	EUR 25 million (USD 28 million)	*Enacted* Effective from 1 January 2020
Belgium[97]	*Proposed – Waiting for global solutions*				
Bulgaria	–				
Cyprus	–				
Croatia	–				
Czech Republic[98]	5%	Targeted advertising Use of multilateral digital interfaces	EUR 750 million (USD 840 million)	CZK 100 million (USD 4 million)	*Proposed* Delayed until 2021 to wait for agreement at the OECD level
		Provision of user data (additional thresholds apply)			

96. https://www.ris.bka.gv.at/Dokumente/BgblAuth/BGBLA_2019_I_91/BGBLA_2019_I_91.html; bmf.gv.at/en/topics/taxation/digital-tax-act.html, accessed 17 January 2021.
97. https://taxfoundation.org/country/belgium, accessed 17 January 2021.
98. https://taxfoundation.org/country/czech-republic, accessed 17 January 2021.

Country	*Tax Rate*	*Scope*	*Global Revenue Threshold*	*Domestic Revenue Threshold*	*Status*
Denmark[99]	Danish Prime Minister announced Denmark's support to an EU-wide agreement on the DST controversy in case a global consensus is not reached				
Estonia	Rejected The parliament rejected the proposal to impose new reporting obligations for operators of digital platforms.				
Finland	*Waiting for global solutions*				
France[100]	3 %	Provision of a digital interface Advertising services based on users' data	EUR 750 million (USD 840 million)	EUR 25 million (USD 28 million)	*Enacted* Retroactively applicable as of 1 January 2019
Germany	*Rejected* The German Federal Ministry of Finance and the Finance Ministries of the German states have decided that withholding tax should not be imposed on payments for digital advertising services				
Greece[101]	*Enacted* General income tax on digital short-term rental services incomes; Income from short-term rentals in the sharing economy through digital platforms				

99. https://www.bloomberg.com/news/articles/2020-01-28/frederiksen-says-denmark-supports-eu-wide-deal-on-digital-tax, accessed 17 January 2021.
100. https://www.legifrance.gouv.fr/jorf/id/JORFTEXT000038811588/, accessed 17 January 2021.
101. Greece – Tax treatment of income earned in the context of sharing economy through digital platforms (22 July 2019), News IBFD.

Country	*Tax Rate*	*Scope*	*Global Revenue Threshold*	*Domestic Revenue Threshold*	*Status*
Hungary[102]	7.5%	Advertising revenue	HUF 100 million (USD 344,000)	N/A	*Enacted* As a temporary measure, the advertisement tax rate has been reduced to 0%, effective from 1 July 2019 through 31 December 2022
Ireland	–				
Italy[103]	3%	Advertising on a digital interface Multilateral digital interface that allows users to buy/sell goods and services; transmission of user data generated from using a digital interface	EUR 750 million (USD 840 million)	EUR 5.5 million (USD 6 million)	*Enacted* Effective from January 2020
Latvia[104]	*Announced/Shows Intentions* The Latvian Government commissioned a study to determine the increase of tax revenue based on the assumption that the country levies a 3% DST				
Lithuania	–				

102. https://taxfoundation.org/country/hungary/, accessed 17 January 2021.
103. https://www.gazzettaufficiale.it/eli/id/2019/01/18/19A00318/sg, accessed 17 January 2021.
104. https://taxfoundation.org/country/latvia/, accessed 17 January 2021.

Country	*Tax Rate*	*Scope*	*Global Revenue Threshold*	*Domestic Revenue Threshold*	*Status*
Luxembourg	–				
Malta	–				
Netherlands	–				
Poland[105]	1.5%	Audiovisual media service and audiovisual commercial communication	–	–	*Implemented* Effective from July 2020
Portugal	–				
Romania[106]	Announced/Shows Intentions Romania had published a decision approving the EU proposal on the corporate taxation of significant digital presence, but no further steps have been taken since that moment				
Slovakia[107]	Proposed The Ministry of Finance opened a consultation on a proposal to introduce a DST on revenue of non-residents from the provision of services such as advertising, online platforms, and sale of user data; however, there were no further steps taken, and none of the political parties has put forward digital tax as their priority agenda				
Slovenia[108]	Announced/Shows Intentions The ministry of finance announced a government proposal to submit a draft bill to the national assembly introducing a DST by 1 April 2020; however, there has been no development so far				

105. https://taxfoundation.org/country/poland, accessed 17 January 2021.
106. Romania – European Commission proposals on taxation of digital economy – Parliament decisions published (12 June 2016) News IBFD.
107. https://taxfoundation.org/country/slovak-republic/, accessed 17 January 2021.
108. https://taxfoundation.org/country/slovenia, accessed 17 January 2021.

Country	*Tax Rate*	*Scope*	*Global Revenue Threshold*	*Domestic Revenue Threshold*	*Status*
Spain[109]	3%	Online advertising services; Sale of online advertising; Sale of user data	EUR 750 million	EUR 3 million	Enacted Effective from 1 January 2021
Sweden	Waiting for global solutions				

109. https://www.hacienda.gob.es/Documentacion/Publico/GabineteMinistro/Notas%20Prensa/2019/CONSEJO%20DE%20MINISTROS/18-01-19%20NP%20IMPUESTOS%20ITF%20e%20IDSD.pdf, accessed 17 January 2021.

The following table shows the recent developments on DSTs and other indirect taxes in the rest of the world.

Table 1.4 Recent Developments on DSTs and Other Indirect Taxes in the Rest of the World

Country	*Status*	*Latest Development*	*Description*
African Tax Administration Forum (ATAF)	Proposed	11 October 2020	The ATAF has announced a paper on the 'Suggested Approach to Drafting Digital Services Tax Legislation'
Argentina[110]	Enacted	23 December 2019	Resident individuals and legal entities are subject to a temporary tax (PAIS) on the acquisition of goods and services from non-resident persons. The PAIS applies at a rate of 30% or 8% to digital services
	Enacted	28 December 2020	Effective 15 December 2020, a 5% tax is imposed on bets made through a digital platform in or from Argentina. The standard tax rate is increased to 10% when a non-resident participates directly or indirectly in the exploitation of the gambling platform and to 15% when the non-resident is in a non-cooperative or low/no tax jurisdiction
Australia[111]	Announced	20 March 2019	Australia will not proceed with an interim measure for the taxation of the digital economy

110. https://www.taxnotes.com/tax-notes-international/digital-economy/taxation-digital-services-argentina/2020/10/05/2czbk, accessed 17 January 2021.
111. https://treasury.gov.au/consultation/c2018-t306182, accessed 17 January 2021.

Country	*Status*	*Latest Development*	*Description*
Brazil[112]	Proposed	4 May 2020	Brazil proposed to introduce a DST on digital revenue from advertising to Brazilian users making a digital platform available that permits users to interact with the objective of the sale of goods or services directly between such users if one user is located in Brazil and transfer of data from users located in Brazil collected during the use of a digital platform or generated by these users. The tax would apply to legal entities domiciled in Brazil or abroad with previous-year global revenues exceeding BRL 3 billion and with gross revenue in Brazil that exceeds BRL 100 million. Brazil's DST will be levied progressively with 1 % levied on amounts up to BRL 150 million; 3 % on amounts exceeding BRL 150 million and under BRL 300 million; and 5 % on the amount exceeding BRL 300 million
	Proposed	7 July 2020	On 19 August 2020, a bill was submitted to the chamber of deputies. The bill would create a contribution on digital services (Contribuição Social Sobre Serviços Digitais, CSSD) to be levied on gross revenue derived by resident and non-resident companies from digital services targeting the Brazilian market provided that they belong to a group with annual global revenue exceeding BRL 4.5 billion. The CSSD would be levied at a 3 % rate upon the receipt of revenue from: – the display of advertisements on a digital platform for users located in Brazil;

112. https://www.ey.com/en_gl/tax-alerts/brazilian-congressman-proposes-digital-services-tax, accessed 17 January 2021.

Country	*Status*	*Latest Development*	*Description*
			– making digital platforms available that allow users to contact and interact with each other to sell goods or provide services directly between each other, provided that one of the users is located in Brazil; and – the transmission of data from users located in Brazil that has been generated by such users or collected while they were using digital platforms.
Cambodia	announced	11 January 2021	The Cambodian Government has already signalled a willingness to consider ways to tax cross-border digital activity. However, the nature of the tax is unclear
Canada	announced	30 November 2020	The government expressed the willingness to introduce a federal 3 % DST on the income of specific digital economy sectors
Chile	rejected	14 January 2020	The proposal to introduce a 10 % digital tax on foreign platforms' digital services has been abandoned
China	announced	17 November 2020	The government should conduct an in-depth study to determine whether a DST based on the concept that users create value should be implemented
Mexico	Enacted	1 June 2020	Payments for non-residents for certain digital services such as downloads or access to images, movies, text, information, video, audio, music, games (including gambling), other multimedia content, multiplayer environments, mobile tones, online news, traffic information, weather forecasts and statistics, online clubs, dating websites, and long-distance teaching or testing

Country	Status	Latest Development	Description		
Norway[113]	Announced/Shows Intentions Norway plans to introduce a unilateral measure in 2021 if the OECD did not reach a consensus solution in 2020				
Turkey[114]	7.5%	Online services including advertisements, sales of content, and paid services on social media websites	EUR 750 million (USD 840 million)	TRY 20 million (USD 4 million)	Enacted Effective from March 2020; the president can reduce the DST rate as low as 1% or increase it as much as 15%
United Kingdom[115]	2%	Social media platforms; Internet search engine; Online marketplace	GBP 500 million (USD 638 million)	GBP 25 million (USD 32 million)	Enacted Retroactively applicable as of 1 April 2020
Vietnam[116]	The DST Communiqué was published in the Official Gazette of 20 March 2020. The Communiqué describes the implementation of the DST, which came into force by Law No. 7194, applicable from 1 March 2020, and the determination of its procedures and principles. The main features of the Communiqué are as follows:				

113. https://taxfoundation.org/country/norway, accessed 17 January 2021.
114. https://taxfoundation.org/country/turkey, accessed 17 January 2021.
115. https://www.gov.uk/government/publications/introduction-of-the-digital-services-tax/digital-services-tax, accessed 17 January 2021.
116. https://research.ibfd.org/#/doc?url=/data/tns/docs/html/tns_2020-03-23_tr_2.html, accessed 14 January 2021.

Country	*Status*	*Latest Development*	*Description*
	– the subject of tax, definitions, taxpayer and tax responsibilities; – exemption; – the tax base, tax rate and calculation of the tax base; and – the taxation period, declaration date and payment of tax and tax security.The Communiqué applies retroactively from 1 March 2020.		

Various states worldwide seem interested in introducing DSTs or other tax measures to catch revenues from digital economies. So far, however, it seems that proposed solutions tend to be very country-specific. Therefore, there is much hope in the work conducted by the OECD or the UN to develop a unified solution that could find its application in jurisdictions around the world, preventing possible confusion over entirely different concepts in diverse states.

3.3 Intangibles

After much attention being paid to intangibles in the transfer pricing context in recent years, the year 2020 turned out to be definitely calmer in that regard.

Ghana issued transfer pricing regulations for 2020. Among the other developments, the new regulations introduce an additional requirement in assessing the arm's length nature of charges and fees for the use of intangible assets in line with BEPS's guidance on hard-to-value intangibles.[117]

Taiwan revised its transfer pricing regulations, including more detailed guidance on the allocation of risk, intangible transfers, comparability, and penalties.[118] As far as intangibles are concerned, Article 4 came into force. This provision defines key terms used throughout the regulations. In 2020, it was revised to align the definition of an intangible asset with the one introduced by BEPS Actions 8-10 and added to Chapter 6 of the OECD TPG. The provision now specifies that compensation is required when any asset other than tangible property that can be *'owned or controlled for use in commercial activities'* is used or transferred to a related party.

On 19 November 2020, Sweden added updates to its DAC 6 guidance covering, among other topics: cash pooling participation and the ALP; transactions under unilateral safe harbour rules for TP purposes; transfers of hard-to-value intangibles between related parties; and cross-border transfers of functions, risks, and/or assets.[119]

3.4 Documentation

The increasing importance of documentation for TP was visible in the activities of various jurisdictions also in 2020. New requirements were introduced around the world in both developing and developed economies.

Effective from 1 January 2020, Bulgaria officially requires the submission of transfer pricing documentation. Both the Master File and the Local File can be required depending on the fulfilment of various conditions (i.e., thresholds of the net book value

117. https://home.kpmg/us/en/home/insights/2020/12/tnf-ghana-transfer-pricing-regulations-2020.html, accessed 17 January 2021.
118. Finally, R. *Taiwan Updates Transfer Pricing Rules on Intangibles and Risk*. Tax Notes Int'l, 83 (4 January 2021). *See also* https://www.mof.gov.tw/singlehtml/384fb3077bb349ea973e7fc6f13b6974?cntId=3a16ebc090a14e9f8b59417d58233b79, accessed 5 January 2021; https://www.taxathand.com/article/15178/Taiwan/2020/Proposed-amendments-to-transfer-pricing-guidelines-for-intangible-assets-announced, accessed 17 January 2021.
119. https://www2.deloitte.com/content/dam/Deloitte/lu/Documents/tax/operationaltaxnews/lu-otn-dac6-barometer-issue7.pdf, accessed 6 January 2021.

of assets, average number of personnel being part of a multinational group).[120] Furthermore, due to COVID-19, Bulgaria extended the deadline for transfer pricing documentation.

On 3 December 2020, the Danish Parliament passed a bill that requires taxpayers to submit both the Master File and Local File to the Danish tax authority annually no later than sixty days after the tax return deadline.[121]

On 23 November 2020, following and completing the Ministerial Decree of 14 May 2018 (Ministerial Decree), the Italian tax authority issued new guidelines for preparing Italian TP documentation, replacing the old version published in 2010 and making them more compliant with the OECD TPG.[122] This provision introduces significant changes to the rules related to the appropriate TP documentation that must be prepared to support the application of the ALP to an intercompany transaction. In particular, the following amendments are worth mentioning:

- the obligation to prepare both the Local File and the Master File has been extended to all resident entities belonging to MNE groups, also including subsidiaries of foreign headquartered MNEs;
- the structure of the Local File and the Master File has been amended to comply with the OECD TPG;
- specific documentation requirements have been introduced for low value-adding services for which the taxpayer decides to apply the simplified approach envisaged by the Ministerial Decree;
- it is possible to delimit the perimeter of transactions to be included under the documentation requirements, but, as a consequence, the penalty protection will be granted exclusively concerning the transactions that have been described and for which the information provided is considered compliant with the requirements;
- the tax authorities' different opinions on the method applied by the taxpayer cannot lead to qualification of the documentation as 'non-compliant'. The deadline for providing the transfer pricing documentation after a formal request by the tax administration has been extended to twenty days.

From 1 January 2021, Malaysia's transfer pricing legislation is amended by the Finance Act 2020. In particular, among other changes, penalties are introduced as a consequence of the failure to provide transfer pricing documentation within thirty days after a written request by the tax authorities.[123]

120. https://www.ey.com/gl/en/services/tax/international-tax/alert--bulgaria-adopts-mandatory-transfer-pricing-documentation, accessed 17 January 2021.
121. https://home.kpmg/us/en/home/insights/2020/12/tnf-denmark-new-requirement-annual-submission-transfer-pricing-documentation.html, accessed 17 January 2021.
122. https://www.agenziaentrate.gov.it/portale/documents/20143/2794495/Provv_prot_0360494_del_23112020.pdf/87a55907-b275-a3b5-1bc7-a6e316b70fef.
123. Other important changes concern a surcharge of not more than 5% to be imposed on transfer pricing adjustments and the possibility for the tax authorities to disregard the structure in a controlled transaction if its form is inconsistent with the transaction's economic substance

3.5 CbC Reporting

On 17 October 2020, the third annual peer review of the CbC report was published.[124] The peer review of the Action 13 Minimum Standard proceeded in stages with three annual reviews in 2017, 2018, and 2019. The peer-review process focused on three critical elements of the minimum standard:

(1) the domestic legal and administrative framework;
(2) the EOI framework; and
(3) the confidentiality and appropriate use of CbC reports.

The implementation of CbC reporting is well underway as the peer-review process proves that over 90 jurisdictions have now introduced an obligation for relevant MNE groups to file a CbC report in their domestic legal framework. This third annual peer-review report reflects the third review outcome that considered all aspects of implementation. It contains the review of 131 jurisdictions that provided legislation or information about the CbC reporting implementation. The peer review of the Action 13 minimum standard is an annual process; therefore, work will continue to monitor the implementation and operation of CbC reporting by IF members and highlight progress made by jurisdictions to address the recommendations that are made.[125]

On 1 October 2020, Turkey approved and published the 'CbC Multilateral Competent Authority Agreement on the Exchange of Country-by-Country Reports' (CbC MCAA) and is therefore considered a signatory state as of 30 December 2019. Accordingly, the automatic exchange of CbC reports will be performed between competent authorities of countries that are signatory parties to the CbC MCAA.[126]

On 16 December 2020, Peru's tax administration published new information regarding the filing of CbC reports for 2017, 2018, and 2019. In general, CbC reports must be filed by subsidiaries of MNE groups with consolidated revenues of more than approximately USD 800 million. There is an exception only for the year 2019 if the ultimate parent company is located in one of the fifty-eight countries with which Peru has an agreement to exchange CbC reports to the extent that the parent company has already filed this report in its residence state prior to the CbC filing deadline in Peru.[127]

---

https://home.kpmg/us/en/home/insights/2021/01/tnf-malaysia-transfer-pricing-measures-enacted.html, accessed 13 January 2021.

124. https://www.oecd.org/tax/beps/country-by-country-reporting-compilation-of-peer-review-reports-phase-3-fa6d31d7-en.htm.

125. https://www.oecd-ilibrary.org/docserver/fa6d31d7-en.pdf?expires=1609957040&id=id&accname=guest&checksum=16B0401B0E068915B2257C59207EB3D7.

126. https://home.kpmg/us/en/home/insights/2020/12/tnf-turkey-cbc-reporting-automatic-exchanges-cbc-mcaa.html, accessed 17 January 2021.

127. https://home.kpmg/us/en/home/insights/2020/12/tnf-peru-guidance-for-filing-country-by-country-reports-for-2017-2018-and-2019.html, accessed 17 January 2021.

3.6 Dispute Resolution

Dispute prevention and dispute resolution remain areas of interest for tax authorities around the world. The year 2020 proved to be meaningful for the regulations in the area of APAs as well as MAPs.

As shown by the 2019 MAP statistics,[128] the number of open cases, as well as closed ones, keeps increasing. As far as open cases are concerned, approximately 2,700 new MAP cases were started in 2019 (+ 20% for transfer pricing cases and + 10% for other cases). This amounts to almost seven new cases per day in 2019, among which there are three transfer pricing cases. The OECD does not expect a significant reduction in MAP activity despite the COVID-19 pandemic and explains that this trend is driven by several factors, including increased globalization and growing confidence in and knowledge of MAPs.

In 2019, competent authorities were able to close 50% more transfer pricing cases compared to 2016; however, the increased number of closed cases still cannot keep up with the increased number of new cases. As a result, the inventories are increasing in the majority of jurisdictions.

As far as the outcomes are concerned, MAP statistics showed a general positive trend: around 85% of the MAPs concluded for transfer pricing cases in 2019 fully resolved the issue (compared to 80% in 2018), reflecting an improvement in the collaborative approach taken by competent authorities. Cases still take a long time to be resolved. On average, MAP cases closed in 2019 lasted for thirty-one months in the transfer pricing area.

Japan and the United Kingdom succeeded in closing transfer pricing cases within the shortest time[129] while Belgium 'won' the 2019 MAP awards for the smallest proportion of pre-2016 cases in end inventory[130] and, together with Norway, for the most effective caseload management.[131] The collaborative award for the pairs of jurisdictions that dealt most effectively with their joint transfer pricing caseload was India-Japan, followed by Italy-Spain.[132]

On 24 December 2020, Russia's federal tax authority announced the conclusion of the bilateral APA with the Finnish tax administration concerning controlled export transactions of the taxpayer in relation to its delivery of products to Finland.[133]

On 14 December 2020, Her Majesty's Revenue & Customs confirmed that, after Brexit, the United Kingdom would not be a party to the EU Arbitration Convention and, therefore, MAP requests under the EU Arbitration Convention will not be accepted after

128. http://www.oecd.org/tax/dispute/mutual-agreement-procedure-statistics.htm.
129. http://www.oecd.org/tax/dispute/mutual-agreement-procedure-2019-awards.htm#category1.
130. http://www.oecd.org/tax/dispute/mutual-agreement-procedure-2019-awards.htm#category2.
131. http://www.oecd.org/tax/dispute/mutual-agreement-procedure-2019-awards.htm#category3.
132. http://www.oecd.org/tax/dispute/mutual-agreement-procedure-2019-awards.htm#category4.
133. https://home.kpmg/us/en/home/insights/2021/01/tnf-russia-first-bilateral-apa-concluded.html, accessed 17 January 2021.

2020. On the other hand, mandatory binding arbitration is currently available under a number of the United Kingdom's tax treaties with the EU Member States.[134]

The 2021 Italian Budget Law amended the existing rules for APAs introducing the possibility of extending the effects of APAs under certain circumstances and retroactively include one or more fiscal years still open for assessment under the applicable statute of limitations. Furthermore, it has been stated that enterprises must pay a fee to access the APA process.[135]

On 3 December 2020, the Australian Taxation Office released an updated law administration practice statement[136] regarding the APA program. The updated guidance reflects changes to the APA decision-making process and improved governance across certain stages of the APA process.[137]

According to China's APA annual report for 2019,[138] the number of agreed and signed APAs in 2019 reflects a historical high and reveals new trends in terms of industry types, transaction types, and transfer pricing methods involved in the concluded APA cases.

3.7 Other Developments

In 2021, the MLI enters into force for the following countries: Albania, Bosnia and Herzegovina, Burkina Faso, Chile, Costa Rica, Egypt, Germany, Jordan, Pakistan, and Panama.[139]

In 2020, specific countries worked intensively on remodelling their TP rules. Among the countries with the most important developments are Botswana, Brazil, Ireland, and Poland.

On its way to a full OECD membership, Brazil decided to harmonize its transfer pricing rules with the OECD TP Guidelines. The project foresees two options to achieve this goal – either immediate alignment of the Brazilian rules with the OECD standards or the alignment in stages, allowing a gradual implementation over a more extended time.[140] On 30 July 2020, the OECD and Brazil's Federal Revenue Authority launched a survey to seek public input in order to understand the specific situations and needs of taxpayers and inform the work related to the development of safe harbours as well

134. https://home.kpmg/us/en/home/insights/2020/12/tnf-uk-map-requests-eu-arbitration-convention-no-longer-accepted-after-2020.html, accessed 6 January 2021.
135. Law 30.12-2020, n. 178, Article 1, para. 1101 https://www.gazzettaufficiale.it/atto/stampa/serie_generale/originario.
136. PS LA 2015/4 Advance Pricing Arrangements. https://www.ato.gov.au/law/view/document?docid=PSR/PS20154/NAT/ATO/00001&PiT=20201203000001.
137. https://home.kpmg/us/en/home/insights/2020/12/tnf-australia-updated-guidance-apas.html, accessed 5 January 2021.
138. http://www.chinatax.gov.cn/chinatax/n810214/n810606/c5157990/5157990/files/2c57f30f874b404186444d529ad62f61.pdf, accessed 5 January 2021.
139. Signatories and Parties to the Multilateral Convention to Implement Tax Treaty Related Measures to Prevent Base Erosion and Profit Shifting. Status as of 18 December 2020 https://www.oecd.org/tax/treaties/beps-mli-signatories-and-parties.pdf, accessed 5 January 2021.
140. https://home.kpmg/us/en/home/insights/2019/07/tnf-brazil-project-to-align-brazils-transfer-pricing-rules-to-oecd-guidelines.html, accessed 8 January 2020.

as other simplification measures and measures that can contribute to enhanced tax certainty.

3.8 Significant Domestic Case Law

In 2020, a few significant domestic cases were issued while other investigations were still ongoing.

Australia

On 6 November 2020, the Australian Full Federal Court ruled in favour of *Glencore Investment Pty Ltd.*[141] The case concerned the transfer prices that Glencore used on certain cross-border related-party transactions associated with its copper mining operations. The court stated that it was correct that the taxpayer started the analysis for the actual transaction with its Swiss-based trading entity as similar relations to the case at hand were also present in independent companies' practice.

Canada

On 26 June 2020, the Canadian Federal Court of Appeal, rejecting the revenue agency's arguments, upheld the 2018 decision of the Canadian Tax Court[142] in *Cameco Corporation, Canadian Federal Court of Appeal.*[143] In particular, the court stated that it had not been shown that the arrangements between Cameco Corp. and its Swiss subsidiary would not have been entered into by arm's length parties. This case has been the first to consider the recharacterization provision in Canada's Income Tax Act. On 30 October 2020, the tax administration announced that it would appeal the decision to the Supreme Court.[144]

New Zealand

In *Oracle Corp. NZ*, the inland revenue department issued an NZD 20.3 million (around USD 14.4 million) tax assessment covering the 2013-2015 income years. While the company considers the inland revenue department's claims to be baseless and has challenged the high court assessment, it has also stated that it is working with that department to explore remedies to resolve the matter. The dispute followed other assessments issued to major US tech companies' affiliates in the last few years.[145]

141. https://www2.deloitte.com/au/en/pages/tax/articles/glencore-wins-transfer-pricing-case-in-full-federal-court-decision.html; https://www2.deloitte.com/au/en/pages/tax/articles/glencore-wins-transfer-pricing-case-in-full-federal-court-decision.html, accessed 17 January 2021.
142. 2018 TCC 195.
143. Case No. 2020 FCA 112.
144. Beeton, D. *Transfer Pricing Cases of 2020: Case Summaries*. Daily Tax Report (15 January 2021).
145. In 2020, a New Zealand affiliate of Cisco Systems Inc. recorded an NZD 4.7 million charge for the settlement of a transfer pricing audit by the IRD while, in 2019, Microsoft New Zealand Ltd. settled a long-running TP dispute with the IRD by paying NZD 24.7 million in back taxes.

United States[146]

In US *Altera* dealing with stock-based compensation – and, in particular, on whether it must be included in a cost-sharing payment – the US Supreme Court declined to issue a writ of certiorari and let the government's favourable decision stand.[147]

Coca-Cola involved the remuneration of Coke Supply Points, offshore manufacturing operations that are principally responsible for mixing the flavours that Coke sells to third party bottlers around the world. Based on the 1996 closing agreement (covering the years 1987-1995 but applied by Coke also for the following years), the Supply Points received a 10% operating margin and then split the remaining residual 50:50 with Coke. The IRS, with the 2007-2009 audit cycle, challenged the 10:50:50 methodology. The tax court agreed with the IRS and rejected Coke's arguments.

The Whirlpool decision involved both the US CFC regime and transfer pricing issues. In particular, as a result of the 2007-2009 restructuring of its Mexican manufacturing operations, Whirlpool used the 'Mexican maquiladora regime' to have Whirlpool Luxembourg as the manufacturer of appliances in Mexico and a disregarded Mexican subsidiary benefitting from tax incentives in Mexico. Additionally, in this case, the tax court ruled in favour of the IRS.

3M concerns the validity of blocked income rules to royalties that cannot be paid by a Brazilian subsidiary. The company argued that this rule is so restrictive that it is invalid. The case has been awaiting a decision since 2016. Interestingly, the court in *Coca-Cola* had the same issue and stated that it would apply the outcome in *3M*, so this may mean that this decision will eventually be issued very soon.

Eaton is another long-pending decision. In this case, the IRS cancelled two APAs arguing the taxpayer had not complied with their terms. The tax court issued a very strong opinion in favour of the taxpayer in 2017, but the final decision is still pending, awaiting parties' calculation of the tax impact. It will be learned if the IRS will appeal that case only once the opinion is finalized.

In addition to the cases mentioned above, the following countries issued decisions that are significant for domestic practice and can also be of interest from an international perspective:[148]

Australia

- Commodity transactions: *Australia v. BHP Biliton Limited*, March 2020, High Court Of Australia, Case No. [2020] HCA 5.

146. For a detailed analysis of US transfer pricing cases, please refer to Chapter 3 of this Volume.
147. https://news.bloombergtax.com/transfer-pricing/insight-transfer-pricing-cases-of-2019, accessed 7 January 2020.
148. https://tpcases.com/; https://www.ibfd.org/IBFD-Products/International-Transfer-Pricing-Journal-All-Articles.

Belgium

- Abnormal and gratuitous advantages: *Belgium v. Alcopa N.V*, September 2020, Supreme Court, Case No. RG F.19.0056.N.

Canada

- Standard of documentation required: AgraCity Ltd., Tax Court of Canada (Case No. 2020 TCC 91).
- TP Documentation: *Canada v. Bayer Inc.*, July 2020, Federal Court, T-272-19.
- Determine the jurisdiction for the appeal of the Minister of National Revenue's decision to deny a taxpayer's request for a downward transfer pricing adjustment: *Canada v. Dow Chemical Canada ULC. Dec 2020, Tax Court,* Case No. 2020 TCC 139.
- Financial transactions: *Canada v. Loblaw Financial Holdings Inc.*, April 2020, Federal Court of Appeal, Case No. 2020 FCA 79.

Denmark

- Recognition of actual transaction: *Denmark v. Engine branch*, January 2020, Tax Tribunal, Case No. SKM2020.30.LSR.
- TNMM, Goodwill Amortizations: High Court of Eastern Denmark (Østre Landsret, ØLR), 13 January 2020, SKM2020.105.ØLR.
- Intangibles, TP Methods: *Denmark v. Pharma Distributor A A/S*, March 2020, National Court, Case No. SKM2020.105.OLR.
- Trademark Licence Agreement: HR [Supreme Court], 25 June 2020, Case BS-42036/2019-HJR, *Adecco A/S v. the Ministry of Taxation*, SKM2020.303. HR.
- Burden of Proof, Transfer Pricing Documentation: *Denmark v. ECCO A/S*, October 2020, High Court, Case No. SKM2020.397.VLR.
- Business Restructuring, Intangibles: *Denmark v. Software A/S*, September 2020, Tax Court, Case No. SKM2020.387.LSR.
- TP Documentation, TP Methods: *Denmark v. Ice Machine Manufacturer A/S*, June 2020, National Court, Case No. SKM2020.224.VLR.

Finland

- Prohibition to Recharacterize Transactions: *KHO: 2020: 35.*
- Compensating adjustments, Losses, TNMM: *Finland v. A Oy*, April 2020, Supreme Administrative Court, Case No. KHO:2020:34.

France

- Services and Fees: *France v. SAS Groupe Lagasse Europe*, January 2020, CCA de VERSAILLES, Case No. 18VE00059 18VE02329.
- Intangibles, Royalties and Licence payments: *France v. SA Sacla*, February 2020, CAA de Lyon, Case No. 17LY04170.
- Losses, TP Methods: *France v. SAS RKS (AB SKF Sweden)*, June 2020, CAA of VERSAILLES, Case No. 18VE02848.

India

- *India v. M/s Redington (India) Limited*, December 2020, High Court of Madras, Case No. T.C.A.Nos.590 & 591 of 2019.
- Permanent establishment: *India v. Samsung Heavy Industries*, July 2020, Supreme Court, Case No. 12183 OF 2016.
- Unrecognized Transactions: Kellogg India Private Limited, Mumbai Income Tax Appellate Tribunal (Case No. ITA 1906/MUM 2016,2262/MUM/2016 & 2314/MUM/2017); Corbus (India) Private Limited, Delhi Income Tax Appellate Tribunal (Case No. ITA No. 2745/Del/2015).
- Use of the Profit Split Method: Toyota Kirloskar Auto Parts Private Limited, Bangalore Income Tax Appellate Tribunal (Case No. IT (TP)A No.1915/Bang/2017).
- Standard of documentation required: Federal-Mogul Anand Bearing India Ltd., Mumbai Income Tax Appellate Tribunal (Case No. TS-580-ITAT-2020(MUM)-TP).

Indonesia

- Royalties and license payments: *Indonesia v. PK manufacturing Ltd*, March 2020 Supreme Court, Case No. 366/B/PK/Pjk/2020.

Ireland

- Business Restructuring, Intangibles – Goodwill Know-how Patents: *Ireland v. Perrigo*, November 2020, High Court, Case No. [2020] IEHC 552 (Juridical Review).

Israel

- Financial Transactions, Non-Recognition and Recharacterization: *Israel v. The Barzani Brothers (1974) Ltd.*, October 2020, Jerusalem Court of Appeal, Case No. 54727-02-17.

Italy

- Financial Transactions: *Italy v. 'Lender' SpA*, February 2020, Regional Tax Tribunal for Umbria, No. 56, 18/02/2020.
- Intra-group services and fees: *Italy v. Rohm and Haas Italia s.r.l*, February 2020, Corte di Cassazione, No. 3599, 13/02/2020.
- Attribution of profits to PE: *Italy v. Citybank*, April 2020, Corte di Cassazione, No. 7801/2020.
- TP Methods: Società Italiana Per L'Oleodotto Transalpino SPA, Italian Corte di Cassazione, Sez. 5, No. 11837/2020.

Luxembourg

- Hybrid debt instruments and lack of Transfer Pricing Documentation: *Luxembourg v. L SARL*, January 2020, Luxembourg Administrative Tribunal, Case No. 41800.

Mexico

- Commodity Transactions, MAP – APA: *Mexico v. Majestic Silver Corp*, September 2020, Federal Administrative Court.

Netherlands

- Financial Transactions: *Netherlands v. [X] B.V.*, legal successor to [Y] U.A., March 2020, Pending before the Supreme Court, Case No. ECLI: NL:PHR:2020:102.
- Business restructuring: *Netherlands v. Zinc Smelter B.V.*, March 2020, Court of Appeal, Case No. ECLI:NL:GHSHE:2020:968.
- Intercompany loan: *Netherlands v. X B.V.*, July 2020, Supreme Court (Preliminary ruling by the Advocate General), Case No. ECLI:NL:PHR:2020:672.

New Zealand

- Financial Transactions: *New Zealand v. Frucor Suntory*, September 2020, Court of Appeal, Case No. [2020] NZCA 383.

Nigeria

- TP Methods: *Nigeria v. Prime Plastichem Nigeria Limited*, February 2020, Tax Appeal Tribunal, Case No. TAT/LZ/CIT/015/2017.

Norway

- TP Methods: *Norway v. Orange Business Norway A/S*, January 2020, Borgarting Lagmannsrett, Case No. 2018-84331.
- ALP, Cost contributions arrangements: *Norway v. A/S Norske Shell*, May 2020, Supreme Court, Case No. HR-2020-1130-A.

Panama

- Royalty and Licence Payments: *Panama v. 'AC S.A.'*, January 2020, Administrative Tribunal, Case No. TAT-RF-002.
- Transfer Pricing Documentation: *Panama v. 'Glass Corp'*, February 2020, Administrative Tribunal, Case No. TAT-RF-015.
- Transfer Pricing Methods: *Panama v. 'Petroleum Wholesale Corp'*, September 2020, Administrative Tribunal, Case No. TAT-RF-062.

Poland

- Transfer Pricing Methods: *Poland v. K. sp. Z o.o.*, January 2020, Supreme Administrative Court, Case No. II FSK 191/19 - Wyrok.
- Services and fees, GAAR: *Poland v. Shared Service Center*, February 2020, Administrative Court, SA/PO 935/19.
- Losses, TP Methods: *Poland v. Cans Corp Sp z.o.o.*, August 2020, Administrative Court, I SA/Sz 115/20.

Sweden

- Intangibles, PE, Goodwill know-how: *Sweden v. Flir Commercial Systems AB*, March 2020, Stockholm Administrative Court, Case No. 28256-18.

Switzerland

- Delineation, Substance over form: *Switzerland v. Swiss Investment AG*, February 2020, Administrative Court Zurich, Case No. SB.2018.00094 and SB.2018.00095.

United Kingdom

- Financial transactions: *UK v. Union-Castle Ltd*, April 2020, UK Court of Appeal, Case No. A3/2018/3003 and 3004.
- Commercially Irrational Transactions: *UK v. Total E&P North Sea UK Ltd*, October 2020, Court of Appeal, Case No. A3/2019/1656; *UK v. General Electric*,

July 2020, High Court, Case No. RL-2018-000005; *UK v. Blackrock*, November 2020, First-tier Tribunal, Case No. TC07920.
- Attribution of profit to permanent establishments: Irish Bank Resolution Corporation Limited and Irish Nationwide Building Society, Court of Appeal (Civil Division)(Case No. A3/2019/3060 [2020] EWCA Civ 1128).

United States

- *Whirlpool Financial Corp. v. Commissioner*, 154 TC. No. 9 (5 May 2020).
- Cost contributions arrangements: *US v. Altera Corp*, June 2020, Supreme Court - review denied, Case No. 19-1009.
- Aggressive tax planning, 'Stateless income': *US v. Whirlpool*, May 2020, US tax court, Case No. 13986-17.
- *US v. Coca-Cola*, November 2020, US Tax Court, 155 T.C. No. 10.

Zambia

- Commodity transactions: *Zambia v. Mopani Copper Mines Plc.*, May 2020, Supreme Court of Zambia, Case No. 2017/24.

4 CONCLUSIONS AND INSIGHTS

The year 2020 saw significant steps taken on the international level to continue the fight against BEPS and make the contemporary tax rules relevant in the era of increasingly digitalized business models. Intensive works were undertaken by both international organizations and domestic legislators. Undoubtedly, the single event that most affected the tax and TP landscape in 2020 was COVID-19. The pandemic raised new issues and forced states to cooperate and undertake concerted efforts to build common and appropriate solutions to face the challenges posed by the pandemic. Indeed, the economic crisis caused (and will continue to trigger) unexpected adverse economic consequences for multinationals that will have to wrestle with transfer pricing complications created by the global crisis. Considering the lack - at the domestic level - of detailed guidance on the specific challenges for transfer pricing policies resulting from the COVID-19-pandemic, the authors expect that a significant issue in 2021 will be how (and if) national tax administrations will interpret and/or implement the respective OECD Guidance. Furthermore, the pandemic and related restrictive measures leading to global lockdowns have boosted the digitalization of the economy and highlighted the need to find global solutions for taxing it.

In this context, the OECD kept working on Pillar One and Pillar Two proposals and, on 12 October 2020, the IF released a package consisting of the Report on the Pillar One Blueprint and the Report on the Pillar Two Blueprint. Considering the significant changes at stake, consensus will require many politically influenced negotiations.

Indeed, the United States has already called on the OECD to 'pause' discussions on Pillar One, confirming the disagreement on DSTs and similar unilateral measures. On the other hand, the US Treasury Secretary declared fully supporting bringing negotiations on Pillar Two to a successful conclusion by 2020. The works on the Unified Approach were not the only ones undertaken by the OECD. In February 2020, the OECD released the report *'Transfer Pricing Guidance on Financial Transactions: Inclusive Framework on BEPS: Actions 4, 8-10'*.[149]

The latter development – which was long-awaited and includes, for the first time in the OECD TPG, guidance on the transfer pricing aspects of financial transactions – can undoubtedly be perceived as being of significant importance to the practice as it will contribute to consistency in the interpretation of the ALP and help prevent TP disputes.

In the transfer pricing realm in the EU, the year's highlight was undoubtedly the decision of the GCEU in the high-profile case of *Apple* even though *Impresa Pizzarotti* covers a hot topic and practitioners and academics have welcomed the relevant CJEU's decision.

Investigations initiated by the Commission in 2019 on the *Nike* and *Huhtamäki* rulings, as well as the resumed investigation of the Belgian excess profit regime, prove that the era of intensive state aid investigations in the EU will not end soon.

When it comes to developing countries, the UN was focusing primarily on updating the Practical Manual on Transfer Pricing, with the most significant change being drafting the new chapter on financial transactions. Other changes, although smaller and mainly focusing on the revisions of the already existing content of the manual, serve further clarification of the most important transfer pricing issues.

In domestic law, the taxation of the digital economy realm saw specific domestic initiatives remaining on a drafting level or their entry into force being delayed while waiting for global consensus. This situation raises questions about the compatibility of such solutions with the possible internationally approved concept, and it seems that these questions will have to be answered sooner rather than later.

When it comes to general transfer pricing legislation, several countries adopted or updated their TP rules. An increasing number of countries also require detailed TP documentation, and APAs are slowly becoming the most favourite way of preventing potential tax disputes among both tax authorities and taxpayers. Finally, transfer pricing remained a vital subject in litigation. With many significant cases from around the world (including high-profile cases decided in the United States and at the EU level), it can be confirmed that transfer pricing rules are definitely not crystal clear and still create interpretational issues.

The year 2020 turned out to be a year in which significant works towards the new taxation model were undertaken. Despite the international discord of overtaxing the digital economy, major TP cases were settled, and states and international organizations worked to find solutions to COVID-19-related issues. Undoubtedly, transfer pricing will continue to be a high-profile topic in 2021. As the system of global taxation is in urgent need of adaption to the changed reality relying heavily on digital business

149. http://www.oecd.org/tax/beps/transfer-pricing-guidance-on-financial-transactions-inclusive-framework-on-beps-actions-4-8-10.pdf.

models, it seems that all stakeholders will be interested in delivering a final solution as soon as possible. However, given the global economy's uncertain environment, the question remains of what the most effective system would be for both countries and taxpayers and how to manage current challenges. Perhaps the OECD will require a little bit more time to deal with unsolved political and technical issues before coming up with a solution that would otherwise risk being an empty agreement that is subject to different interpretations.

CHAPTER 2

Transfer Pricing Developments in the European Union

Isabel Verlinden, Stefaan De Baets & Jean-Philippe Van West

1 INTRODUCTION

A recent economist magazine briefing on Brexit mentions: 'The world is returning to an era of great-power competition: deepening rivalry between America and China, Russia's brazen opportunism and the EU's stubborn assertiveness, at least in economic policy.'[1] Criticizing the European Union (EU) has become a 'bon ton' for some. As Brussels-based advisers, it is for the authors, though far less evident, to cry wolf with allegations on the EU 'punching above its weight' when looking at demographic and societal evolutions as foundations for economic and social progress. Unfettered access to the EU single market is and will remain for the foreseeable future a precious ambition for many and worth the price of having to comply with regulations that can be felt as (overly) inflexible. Within the EU, there is the balancing act of decision-making through the lens of the 'level playing field' for EU labour as well as environmental and state-aid standards. Conceding on the principle of full sovereignty is hard, and there is yet another catalyst for accelerated disruption and transformation. Indeed, as an overlay to all discussions and speculation on geopolitical dominance, something so small that is not even visible under a regular microscope shook the world. During the 2019-2020 New Year's celebrations, nothing could have anticipated that the Sars 2 COVID-19 virus (COVID-19) would become a global pandemic and grind some economies almost to a halt. Still, it has.

It would therefore not come as a surprise that the COVID-19 virus plays a leading role in the tax and TP developments in the EU. However, the COVID-19 virus is not the only thread that runs through the activities and projects that impact Europe or that the European Commission (EC) launched or at least announced. There is, of course, the digitalization of the economy with a regulatory and fiscal angle. On the latter, although this is originally an Organisation for Economic Co-operation and Development (OECD)/Inclusive Framework (IF) project, reaching a multilateral solution will be anything other than a walk in the park. A quick look at the unilateral measures issued or considered by several European countries with Austria, France, Spain, or Italy taking a prominent role illustrates it all.

Another lead part is reserved for the fight against what would be called 'illegitimate ways that companies can choose to manage their tax affairs'. Indeed, the increasing blurring of the boundaries between tax policy and tax politics implies that illegal acts such as tax evasion and tax fraud are (conveniently) thrown in one bag with perfectly legal ways to minimize the tax bill, aka tax avoidance. An undesirable corollary of that

1. The Economist, *Britain and the world: Amazing journey?*, 2 January 2021.

is the temptation for tax officials to forego a deep technical analysis and to jump straight away on the anti-avoidance bandwagon. This may ease the potential downsides of the mounting pressure for increasing transparency by companies. The environmental, social, and governance (ESG) imperative to properly inform multi-stakeholders is a noble cause. As public country-by-country reporting (CbCR) may soon be given the kiss of life, the question remains of whether the quality of such information reaches the standard needed to meaningfully comment on where value is actually created.

Additionally, for those enjoying a healthy bite every now and then ... someone must have bitten through a very sour apple in 2020 ... it does not mean that state aid procedures are now off the table.

Let the authors be the guide on this rollercoaster of what happened in Europe in 2020 and unveil a bit of what they believe is worthwhile addressing in more depth as part of its agenda for 2021.

2 A NEW DIGITAL LEVY

It would seem as if the recovery from COVID-19 and the taxation of the digital economy got connected. In its communications of 27 May 2020,[2,3] the EC presents its ambitious, innovative, and comprehensive plans for the European recovery from the COVID-19 pandemic. These bold plans should 'kick-start the European economy, boost the green and digital transitions, and make it fairer, more resilient and more sustainable for future generations'. It would cost at least EUR 1.5 trillion to repair the immediate social and economic damage caused by the COVID-19 pandemic. The plan is based on:

- An emergency European Recovery Instrument (Next Generation EU) for EUR 750 billion. This will be enforced through a recovery and resilience facility (RRF) as the centrepiece of the recovery.
- A reinforced multiannual financial framework for 2021-2027 of EUR 1,100 billion.
- The exceptional measures taken at the EU level even reach EUR 1,290 billion when the package of EUR 540 billion supporting workers, business, and sovereigns is considered in the equation.[4]

This contribution will not go into detail on how these vast amounts of assistance to the recovery will be allocated over the different projects.

2. Communication from the Commission to the European Parliament, the European Council, the Council, the European Economic and Social Committee and the Committee of the Regions – COM(2020) 442 Final – 27.5.2020, https://eur-lex.europa.eu/legal-content/EN/TXT/PDF/?uri=CELEX:52020DC0442&from=EN (accessed 14 December 2020).
3. Communication from the Commission to the European Parliament, the European Council, the Council, the European Economic and Social Committee and the Committee of the regions – Europe's moment: Repair and Prepare for the Next Generation – COM(2020) 456 Final – 27.5.2020, https://eur-lex.europa.eu/legal-content/EN/TXT/?uri=COM:2020:456:FIN (accessed 14 December 2020).
4. *Supra* n. 2, p. 1.

Spending is one thing, but these aid measures must also be financed. When looking at the Next Generation EU project, the Council mandated that the EC reform its own resources system by supplementing the traditional own resources (mainly customs duties, sugar levies, percentage of Value-added tax (VAT), and resources based on the gross national income of Member States).[5] These supplemental own resources, allowing for a potential decrease of Member States' contributions, could come from a myriad of levies such as:

- non-recycled plastics packaging waste;
- 'green' own resources, combining the recovery effort with the green transition of the European economy and society based on, for example, an emissions trading system (possibly extended to shipping and air transport sectors) as well as a carbon border adjustment system;[6] and
- a financial transaction tax.

On 18 December 2020, a political agreement was reached on the RRF between the European Parliament (EP) and the Council of the EU (the Council). The EC welcomed this political agreement as a key instrument at the heart of the Next Generation EU plan. It will make EUR 672.5 billion available to support the reforms and investments undertaken by the Member States.[7]

The new own resource for the EU that might be of particular interest, however, is a *European digital levy*. The EC phrases it:

> A digital tax would build on OECD work on corporate taxation of a significant digital presence; the Commission actively supports the discussions led by the OECD and the G20 and stands ready to act if no global agreement is reached. A digital tax applied on companies with a turnover above EUR 750 million could generate up to EUR 1.3 billion per year for the EU budget.[8]

What can be learned from this European digital levy?

(1) It repeats a well-known mantra: support of a global solution[9] with regard to the digitalization of the economy but, if no global solution is reached, then the EU will go on its own.
(2) The EC is considering a digital levy for its own resources; it is unclear whether this digital levy will be repealed when a global solution on the digitalization of the economy is reached.

5. European Commission, *EU Budget own resources*, https://ec.europa.eu/info/strategy/eu-budget/long-term-eu-budget/eu-budget-2014-2020/revenue/own-resources_en (accessed 14 December 2020).
6. *Supra* n. 2, p. 15.
7. European Commission, *Press release of the EC – Commission welcomes political agreement on Recovery and Resilience Facility*, https://ec.europa.eu/commission/presscorner/detail/en/IP_20_2397 (accessed 21 December 2020).
8. *Supra* n. 2, p. 15.
9. OECD/Inclusive Framework project on the digitalization of the economy – *See* (Chapter 1) on Global developments in transfer pricing.

(3) The proceeds of such a digital levy could (only) generate up to EUR 1.3 billion for the EU budget.[10]
(4) It is unclear who should be liable to the levy as the text indicates 'companies' with a turnover of EUR 750 million.[11]

The Next Generation EU document repeats the same kind of message on introducing a number of new resources but with a slight twist: an emission trading scheme, a carbon border adjustment mechanism, and an own resource based on the operation of large companies. A question is whether this own resource based on large companies undertaking qualifies as something other than taxation of a digital economic presence. The document states that 'it could also include a new digital tax, building on the work done by the OECD'.[12] It may hence be wondered whether this is the same as - say, Pillar One - or instead something that would coexist with Pillar One.

In any way, the EC appears to be very much engaged and committed to digital tax. The pursuit of fair digital taxation is once more mentioned as a legislative priority for 2021 in the Joint Declaration of the EP, the Council, and the EC released on 10 December 2020.[13] In the Programme for the Portuguese Presidency of the EU during the first half of 2021, only a (remarkably) short mention on a digital tax was made: 'The Presidency will address the challenges of European taxation, including the model for taxation of the digital economy, under the principles of fairness and tax efficiency.'[14] When putting all of the pieces of the jigsaw puzzle together, it can indeed be unveiled that the EC is mandated to introduce a digital levy as an element of its own resources in a legislative proposal by June 2021,[15] hence, sooner rather than later. According to Mr Gerassimos Thomas,[16] the digital tax could be compatible with a future OECD solution.[17] It is still not clear, however, if and if so, how this digital tax would coexist in one way or another with the OECD solution.

French Finance Minister Bruno Le Maire clearly put an ultimatum before President Biden by indicating that, if no global agreement is reached by the Summer of 2021, '*we will have to come back for a European solution*'.[18] Strangely enough, this ultimatum comes shortly after the United States (US) indicated that it stands down on tariff retaliation against the French unilateral digital services tax (DST).[19] Furthermore, the

10. The Multiannual Financial Framework 2021-2027 is set at EUR 1,074.3 billion.
11. The authors believe that 'companies' should be read as multinational enterprises.
12. *Supra* n. 3, p. 4.
13. Joint Declaration of the European Parliament, the Council of the European Union and the European Commission EU – Legislative Priorities for 2021 – p. 3, https://www.consilium.europa.eu/media/47644/st_13546_2020_rev_1_en.pdf (accessed 18 December 2020).
14. *See* 2021 Portugal.eu – Programme for the Portugues Presidency of the Council of the European Union – p. 17.
15. S. Paez, *A Look Ahead: How Will the EU Pay for the Pandemic,* Tax Notes Today International (2020).
16. Director-general of the Directorate-General for Taxation and Customs Union (DG Taxud).
17. E. Lamer, *EU and OECD Digital Taxes Could Coexist, Commission Says,* Tax Notes Today International (2 December 2020).
18. Biden has until Summer to Agree on OECD Tax Plan, Le Maire Says – Law 360 – 12 January 2021.
19. S. Soon Johnston, *US Stands Down on Tariff Retaliation Against French Digital Tax,* Tax Notes Today International (2021).

EC launched a public consultation and Inception Impact Assessment on 14 January 2021 on the introduction of a digital levy to address the issue of fair taxation of the digital economy.[20] The public consultation document indicates that the prospective timeline is to introduce a legislative proposal in the second quarter of 2021. On 18 January, the EC published a seventeen-page questionnaire[21] on the digital levy. Browsing through the questionnaire learns that its introduction is an almost sure thing.

It is difficult to gauge how the unilateral and EU digital taxes should be viewed in an international context. On the other side of the ocean, US (tech) companies and legislators could have the impression they are being disproportionally or even unfairly hit. Another view could be that it is just levelling out a situation in which taxing rights were lost.[22]

3 SOME OTHER ACTIONS UNDER THE RECOVERY STRATEGY

The two documents that the EC published in May were followed by the Action Plan for Fair and Simple taxation supporting the recovery strategy (the action plan).[23]

In the action plan, the EC stresses the importance of fair and efficient taxation for the recovery of the COVID-19 pandemic and crisis. The EC announces it *will step up the fight against tax fraud and other unfair practices* to help the Member States recover the tax that will allow them to finance the bailout of the COVID-19 crisis. Not less than twenty-five actions are mentioned in the document. Besides the communication itself, the action plan consists of the following two elements:[24]

(1) The first element is the sixth revision of the Directive on Administrative Cooperation (informally known as DAC7) and introduces an automatic exchange of information requirement for income or revenue generated by platform operators. Further, the revision contains some clarifying rules on joint/simultaneous audits. DAC7 is discussed in more detail later in this contribution.
(2) The second element stresses the importance of acting at both European and global levels. The EC will do so by focusing on, for example:
   - reforming the Code of Conduct for Business Taxation;[25]

20. *See* Inception Impact Assessment on Digital Levy, https://ec.europa.eu/info/law/better-regulation/have-your-say/initiatives/12836-Digital-Levy (accessed 15 January 2021).
21. Questionnaire available at, https://ec.europa.eu/eusurvey/runner/digital_levy?surveylanguage=en – registration is required to access the questionnaire.
22. The Economist Schumpeter, *A tech CEO's guide to taxes*, 9 January 2021.
23. European Commission, *Communication from the Commission to the European Parliament and the Council – An Action Plan for Fair and Simple Taxation Supporting the Recovery Strategy – 15.7.2020 – COM(2020)* 312 final, https://ec.europa.eu/taxation_customs/sites/taxation/files/2020_tax_package_tax_action_plan_en.pdf (accessed 14 December 2020).
24. *Supra* n. 23, p. 3.
25. The Code of Conduct for Business Taxation is a political commitment to amend, abolish or refrain from introducing harmful tax practice regimes. *See*, https://www.consilium.europa.eu/en/council-eu/preparatory-bodies/code-conduct-group/ (accessed 14 December 2020).

- reviewing the EU-list of non-cooperative jurisdictions for tax purposes;
- reinforce tax good governance vis-à-vis EU funds and improve the coordinated defensive measures by the Member States; and
- support developing country partners for enhancing good tax governance.

The authors will take a closer look at some of the actions that might be of particular interest. This does not mean that the other actions mentioned in the paper are not important, of course. As the EC is putting it, the action plan for fair and simple taxation 'will be front and centre in 2021'.[26]

3.1 Building an EU Cooperative Compliance Framework

The first item worthwhile mentioning falls under the header of Reporting under the action plan, though 'taxpayer transparency' might have better served as a header. Under action item three, the EC plans to introduce an EU cooperative compliance framework based on 'greater cooperation, trust, and transparency amongst tax administrations'.[27] The intention is to launch a pilot project in 2021 to cover both SME and larger companies. It would complement the already existing national and international programmes on cooperative compliance (e.g., the International Compliance Assurance Programme - ICAP). The authors are of the opinion that investing in multilateral cooperative compliance programmes indeed has advantages such as increased transparency and certainty, avoidance of double (or multiple) taxations and lengthy disputes, as well as the development of common views and approaches between the concerned taxpayer(s) and tax authority(ies). The pilot would allow for an opportunity to build on existing programmes and experiences as well as strengthen the positive features thereof. It can also remedy some downsides of national programmes, such as differences in approaches, different timelines, and different documentation requirements.

In 2020/2021, the EC will prepare an initiative in cooperation with the Member States for facilitating and promoting tax compliance for businesses. This initiative, the *EU cooperative compliance framework,* will be based on greater cooperation, trust and, transparency among tax administrations. It will provide tax administrations with a clear framework for preventive dialogue in the field of the common resolution of cross-border tax issues in the area of corporate income tax.[28]

The authors welcome this framework as it would fit in nicely with other international initiatives such as the ICAP or national cooperative compliance programmes. The key is to be able to discuss in full mutual transparency the issues that might be of interest to the taxpayer and the tax authorities. What will be important for the success

26. E. Lamer, *A Look Ahead: 2021 to Be Pivotal Year for EU Taxation*, Tax Notes Today International (2021).
27. *Supra* n. 23, pp. 8-9.
28. *Supra* n. 23, p. 8.

of such a program is that all parties sitting around the table are convinced of the role that such a cooperative compliance framework has to play and that it has clear benefits for all, including compliance for tax authorities and more certainty for taxpayers.

3.2 The EU List of Non-cooperative Countries

As of 2020, the EU list of non-cooperative countries, in common parlance referred to as the 'blacklist', is updated twice a year. It is becoming increasingly relevant as deductible cross-border payments made to an associated enterprise in a blacklisted country should be reported under DAC6 as a potentially harmful arrangement.[29] Further, certain EU Member States make the allocation of support to enterprises related to the COVID-19 recovery dependent on refraining from engaging with blacklisted countries.

The exact composition is expected to stay in a flux for a while at the very minimum. Only four countries (American Samoa, Guam, Samoa, and Trinidad and Tobago) have been on the list continuously since December 2017. The further evolution to the latest four reviews gives the following picture:

October-2020	*February-2020*	*March-2019*	*December-2017*
American Samoa	*American Samoa*	*American Samoa*	*American Samoa*
Anguilla			
		Aruba	
			Bahrain
Barbados		Barbados	Barbados
		Belize	
		Bermuda	
	Cayman Islands		
		Dominica	
Fiji	Fiji	Fiji	
			Grenada
Guam	*Guam*	*Guam*	*Guam*
			South Korea
			Macao
		Marshall Islands	Marshall Islands
			Mongolia
			Namibia
	Oman	Oman	
Palau	Palau		Palau

29. Directive on Administrative Cooperation #6, Annex, Hallmark C.1. (b) (ii).

October-2020	*February-2020*	*March-2019*	*December-2017*
Panama	Panama		Panama
			Saint Lucia
Samoa	*Samoa*	*Samoa*	*Samoa*
Seychelles	Seychelles		
Trinidad and Tobago	*Trinidad and Tobago*	*Trinidad and Tobago*	*Trinidad and Tobago*
			Tunisia
		United Arab Emirates	United Arab Emirates
US Virgin Islands	US Virgin Islands	US Virgin Islands	
Vanuatu	Vanuatu	Vanuatu	

The list has gained significant interest from the EP through the newly established subcommittee on tax (FISC Committee – *see* section 5). The removal of the Cayman Islands in October 2020, in particular, fuelled the debate on reorganizing the working of the code of conduct group and the blacklisting process. With the EP resolution of 10 December 2020[30] on the changes to be made to the system used to draw up the EU list of tax havens to make the compilation of the blacklist more transparent, the EP wants to grasp how the list is compiled. Moreover, the resolution seeks to widen the scope. For example, the chair of the FISC Committee on tax refers to the removal of the Cayman Islands despite its zero-tax rate. To the authors' best knowledge, however, this was never a criterion to consider a jurisdiction as non-cooperative. It was instead the absence of exchange of information. On 21 January 2020, the EP accepted a resolution on reforming the EU list of tax havens.[31] EU Tax Commissioner Paolo Gentiloni stated during an EP hearing held on 20 January 2021 that the blacklist must be strengthened.[32]

3.3 Transparency

Transparency of MNEs is one of the items that is also on the priority list of the EC.[33] What is of importance in the transparency debate is the evolution in the DAC. When transparency and the EU are thought of, the idea of public CbCR is never far away.

30. European Parliament, *Press release 10 December 2020 Resolution setting out changes to be made to the system used to draw up the EU list of tax havens*, https://www.europarl.europa.eu/news/en/press-room/20201208IPR93318/eu-tax-haven-blacklist-not-catching-worst-offenders (accessed 13 January 2021).
31. European Parliament, *European Parliament resolution of 21 January 2021 on reforming the EU list of tax havens (2020/2863(RSP))*, https://www.europarl.europa.eu/doceo/document/TA-9-2021-0022_EN.html (accessed 21 January 2021).
32. S. Paez, *EU Tax Haven Blacklist Must Be Strengthened, Gentiloni Says*, Tax Notes Today International (2021).
33. *Supra* n. 13, p. 2.

Although the proposal for a directive on it was dormant for quite some time, it has recently been given the kiss of life under the Portuguese presidency.[34]

3.3.1 Directive on Administrative Cooperation

Since its inception in 2011, the DAC has already undergone several changes:

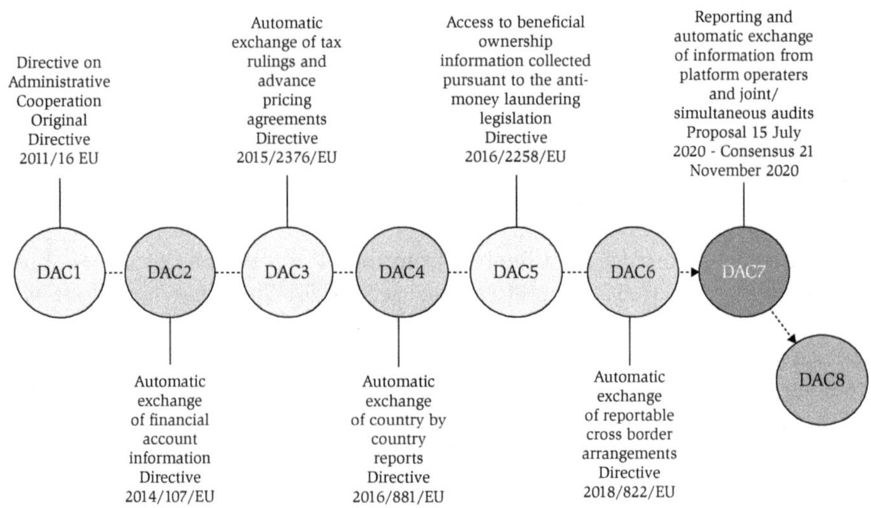

There are few recent evolutions in this Directive that merit further attention.

3.3.1.1 Directive on Administrative Cooperation #6

Three hallmarks under DAC6 relate in particular to transfer pricing and address: (1) the use of unilateral safe harbours, (2) transfers of hard-to-value intangibles, and (3) business restructurings with a substantial impact on the EBIT level post-restructuring.[35]

With the COVID-19 pandemic hitting hard, several EU countries opted to defer the filing deadlines as laid down in DAC6.[36] The new reporting deadlines – if the Member State opted for deferral – were as follows:

34. *See* Proposal for a Directive of the European Parliament and of the Council amending Directive 2013/34/EU as regards disclosure of income tax information by certain undertakings and branches, https://eur-lex.europa.eu/legal-content/EN/TXT/PDF/?uri=CELEX:52016PC0198&from=EN (accessed 5 January 2021).
35. *See also* Transfer Pricing Developments Around the World 2020 – edited by Michael Lang and Raffaele Petruzzi – p. 49.
36. Council Directive (EU) 2020/876 of 24 June 2020 amending Directive 2011/16/EU to address the urgent need to defer certain time limits for the filing and exchange of information in the field of taxation because of the COVID-19 pandemic, https://eur-lex.europa.eu/legal-content/EN/TXT/PDF/?uri=CELEX:32020L0876&from=EN (accessed 21 December 2020).

- for reportable cross-border arrangements, the first step of which was implemented between 25 June 2018 and 30 June 2020, the new filing deadline is 28 February 2021;
- when the triggering event for the reporting took place between 1 July 2020 and 31 December 2020, the period of thirty days for filing information started on 1 January 2021; and
- for marketable arrangements, the first periodic report had to be made by the intermediary by 30 April 2021.

The first automatic exchange of information that had to take place by 30 April 2021 is also delayed.

Germany, Finland and Austria did not opt for deferral. The other Member Countries have now joined the actual reporting under DAC6.

3.3.1.2 Directive on Administrative Cooperation #7

On 15 July 2020, as part of its recovery plan,[37] the EU Commission published its proposal for again amending the DAC.[38,39] It is the sixth amendment in a row of the DAC since its inception in 2011. The consensus at the Member States' level on the draft was reached on 21 November 2020.[40] In its press release of 1 December 2020, the EC stressed that the agreed proposal would ensure that the Member States automatically exchange information on the revenues generated by sellers on digital platforms whether the platform is located in the EU or not. Although the EC further indicated that the proposal also strengthens and clarifies the rules in other areas in which the Member States work together to fight tax abuse (referring to joint audits and simultaneous controls), it did not mention the potential benefits that such joint audits or simultaneous controls could bring to multinational enterprises.[41] These benefits were addressed, however, in the Report of the Joint Transfer Pricing Forum on A Coordinated Approach to Transfer Pricing Controls within the EU,[42] such as a cooperative approach, improved communication between stakeholders, and in particular respect of taxpayers

37. *Supra* n. 23, p. 3.
38. Proposal for a Council Directive amending Directive 2011/16/EU on administrative cooperation in the field of taxation of 15 July 2020 {SEC(2020) 271 final} – {SWD(2020) 129 final} – {SWD(2020) 130 final} – {SWD(2020) 131 final}, https://ec.europa.eu/taxation_customs/sites/taxation/files/2020_tax_package_dac7_en.pdf.
39. Annex to the Proposal for a Council Directive amending Directive 2011/16/EU on administrative cooperation in the field of taxation of 15 July 2020, https://ec.europa.eu/taxation_customs/sites/taxation/files/2020_tax_package_dac7_annex_en.pdf contains the reporting rules for platform operators.
40. Draft Council Directive amending Directive 2011/16/EU on administrative cooperation in the field of taxation (DAC7) – Endorsement – of 25 November 2020, https://data.consilium.europa.eu/doc/document/ST-13130-2020-REV-1/en/pdf (accessed 21 December 2020).
41. European Commission, *Press release 1 December 2020 Fair Taxation: Member States agree on new tax transparency rules on digital platforms*, https://ec.europa.eu/commission/presscorner/detail/en/ip_20_2253 (accessed 21 December 2020).
42. European Union Joint Transfer Pricing Forum, https://ec.europa.eu/taxation_customs/sites/taxation/files/jtPf_report_on_a_coordinated_approach_to_transfer_pricing_controls_within_the_eu_en.pdf (accessed 21 December 2020).

rights.[43] The question is hence whether the EC allots more weight to the tax authorities' expectations than to what can help taxpayers meeting compliance requirements while minimizing administrative complexity and waste of valuable management time. Taxpayers may have welcomed the Belgian Finance Minister's suggestion to evaluate the practical use of the information exchanged under all of the administrative cooperation directives when thinking about the next one. The Luxembourg Finance Minister sees similarities between DACs and wine launches as they both seem to follow an annual pattern.[44]

Formal adoption of DAC7 will follow once the EP and the Economic and Social Committee have given their opinion. DAC7 addresses the following main issues:

- reporting requirements for digital platform operators on sharing information on sellers that make use of the digital platform and their income;
- rules on joint audits and simultaneous controls; and
- presence and participation of tax officials of a Member State in audits conducted in another Member State.

3.3.1.2.1 Digital Platform Operators

Although the Directive is inspired by the OECD work on the Sharing and Gig Economy that was released on 3 July 2020,[45] its scope and application are broader than the OECD Report.

The mandatory reporting imposed on platform operators of certain items such as income earned by the sellers through the platform is believed – according to the EC – to be a workable solution against tax evasion through the automatic exchange of information mechanisms that already exist between the Member States.[46] A platform is defined as any software (including a website or a part thereof) and (mobile) applications allowing sellers to be connected to other users for the purpose of directly or indirectly carrying out an in-scope activity.[47] The directive is applicable to platform operators that perform commercial activities in the EU and is hence extended to non-resident platforms (non-incorporated or managed or without a permanent establishment in the EU).[48]

The reporting under DAC7 is organized as a three-step approach:[49]

43. *See* Transfer Pricing Developments Around the World 2019 – edited by Michael Lang, Raffaele Petruzzi and Alfred Storck – p. 80 and *supra* n. 18, p. 45.
44. E. Lamer, *EU Sees Stars Aligning on Digital Taxation*, Tax Notes (2020).
45. OECD, Model Rules for Reporting by Platform Operators with respect to Sellers in the Sharing and Gig Economy, OECD, Paris, https://www.oecd.org/tax/exchange-of-tax-information/model-rules-for-reporting-by-platform-operators-with-respect-to-sellers-in-the-sharing-and-gig-economy.htm (accessed 21 December 2020).
46. *Supra* n. 38, p. 7.
47. *Supra* n. 39, para. A.1.
48. *Supra* n. 38, para. 13.
49. *Supra* n. 39, sections II, III and IV.

(1) Obligation on the reporting platform operators to collect and verify the information in line with due diligence procedures.
(2) Report information on the reportable sellers that use the platform.
(3) Communicate the reported information to the competent authority (CA) of the Member State where the reportable seller is a resident or to the CA of the Member State where the immovable property is located.

The relevant activities performed through the platform that are within the scope of the proposal are also broad:[50]

- The rental of immovable property.
- The provision of personal services (which is described as services involving time- or task-based work performed by one or more individuals that act either independently or on behalf of an entity, carried out at the request of a user either online or physically offline after having been facilitated via a platform).
- The sale of goods.
- The rental of any mode of transport.

The proposal for the directive is also assorted with several administrative measures. For example, a platform operator that is not incorporated, managed, or having a PE in a Member State must register in the Member State where it commences its operations (unless it is already registered for VAT purposes). The platform must collect, verify, and have the required information available by 31 December of the reportable period and communicate the information through a one-stop-shop one month later. Records have to be kept for a period of five to seven years. As usual, the proposal for the directive provides that the Member States must introduce effective proportionate and dissuasive penalties. Member States should transpose this part of the directive by 31 December 2022 with an application as from 1 January 2023 for platform operators.

With this DAC7 amendment, another layer of compliance measures under the transparency banner is put on the shoulders of certain taxpayers.

In its EU-US agenda for global change[51] (*see also* section 4), the EC also addresses online platforms and big tech. The agenda mentions that the EU and the US should 'open a transatlantic dialogue on the responsibility of online platforms and Big Tech – to find global solutions for fair taxation and market distortions in the digital economy'. According to the EC, a growing consensus arises that online platforms and big tech threaten our societies and democracies through harmful market behaviour, illegal content, or algorithm-fuelled proliferation of hate speech and fake news. On the tax side, the EC invites the US to commit strongly to a timely global solution on the OECD digitalization of the economy project.

For some, the proposal with regard to platforms does not go far enough. Members of the EP have already laid down amendments that focus on more enforcement and,

50. *Supra* n. 38, para. 14 and *supra* n. 39, para. A.5.
51. European Commission, *Joint Communication to the European Parliament, the European Council and the Council – A new EU-US agenda for global change*, https://ec.europa.eu/info/sites/info/files/joint-communication-eu-us-agenda_en.pdf (accessed 21 December 2020).

among others, to expand the directive and provide penalties for non-cooperative platforms.[52]

3.3.1.2.2 Joint Audits and Simultaneous Controls

Simultaneous controls are already covered under Article 12 of DAC1. A simultaneous control is a tax inspection for which each Member State that is involved simultaneously audits, in its own territory, one or more persons of common or complementary interest to them with a view to exchanging the information that is obtained. A new Article 12A introduces the concept of a joint audit. A joint audit under the directive is defined as an administrative enquiry jointly conducted by the CAs of two or more Member States and linked to one or more persons of common or complementary interest to the CAs of these Member States.

The information gathered and exchanged may be used not only for direct tax purposes but also for VAT and other indirect taxes. Such information could also be used for other purposes if the internal law of both (sending and receiving) Member States so allows.[53]

The directive is applicable for joint audits as of 1 January 2024.

3.3.1.2.3 Presence and Participation of Foreign Tax Officials in Audits

The Directive has made it clear that, under a joint audit, foreign tax officials cannot only be present during an examination but effectively take an active part in the audit. According to the directive, the role of the foreign tax official includes interviewing individuals and examining records together with the officials of the Member State where the activities of the joint audit take place.[54] This approach gives the tax auditors extra-territorial powers and means in their investigations.

3.3.1.3 Directive on Administrative Cooperation #8

Together with the communication that an agreement was reached on DAC7, the EC announced it started working on DAC8. This revision of the DAC should also be viewed from the angle of the fight against tax fraud and evasion. It should cover the exchange of information with respect to cryptocurrencies and the harmonization of penalties. Although the drafting process is still at an early stage, it illustrates the trend towards full transparency.[55] The project is part of the action plan for fair and simple taxation[56]

52. European Parliament, *DRAFT REPORT on the proposal for a COUNCIL DIRECTIVE amending Directive 2011/16/EU on administrative cooperation in the field of taxation – Committee on Economic and Monetary affairs*, https://www.europarl.europa.eu/doceo/document/ECON-PR-658793_EN.pdf (accessed 4 January 2021).
53. *Supra* n. 38, paras 25 and 25A.
54. *Supra* n. 38, Article 12a(4).
55. *See* Tax fraud & evasion – strengthening rules on administrative cooperation and expanding the exchange of information, https://ec.europa.eu/info/law/better-regulation/have-your-say/

supporting the recovery strategy and should ensure consistency with ongoing work such as the digital finance strategy adopted on 24 September 2020 and the proposal for a regulation on markets in crypto assets.

According to the EC, tax authorities face two issues, i.e., (1) uncertainty about the legal status of crypto assets and (2) the tax treatment of transactions using crypto assets. Connected thereto, at least according to the EC, is that the possibility for avoiding the tax is made easier by using crypto assets.[57]

In 2021, a new chapter of the DAC will undoubtedly be seen.

3.3.2 *Public CbCR*

The proposal for a directive on public CbCR has received quite some headwind since its inception in 2016.[58] The apparent lack of support among the Member States implied limited evolution over the last years. However, within the ambit of the EU tax package, public CbCR again received a more prominent place on the agenda, and, under the Portuguese EU Presidency, a new draft proposal for a directive introducing public CbCR was published on 13 January 2021.[59] It remains to be seen whether an agreement can be reached this time among the Member States.

Just as a reminder, the directive on public CbCR aims at making general information such as the name, the activities, and an average number of employees publicly available on the website of the company or branch. This would include financial information such as turnover or income, profit or loss before income tax, income tax accrued and paid (on a cash basis), and accumulated earnings.

It would seem that, during the Portuguese Presidency (January-June 2021), some initiatives were taken to revive public CbCR, although it is described rather cryptically as: 'The Presidency will seek to create the conditions for reaching a political agreement on the revision of the rules on disclosure of information concerning tax on revenues for

initiatives/12632-Tax-fraud-evasion-strengthening-rules-on-administrative-cooperation-and-expanding-the-exchange-of-information (accessed 21 December 2020), and Taxation: Commission published roadmap to extend the scope of the Directive on Administrative Cooperation to crypto assets and e-money | EU Commission Press, https://www.pubaffairsbruxelles.eu/taxation-commission-published-roadmap-to-extend-the-scope-of-the-directive-on-administrative-cooperation-to-crypto-assets-and-e-money-eu-commission-press/ (accessed 21 December 2020).

56. *Supra* n. 23, p. 12.
57. Inception Impact Assessment – Proposal for a Council Directive amending Directive 2011/16/EU as regards measures to strengthen existing rules and expand the exchange of information framework in the field of taxation to include crypto assets and e-money, https://eur-lex.europa.eu/legal-content/EN/TXT/HTML/?uri=PI_COM:Ares(2020)7030524&from=EN (accessed 13 January 2021).
58. For a discussion on the proposal on public CbCR, *see* Transfer Pricing Developments Around the World 2017 – edited by Michael Lang, Raffaele Petruzzi and Alfred Storck – p. 61.
59. Proposal for a Directive of the European Parliament and of the Council amending Directive 2013/34/EU as regards disclosure of income tax information by certain undertakings and branches – consolidated compromise proposal, https://eur-lex.europa.eu/legal-content/EN/TXT/PDF/?uri=CONSIL:ST_5183_2021_INIT&from=EN (accessed 14 January 2021).

certain companies and branches.'[60] The chair of the FISC Committee[61] has also indicated that it plans to advance the issue of public CbCR.[62] There is certainly more to come in the course of 2021!

The aim of the presidency proposal seems to be centred around:

- enhancing public scrutiny of MNEs that are active in the EU;
- third-party interest protection (including the general public and competitors);
- enhancing compliance and transparency; and
- regaining trust in the fairness of national tax systems.

The authors wonder why compliance, transparency, and trust in the tax systems should depend on making information publicly available that is already in the hands of the tax authorities?[63] It seems instead to be riding the waves of mere populist approaches of putting companies in the spotlight based on perceptions stemming from the interpretation of incomplete information to meaningfully comment on fair profit allocation throughout the value chain.

What is remarkable is that the proposal suggests that the Member States delete the following paragraph in the preamble of the proposed directive:

> (6b) At the same time it is stressed that, as concluded by the G20 and the OECD, country-by-country reports will be helpful for high-level transfer pricing risk assessment purposes only. The information in the Country-by-Country Report on its own does not constitute conclusive evidence that transfer prices are or are not appropriate and that information should not be used as a substitute for a detailed transfer pricing analysis of individual transactions and prices based on a full functional analysis and comparability analysis.

The authors believe that this paragraph is absolute key and cannot help but wonder why the Portuguese Presidency is proposing to strike it. This contradicts the wording of BEPS 13 CbCR, where such limitations are clearly indicated. Those seeing the glass half empty rather than half full may feel tempted to start speculating about this serving as a door opener to the use of public CbCR for unitary taxation.

3.3.3 Global Reporting Initiative on Public CbCR

The EC is not the only player that has engaged with public CbCR. For example, on 5 December 2019, the Global Reporting Initiative (GRI) – an independent international organization that develops and publishes voluntary standards for sustainability reporting – published its standard on tax, including CbCR.[64]

60. *See* 2021Portugal.eu – Programme for the Portuguese Presidency of the Council of the European Union – p. 17.
61. *See* section 5 of this contribution on the FISC Committee.
62. *See* Conversations: N.A. Sarfo, *Paul Tang Discusses the Future of EU Tax*, 100 Tax Notes International, 879-880 (2020).
63. *Supra* n. 57, p. 3.
64. *See* GRI 207: Tax, https://www.globalreporting.org/how-to-use-the-gri-standards/gri-standards-english-language/ (accessed 5 January 2021).

If an MNE has opted to apply the GRI-207 standard, it becomes applicable for materials and records published from 1 January 2021 (i.e., reporting periods covering 2020). Although there is a discernible link between the OECD (and EU) CbCR, there are also quite some differences, for example (not exhaustive):[65]

GRI-207 – CbCR	BEPS 13/DAC4 (COUNCIL DIRECTIVE (EU) 2016/881)
Voluntary disclosure	Mandatory disclosure for MNE with consolidated group revenues exceeding EUR 750 million
Committed to regularly providing a consolidated disclosure statement of the economic, environmental, and social impacts	Filing: twelve months after the last day of the reporting period of the MNE
Flexibility in calculation method for a number of employees	Number of employees reported on Full time equivalents basis
Revenue from related parties situated in other jurisdictions required	Revenue from related parties required
Corporate income tax paid with the possibility to report withholding tax separately	Corporate income tax paid (including withholding tax)
Reasons for the difference between corporate income tax accrued on profit/loss and the tax due if the statutory tax rate is applied to profit/loss before tax	NA
NA	Reporting of stated capital
NA	Reporting of accumulated earnings

The authors are convinced that the voluntary disclosure of records and information on the grounds of sustainability can have particular merits and will increase in relevance given its link to ESG criteria. Paying taxes is hence evolving from settling a cost of doing business to a company's contribution to society from which it obtained its license to operate.

4 RELATIONSHIP BETWEEN THE EU AND THE US

With the recent change of US administration and President Joe Biden getting settled in the White House, the High Representative of the Union for Foreign Affairs and Security

65. *See* Comparison of GRI 207: Tax 2019 & OECD Action 13 BEPS Country-by-Country Report, https://www.globalreporting.org/search/?query=207 (accessed 5 January 2021).

Policy took the initiative to rejuvenate the transatlantic relationship between the US and the EU. On 2 December 2020, an ambitious agenda was proposed.[66] The communication is built on key principles such as finding solutions that respect common values, the pursuit of common interests, and stronger multilateral actions, just to name a few.

In this ambitious agenda, four main policy areas can be distinguished. They focus on working together:

- for a healthier world – COVID-19 and beyond;
- to protect our planet and prosperity;
- on technology, trade, and standards; and
- towards a safer, more prosperous, and more democratic world.

The EC proposes to work closely together on emissions trading, carbon pricing, and taxation.

Referring to the works of the OECD and the G20, the EC proposes to commit to a timely conclusion on the OECD/IF project on the digitalization of the economy. As a first step, the agenda indicates that 'the EU and the US should open a transatlantic dialogue on the responsibility of online platforms and Big Tech – starting by working together to find global solutions for fair taxation and market distortions in the digital economy'.

It is clear that the EC wants to bring a message of sustainability combined with a discussion on taxation. The authors would welcome a renewed sound and sustainable cooperation between the EU and the US. The question, however, is whether a healthy separation between fiscal policy and tax politics can also be achieved in this matter. Policies are developed in a bilateral way; politics are determined unilaterally. It will be interesting to see the reaction from the US on the agenda.

5 EP SUBCOMMITTEE ON TAX MATTERS: THE FISC COMMITTEE

In September 2020, the EP created a new subcommittee on tax matters, the FISC Committee, presided by Mr Paul Tang.[67] With his election as chair comes a 'politically loaded jargon' such as '*tax dodging, practices that cannot bear the light of day* and *ensuring that huge corporations and high-fortune individuals contribute more fairly to society*'.

On the agenda of the FISC Committee is a discussion of what the chair calls the 'empty blacklist' of non-cooperative countries. It is his attempt to expand the blacklist. The FISC Committee adopted a motion for resolution to reform the EU tax blacklist on

66. Joint Communication to the European Parliament, the European Council and the Council, *A new EU-US agenda for global change*, https://ec.europa.eu/commission/presscorner/detail/en/ip_20_2279 (accessed 22 January 2021).
67. *See*, https://www.europarl.europa.eu/news/en/press-room/20200918IPR87429/paul-tang-elected-as-chairperson-of-the-new-subcommittee-on-tax-matters (accessed 6 January 2021).

10 December 2020, containing changes to make the listing or delisting of countries on the blacklist more '*transparent, consistent and impartial*'.[68]

The chair indicated that the blacklisted countries only account for 2% of corporate tax avoidance, adding that 36% of EU Member States are also tax havens. He mentioned that the FISC Committee will examine all Member States that are responsible for tax avoidance.[69] *See also* section 3.2 for a discussion of the blacklist.

Other topics for the FISC Committee are public CbCR (*see* section 3.3.2) and tax measures that would serve as own resources for the EU. For the chair, for purposes of taxation, '*big polluters* or *big tech* should be in scope *because they don't pay enough taxes or they don't pay taxes at all. And in fact the big companies are the main beneficiaries of the internal market*'.[70] The priorities of the FISC Committee are hence clear.

6 THE EU TAX OBSERVATORY

A European body that saw the light of day in 2020 is the EU Tax Observatory (the Observatory). According to the action plan, the Observatory will monitor and quantify trends in the level and scope of tax abuse to contribute to evidence-based policy-making in order to stimulate a European debate on international tax issues.[71]

The Observatory is led by Mr Gabriel Zucman,[72] who pledged to conduct, promote, and share innovative, high quality, and impactful research on EU taxation with a focus, a.o., on high-quality research with regard to corporate tax avoidance, tax evasion, money laundering, and possible solutions to these problems. The Observatory will also launch a website where the impact of ongoing or projected corporate tax reforms could be tested and visualized, such as the Common Consolidated Corporate Tax Base (CCCTB). The Observatory will also disseminate a public repository of data and analysis on tax evasion and avoidance as well as aggressive tax planning with a focus on corporate tax.[73]

7 UNILATERAL MEASURES: DSTs

More and more countries, in particular, but not only European countries, have introduced or are in the process of introducing new levies to tax the 'digital presence' of enterprises in their jurisdiction, commonly known as digital services taxes or 'DSTs',

68. European Parliament, *Press release 10 December 2020 – EU tax haven blacklist not catching worst offenders*, https://www.europarl.europa.eu/news/en/press-room/20201208IPR93318/eu-tax-haven-blacklist-not-catching-worst-offenders#website-body (accessed 12 January 2021).
69. *Supra* n. 67.
70. N.A. Sarfo, *Paul Tang Discusses the Future of EU Tax*, 100 Tax Notes International, 878-880 (2020).
71. *Supra* n. 23, p. 12.
72. S. Paez, *Economist Gabriel Zucman to Lead EU Tax Think Tank*, Tax Notes Today International (2020).
73. Preparatory action 'EU TAX OBSERVATORY', https://ec.europa.eu/taxation_customs/sites/taxation/files/2020_cfp01_publication_of_call_results.pdf (accessed 13 January 2021).

because of the digitalization of the economy. The aim of the DSTs is to allow the tax authorities of a country to tax the activities of large digital companies that may or may not have a physical presence (i.e., nexus) in that country. Even without a physical presence, digital companies can have a large economic reach in a country.

Each of these DSTs has its own characteristics and design features (e.g., the scope of taxpayers and services or goods covered, rates, tax base, effective implementation, the definition of users, compliance measures, etc.). The lack of uniformity makes compliance burdensome and complex. It is not the intention of this contribution to discuss each individual DST.

The first element that comes to mind is whether a DST is considered to be an income tax (e.g., as a corporate income tax) or should rather be labelled a sales tax (e.g., VAT).[74] The qualification as an income tax or as a sales tax is important because that qualification will indicate whether the treaties for the avoidance of double taxation are applicable.

The point is that DSTs have a hybrid character; they have the features of both income taxes and sales taxes. Perhaps the most relevant criterion for the qualification of DSTs is that taxes on income, in principle, focus on the recipient of the payment instead of on the consumer.[75] Based on this criterion, a distinction can be drawn between taxes on income and turnover taxes.[76] In practice, a clear classification is not possible because of the hybrid nature of DSTs. The more features resembling those of an income tax, the more a DST is likely to qualify as a tax on income, and the tax treaties will be applicable. On the contrary, the more the DST has features of a sales tax, the less likely the tax treaties will be applicable. This will, e.g., be the case if they are imposed on the supply of a certain defined category of digital services that are charged at a fixed rate while the personal characteristics of the supplier are not taken into account; or if they are not creditable against any income tax or eligible for any other type of relief against income tax.[77] However, the economic incidence and the legislative or political intent of the tax should not be determined for the qualification of a tax as an income tax under Article 2 OECD Model.[78]

It is, at the time of drafting, still uncertain what the features will be of the European digital levy and whether it could be offset against other taxes. One element that the authors do already see is that the enterprises that are liable to DSTs or digital levies may

74. It is unlikely that a DST will be qualified as tax on capital.
75. OECD, Tax Challenges Arising from Digitalisation – Interim Report 2018: Inclusive Framework on BEPS, OECD/G20 Base Erosion and Profit Shifting Project (OECD Publishing 2018) (OECD 2018 Interim Report), paras 415-424. R. Ismer and C. Jescheck, *Taxes on Digital Services and the Substantive Scope of Application of Tax Treaties: Pushing the Boundaries of Article 2 of the OECD Model?*, 46(6-7) Intertax, 575 (2018).
76. *See* for example R. Ismer and C. Jescheck, *The Substantive Scope of Tax Treaties in a Post-BEPS World: Article 2 OECD MC (Taxes Covered) and the Rise of New Taxes*, 45(5) Intertax, 384-385 (2017).
77. OECD, Tax Challenges Arising from Digitalisation – Interim Report 2018: Inclusive Framework on BEPS, OECD/G20 Base Erosion and Profit Shifting Project (OECD Publishing 2018) (OECD 2018 Interim Report), para. 421.
78. D. Hohenwarter, et al., *Qualification of the Digital Services Tax under Tax Treaties*, 47 Intertax, 140-147 (2019).

(try to) pass on the tax invoice to the customers or users depending on price elasticity and corporate policy.

7.1 Office of the United States Trade Representative

In early January 2021, the Office of the United States Trade Representative (USTR) issued findings in section 301 investigations of DSTs as adopted by Austria, Spain, and the United Kingdom. The findings conclude that each of the DSTs discriminates against US companies, is inconsistent with prevailing principles of international taxation, and burdens or restricts US commerce.[79] The USTR also indicated that India's equalization levy and the Italian and Turkish DSTs are unfair to US businesses, but no immediate reactions are expected. It will have to be seen how the newly appointed Biden administration will tackle the issue going forward.

8 STATE AID

8.1 Apple

A dispute on EUR 13 billion can hardly be swept under the carpet when touching on relevant European tax matters. The amount at stake in the state aid case between the EC and Ireland related to Apple is astronomic. On 15 July 2020, the General Court (GC) of the European Union published its (lengthy) ruling regarding the action brought by Apple Sales International, Apple Operations Europe, and Ireland[80] for the annulment of the state aid decision of the EC of 30 August 2016.[81] The GC annulled the decision because the EC did not demonstrate the existence of an economic advantage within the meaning of EU state aid rules. In the ruling, the GC gave a reasoned opinion on the EC's use of profit allocation rules, OECD transfer pricing guidelines, and the authorized OECD approach (AOA).

The EC is not formally bound by the OECD transfer pricing guidelines or the AOA. The EC could rely on the AOA, however, because there was an overlap between the functional and factual analysis under the first step of the AOA and the application of Irish domestic tax law. The GC also ruled that the EC rightly used the ALP in the selectivity analysis. The question is hence – where did it go wrong for the EC?

The authors' elevator speech would be 'facts, facts, facts … there is no substitute for taking a deep dive in the facts pattern'.

The EC limited itself to identifying the functions performed by the enterprises as such but did not conduct an analysis of the functions performed, assets used, and risks assumed by the Irish branches. The EC only presumed that the functions of the

79. Office of the United States Trade Representative, USTR Releases Findings and Updates in DST Investigations, 14 January 2021, https://ustr.gov/about-us/policy-offices/press-office/press-releases/2021/january/ustr-releases-findings-and-updates-dst-investigations.
80. Cases T-778/16 and T-892/16.
81. Commission Decision of 30.8.2016 On State Aid – Sa.38373 (2014/C) (Ex 2014/Nn) (Ex 2014/Cp) Implemented by Ireland to Apple.

enterprise as a whole were conducted by the branches as they could not have been allocated to a head office. The EC failed to conduct an analysis of the branches and thus failed to apply the AOA correctly according to the GC. What the EC did was akin to an exclusion approach: the functions cannot be performed by the head office, so they must be performed by the branches, omitting that the boards of directors of the enterprises delegated the powers to persons who were not employed by the Irish branches.

The GC recognized that there were some methodological flaws in the approach that Ireland applied, but these flaws in themselves were not sufficient to demonstrate that the tax measures gave a selective advantage to the Apple affiliates that were concerned. The EC did not demonstrate that the methodological flaws have led to a reduction of the tax burden compared to the normal domestic tax rules.

In the words of the GC, the EC failed to prove '*to the requisite legal standard that there was a selective advantage for the purposes of Article 107(1) TFEU*'.[82]

Although the GC ruled against the state aid decision in this particular case, the GC did confirm the relevance of the arm's length principle and the use of the AOA in a state aid analysis, in particular with regard to the selectivity criteria. The EC appealed the decision of the GC for the reason that the GC judgment raises important legal issues and has made a number of errors of law.[83]

The crusade is far from over, and the next stage will definitely once more trigger attention far beyond EU borders.

8.2 The Belgian Excess Profit Rulings

On 3 December 2020, Advocate General (AG) Kokott of the CJEU delivered her opinion[84] in *Commission v. Belgium and Magnetrol International* (C-337/19 P) on the appeal lodged by the commission in the so-called excess profit rulings (EPR).[85] To refresh memories, the decision of the EC was annulled because the GC ruled it was not an aid scheme.[86] The position that the EPR was an aid scheme was indeed the main argument of the EC. The GC did not examine the other pleas brought forward in this case.

In essence, AG Kokott opined now that the commission was right to consider that the Belgian EPR constituted an aid scheme and that the CJEU should annul the judgment of the GC of 14 February 2019. If the CJEU follows the AG, the procedure will be

82. *See* para. 507 of the Ruling of the General Court.
83. European Commission, *Statement of 25 September 2020 by Executive Vice-President Margrethe Vestager on the Commission's decision to appeal the General Court's judgment on the Apple tax State aid case in Ireland*, https://ec.europa.eu/commission/presscorner/detail/en/STATEMENT_20_1746 (accessed 12 January 2021).
84. Case C-337/19 P – Opinion of Advocate General Kokott delivered on 3 December 2020, http://curia.europa.eu/juris/document/document.jsf;jsessionid=C175E008668FEB07E3F3318F7C8D4738?text=&docid=234967&pageIndex=0&doclang=EN&mode=lst&dir=&occ=first&part=1&cid=23338867 (accessed 13 January 2021).
85. Commission appeal against the 14 February 2019 General Court judgement in the joined cases of *Belgium v. Commission* (T-131/16) and *Magnetrol International v. Commission* (T-263/16).
86. Judgment of the General Court (Seventh Chamber, Extended Composition) of 14 February 2019 in Cases T-131/16 and T-263/16, para. 135.

referred back to the GC that will then proceed by considering the EPR-regime against the state aid criteria and, very likely, this time on a material basis.

According to the AG, the three conditions for the establishment of the state aid scheme qualification are met in the case at hand:

(1) the concept of an act can also encompass a consistent administrative practice. This is the case for the EPR-regime as the commission's sample of a limited number or rulings[87] is found to be a sufficiently representative and adequate sample by the AG to constitute a consistent administrative practice;
(2) aid granted without further implementing measures: according to the AG, this is the case for the EPR-regime as it is found to be a consistent administrative practice; and
(3) identification of beneficiaries in a general/abstract manner that also stems from the consistent administrative practice that does not require further implementing measures. The AG finds identification of the beneficiaries to be inherent to such practice.

In other words, AG Kokott indicates that the GC has interpreted the notion of an aid scheme too restrictively.

Besides this assessment of the state aid scheme qualification, it is interesting to note that AG Kokott also opined on the Belgian corporate income tax regime by stating in paragraph 105, among others, that the Belgian tax authorities have gone '*beyond the wording of Article 185(2) of the CIR 92*'. To quote a cyborg from the future, EPR will be back!

8.3 Inter Ikea

In July 2020, the EC published its decision to extend its formal investigation regarding potential state aid granted by the Netherlands to Inter Ikea.[88] At the centre of the opening investigation of 2017 lies the question on the valuation of the Ikea intellectual property (IP) that was acquired by Inter Ikea Systems BV. A valuation was done for which an advance pricing agreement (APA) from the Dutch tax authorities was obtained. The EC noted, however, that since the publication of the opening decision, Inter Ikea Systems BV started to amortize the IP, and this was in contravention to what had been explicitly agreed upon in the APA. Furthermore, according to the EC, the price of the IP was increased after the opening decision. For these two reasons, the commission decided to extend the scope of its investigation to take into account the tax consequences thereof. The authors felt it premature to expand more in depth on the technical merits of the allegations at this stage.

87. The EC based its decision only on a set of 22 EPR rulings.
88. State aid SA.46470 (2017/C) – Netherlands Possible State aid in favour of Inter IKEA – Extension of the formal Investigation, https://ec.europa.eu/competition/state_aid/cases1/202027/272426_2169565_285_2.pdf.

9 COMMON CONSOLIDATED CORPORATE TAX BASE

A classic among the topics in an overview of the transfer pricing developments in Europe is, of course, an update on the CCCTB. The discussion can be kept relatively short in the absence of noteworthy evolutions on the technical CCCTB front.

There is, however, the political debate around the desirability of group-based taxation that spices up the topic. Indeed, in most of the EC publications and recitals with regard to tax, CCCTB is mentioned. For example, the EC refers to the CCCTB as a means for simplification in the *next generation* document stating that it would provide businesses with a single rulebook to compute the corporate tax base in the EU.[89] The simplification would lead to an improved business environment and contribute to economic growth. This is definitely interesting from a tax technical perspective, particularly as a CCCTB mechanism would be agnostic to factors of economic productivity whatsoever.

Strangely enough, a reference to CCCTB is not found in the action plan for fair and simple taxation supporting the recovery strategy. A reference to a new common corporate tax base is found, however, as a form of new additional own resources in the agreement reached between the EC, the EP, and the Member States on Europe's next long-term budget and the temporary recovery instrument.[90] A proposal is expected by June 2024.

The creeping effect of some of the elements that are embedded in the CCCTB probably deserves continued attention. As is known, the three components of the formula under CCCTB are sales, payroll and employees, and fixed assets.

When looking at the Blueprints on Pillar 1 and Pillar 2 of the OECD/IF Project on the digitalization of the economy, some of these elements can be identified.[91] For example, in the formulaic substance-based carve-out under Pillar 2, reference is made to a payroll component and a tangible asset component to exclude a fixed return for substantive activities from the scope of the rules (the minimum tax) developed under Pillar 2.[92] Under a so-called profitability test to identify the paying entities under Amount A of Pillar 1, reference is made to an alignment with the substance carve-out proposed under Pillar 2.[93] Is it a coincidence that two out of three components under the CCCTB find their way in the OECD/IF proposals, or is it just part of a kind of *green*

89. *Supra* n. 3, p. 11.
90. EU budget: European Commission welcomes agreement on €1.8 trillion package to help build greener, more digital and more resilient Europe, https://ec.europa.eu/commission/presscorner/detail/en/IP_20_2073 (accessed 13 January 2021).
91. A discussion on the Pillar1 and Pillar 2 blueprints fall outside the scope of this contribution of course.
92. OECD, Tax Challenges Arising from Digitalisation – Report on Pillar One Blueprint: Inclusive Framework on BEPS, OECD/G20 Base Erosion and Profit Shifting Project (OECD Publishing, Paris 2020), https://doi.org/10.1787/beba0634-en. – section 4.3. Formulaic Substance-based carve-out.
93. OECD, Tax Challenges Arising from Digitalisation – Report on Pillar One Blueprint: Inclusive Framework on BEPS, OECD/G20 Base Erosion and Profit Shifting Project (OECD Publishing, Paris 2020), https://doi.org/10.1787/beba0634-en. – para. 564.

deal between the EU and the OECD to *recycle* parts of the formula of the CCCTB under the digitalization project?

10 UNANIMITY

One of the difficulties in harmonizing direct taxes within the EU is the requirement of unanimity (or consensus) to adopt directives in the field of direct taxation. Indeed, unlike for VAT for which Article 113 TFEU serves as a specific legal basis, it is generally accepted that Article 115 TFEU serves the same function for harmonization in the field of direct taxation that requires unanimity among all Member States. Given the differences between the Member States and their respective individual interests, several proposals do not go further than the draft stage, or it takes an enormously long time to reach a meeting of the (twenty-seven) minds. The CCCTB proposal serves[94] as a good illustration.

Although discussions on the unanimity requirement are ongoing for years, in order to realize its tax package and to deal with the digitalization of the economy, the topic was again at the centre of the debate in 2020 after the inclusion of the following paragraph by the commission in the tax package:

> To fully deliver on the EU's fair tax agenda, all existing policy levers have to be activated. It is in this context, that the Commission will explore how to make full use of the provisions of the Treaty on the functioning of the EU (TFEU) that allow proposals on taxation to be adopted by ordinary legislative procedure, including article 116 TFEU.[95]

The position of the EC that it will explore whether harmonization in the field of direct taxation can be based on Article 116 TFEU which allows for the adoption of directives by the ordinary legislative procedure instead of the required unanimity under Article 115 received a lot of criticism. The main argument was that Member States did not want to give up their sovereignty in the field of direct taxation when joining the EU, and it was never the intent of Member States to allow for harmonization of direct taxation based on Article 116 TFEU. Taking into account this criticism, it seems that, for now, the EC will try to find unanimity among the Member States to realize its tax package.

In the past, the United Kingdom was often one of the countries with an interest that deviated from the continental European Member States (e.g., regarding the financial transaction tax). It remains to be seen whether, now that the United Kingdom has left the EU, it will be easier to reach unanimity.

94. Proposal for a Council Directive on a Common Consolidated Corporate Tax Base (CCCTB), https://ec.europa.eu/taxation_customs/sites/taxation/files/com_2016_683_en.pdf.
95. *Supra* n. 23, p. 2.

11 STANDING COMMITTEE TO CONTRIBUTE TO THE EFFECTIVENESS OF DISPUTE RESOLUTION AMONG MSS AND A NEW EXPERT GROUP ON TRANSFER PRICING

The EC intends to continue monitoring the dispute resolution mechanism directive.[96,97] The intention is to constitute a permanent body for dispute resolution, a so-called standing committee, the legal basis of which can be found in the dispute resolution directive. What seems to be missing, however, is a monitoring procedure for the arbitration convention.[98] Although its role may be diminishing, it is still an instrument in force. Additionally, the role of the standing committee under the arbitration directive goes beyond simply monitoring. Indeed, according to the arbitration directive, it could serve as an alternative dispute resolution commission in the form of a committee that is of a permanent nature.[99]

Moreover, in 2021 or 2022, the EC will create an expert group on transfer pricing.[100] This expert group will seek non-legislative solutions to practical transfer pricing problems that are relevant for the EU. The group will be composed of representatives from the Member States and participants from businesses and civil society.

These initiatives are, of course, very much welcomed. The combination monitoring dispute resolution and the expert group seeking pragmatic solutions very much resemble the European Union Joint Transfer Pricing Forum (EU JTPF). The impact of the EU JTPF cannot be overstated. Despite the lack of legal mandate, whatsoever it has served as a catalyst for 'effective landing' on a number of most relevant topics such as cross-border benchmarking, low value-adding services, monitoring the remediation of double taxation, and much more, albeit all in the context and in the application of the OECD Transfer Pricing Guidelines. Its swan song in spring 2019 was hence regretful. The authors understand that the role of the standing committee on dispute resolution might be broader than just transfer pricing that is in line with the arbitration directive. The authors do hope that the standing committee will monitor the cases that are submitted under the arbitration directive and under the arbitration convention, as well as the pending APA cases. At least, this is what the EU JTPF did, and monitoring cases proved to be a useful incentive for tax authorities to resolve the cases under dispute or in an APA context in a timely manner. Moreover, given the fast evolution of and surging complexities around sustainable profit allocation throughout global value chains, adding other tasks to the expert group's plate may be considered. For instance, grappling with DAC6 from the trenches teaches that it may be a good idea to share best practices across countries and filter out overly draconic approaches that serve little other purpose than distracting tax authorities and taxpayers from what truly counts:

96. *Supra* n. 23, p. 13.
97. Council Directive (EU) 2017/1852 of 10 October 2017 on tax dispute resolution mechanisms in the European Union.
98. Convention on the elimination of double taxation in connection with the adjustment of profits of associated enterprises (90/463/EEC).
99. *Supra* n. 97, Article 10(1).
100. *Supra* n. 23, p. 15.

demonstrating where 'true' profitability lies in a convincing way that enables tax authorities to focus on 'true' tax risk.

12 CONCLUSION

Embracing the 'Resilient, Green, Digital, Social and Global Europe' ambitions of the Portuguese EU presidency will necessitate investment and effort from all stakeholders. Few will doubt the merits of such a noble cause. Europe deserves praise for keeping up as a crucial economic block defending fundamental rules of the game to keep its twenty-seven members on board. This will come at a cost in terms of 'political capital' to be spent on various matters far beyond the tax agenda. Recovering from COVID-19, migrating to zero-based emissions, and much more will be a costly affair, and funding is unavoidable. Moreover, the global economy is no longer delivering what is (felt) needed as it depends on a system of rules and norms that may not work (appropriately) to generate social progress (anymore). The authors hence very well appreciate that 'tax politics' may complicate the design and implementation of robust and sustainable principle-based tax policy initiatives. This is probably a fair *captatio benevolentiae* to sharpen the authors' tone a bit now. Indeed, when writing this contribution, it was striking to see the easiness and frequency to use terms such as 'tax avoidance' or 'aggressive tax planning' and the like in EC documents. It almost looks like a religion where everyone should salute those notions with little or no critical contemplation. There should obviously be no room for tax fraud or tax abuse. This being said, appreciating the 'legitimacy' of something is a harder nut to crack. Only the initiatives on dispute resolution and the EU cooperative compliance framework respectively can be considered as being in favour of taxpayers, at least those adhering to the broadest transparency standards (and probably further than what is needed for a decent analysis of value creation across borders). Such wording to fuel public sentiment amplified by (social) media about (deemed) improper behaviour by multinational companies may be expected.

The year 2020 also showed that the EU is looking to finance its budget through its own resources via the EU digital levy and other taxes. These levies will, of course, make the EU leaders and the EP responsible (perhaps in part, at first) for balancing the EU budget. The taxes will be levied according to EU rules and no longer according to national rules.[101] The first bites of sovereignty are hence in the process of being chewed off. We enter the era of the dawning of supranational taxes, besides local (e.g., municipal or provincial) taxes and national taxes (e.g., corporate income tax).

The months and years ahead will offer fruitful inspiration for more guidance and rules on taxation to cushion the economy from the pandemic and geopolitical threats. The authors hope that, when inking new rules, the EU legislators empathize with the four key questions on a VP tax's plate:

(1) Are we compliant from a penalty protection perspective?

101. F. Vanistendael, *Remembering 2020*, 101 Tax Notes International, 331 (2021).

(2) Do we pay taxes where value is created?
(3) What are the group's long-term strategic tax priorities, and are these in line with business strategy, including the ESG agenda?
(4) Are tax rates predictable, sustainable, and explainable?

Anti-avoidance rules are here to stay and serve a purpose. They should not, however, become an EU fetish and serve as a substitute for in-depth analysis. While this may not be the intention of the (EU) legislator, it may be the consequence when tax inspectors are fiddling with these concepts in the (field audit) trenches.

There is no doubt that there will not be any dull moment for those practising international taxation in the foreseeable future.

CHAPTER 3

Transfer Pricing Developments in the United States*

Sean F. Foley, Kevin D. Kramer, Thomas D. Bettge, Lillie M. Sullivan & Josh D. McConkey

* The information in this chapter is not intended to be 'written advice concerning one or more federal tax matters' subject to the requirements of section 10.37(a)(2) of Treasury Department Circular 230 because the content is issued for general informational purposes only. The information contained in this chapter is of a general nature and based on authorities that are subject to change. Applicability of the information to specific situations should be determined through consultation with your tax adviser. This chapter represents the views of the author or authors only and does not necessarily represent the views or professional advice of KPMG LLP.

Transfer pricing remains important in the United States, and the past year has brought about significant developments, primarily in the area of transfer pricing litigation. The Internal Revenue Service (IRS) achieved several major victories in 2020 that will have a significant impact on transfer pricing moving forward. This chapter addresses the recent case law highlights as well as some key administrative developments and considers what they mean for transfer pricing in the United States in the future.

1 CASE LAW MILESTONES

The past year was characterized by two major IRS victories beginning with the Supreme Court's denial of certiorari in *Altera Corp. v. Commissioner*, which effectively ended the regulatory challenge mounted by the taxpayer. Additionally, the IRS demonstrated that it can successfully challenge and defend a transfer pricing adjustment on the facts following the large victory in *Coca-Cola Co. v. Commissioner*.

1.1 *Coca-Cola Co. v. Commissioner* (2020)[1]

1.1.1 Background

During the years at issue, the Coca-Cola Co. (Coke) licensed brand and manufacturing intangibles to Supply Points (SPs).[2] All of the SPs were classified as controlled foreign corporations (CFCs) except for the Mexican SP that was a branch of Coke. The SPs manufactured concentrate and sold it to unrelated bottlers. While the SPs manufactured the concentrate, Coke's other foreign activities were carried out by local service companies (ServCos). The ServCos were responsible for local advertising and in-country consumer marketing in addition to liaising with third party local bottlers, among other functions.

The ServCos were generally reimbursed by Coke on a cost-plus basis with the exception of some expenses such as third-party marketing expenses that were reimbursed at cost. The SPs had practically no workers other than those engaged in producing concentrate and their support staff. Most other personnel, including leadership, were employed by the ServCos and Coke. The ServCos leadership acted as the liaison between Coke and the local bottlers while also serving as their advisors.

The SPs reimbursed Coke for a share of the fees earned by the ServCos, including a share of the ServCos' third-party marketing expenses. However, in almost every case, there was no contractual or other documentation in place evidencing an SP's agreement to bear these charges. The royalties the SPs paid to Coke were based on a

1. The *Coca-Cola Co. v. Comm'r*, 155 T.C. No. 10.
2. References to Coke include, when appropriate, its wholly owned domestic subsidiary, Coca-Cola Export Corp.

'10-50-50 method' under which the SPs retained a 10% operating margin and split their residual profit 50:50 with Coke. The 10-50-50 method originated in a 1996 closing agreement between Coke and the IRS, covering the years 1987-1995. Coke applied the method for the next eleven years, and the IRS accepted Coke's transfer pricing without adjustment.

The IRS, upon examination of Coke's 2007-2009 returns, determined that the 10-50-50 method did not reflect arm's length norms because it overcompensated the SPs and undercompensated Coke for the use of its intellectual property (IP). Therefore, the IRS reallocated income to Coke using the comparable profits method (CPM), treating the Coca-Cola bottlers as comparable parties. All of the income received by the SPs in excess of the CPM returns was reallocated to Coke.

1.1.2 Tax Court's Opinion

The tax court, in a reviewed opinion, agreed with the IRS, rejecting Coke's argument that the terms of the closing agreement should apply for future years. While the agreement contained a provision that allowed Coke to avoid penalties if it followed the closing agreement, the court found this provision corroborated its determination as it indicated that the parties knew how to make a prospective agreement on the 10-50-50 method and yet chose not to do so with respect to the 10-50-50 method itself.

The tax court found that the IRS's CPM position was 'conservative' as the independent bottlers identified as comparable companies had more functional responsibility and risk and likely owned their own intangibles. The court determined that the SPs held no rights, express or implied, to guaranteed production of Coca-Cola products. The record reflected that Coke closed or shifted production from over a dozen SPs between 1980 and 2011, which resulted in a loss or a total elimination of income for some SPs. Neither Coke nor the SPs benefitting from the production shifts paid compensation to the SPs that suffered a loss or elimination of income stemming from the production shifts. Additionally, the contracts between Coke and the SPs indicated that the SPs did not have intangibles, and the independent bottlers had long-term contractual arrangements with Coke, whereas the SPs were routinely terminated and consolidated. Thus, the court suggested that, based on these facts, the independent bottlers should arguably earn more income than the SPs.

Coke argued that the SPs possessed unique marketing intangibles due to their funding of consumer marketing expenses, making the use of the CPM for the SPs unreliable. Although the SPs did not perform marketing functions, they did fund consumer marketing expenses, and Coke argued that this funding entitled the SPs to intangible related returns. However, the tax court ruled that the mere allocation of marketing expenses does not create IP, and thus the CPM could be applied.

The tax court also rejected Coke's use of the comparable uncontrolled transaction (CUT) method as the best method. More specifically, it rejected the taxpayer's argument that the CUT was preferred to the CPM and noted that, while the CUT method generally provides a higher degree of reliability than the CPM when the conditions for its application are satisfied, those conditions were not satisfied in this case. Therefore, the CPM provided the most reliable method for determining arm's length prices.

Lastly, given that the parties did not dispute the cost-plus returns earned by the ServCos, the tax court did not need to address these returns.[3] Coke sought to include the functions of the ServCos in its analysis of the appropriate offshore earnings of Coke's foreign affiliates. However, based in part on the parties' stipulation that the ServCos already earned an arm's length return, the tax court rejected this line of argument.

1.1.3 Key Takeaways

Overall, the *Coke* tax court opinion demonstrates the pitfalls of relying on expired IRS agreements for transfer pricing methods and reinforces the necessity of clearly identified and implemented transfer pricing policies and practices. Specifically, being aware of the relative returns earned by affiliates is important to help identify any similarities with the fact patterns at issue in the *Coke* opinion.

Additionally, it is important to be clear on who owns any intangibles and to make sure there is a connection between the funding of intangible development and the ownership of the resulting intangibles. In the case of Coca Cola, the tax court held that the SPs did not acquire any intangible property rights and were not otherwise entitled to non-routine returns as a result of their funding of marketing spend. Importantly, the intercompany agreements and the actions of the parties did not clearly indicate ownership of intangibles by the SPs.

The *Coke* case also raised the question of what effect must be given to foreign legal restrictions on payment for purposes of section 482.[4] Coke's Brazilian SP could not pay royalties in excess of a certain amount because of Brazilian legal restrictions. Instead, during the years at issue, the Brazilian SP paid dividends to Coke and sought to characterize these dividends as royalty payments via dividend offset treatment under the terms of its 1996 closing agreement. The Brazilian legal restriction did not qualify because Treasury Regulation § 1.482-1(h)(2) requires that a foreign legal restriction must prevent the payment of income in any form, and thus Coke was required to include the Brazilian royalties (as adjusted by the IRS) in income.

Although Coke challenged the validity of the regulation, the tax court did not reach a decision on this issue and instead noted that the regulation has been challenged in *3M Co. v. Commissioner* (discussed below) and reserved ruling on the issue until an opinion is issued in *3M*. The court did determine that Coke was entitled to claim dividend offset treatment for the Brazilian dividends, notwithstanding the fact that Coke did not file the statements required by Rev. Proc. 99-32, which the court found – on the particular facts of Coke's case – to be an excusable omission.

3. Note that, while the court did not address the proper arm's length returns for the ServCos, it did address the compensation received by the ServCos to the extent this was affected by split invoicing with the SPs.
4. All section references herein are to the Internal Revenue Code of 1986, as amended.

1.2 *Altera Corp. v. Commissioner* (2015, 2018, 2019)

The *Altera*[5] case involved a challenge to the validity of a regulation that required parties to a qualified cost-sharing arrangement (CSA) to share stock-based compensation (SBC) costs.[6] The taxpayer contended that third parties do not share SBC costs when entering into qualified CSAs with third parties and that the United States Department of the Treasury (Treasury) failed to adequately consider comments to that effect when promulgating the regulation.

1.2.1 Predecessors

The SBC issue predates *Altera* and has been an IRS focus since the 1990s. The 1968 transfer pricing regulations did not mention SBC as such but provided that '[i]n order for the arrangement to qualify as a bona fide [cost sharing] arrangement, it must reflect an effort in good faith by the participating members to bear their respective shares of *all the costs and risks* of development on an arm's length basis'.[7] In *Seagate Technology, Inc. v. Commissioner,*[8] the IRS sought to include SBC costs in the taxpayer's CSA on the basis of the 1968 regulations. Although the tax court denied the taxpayer's motion for summary judgment on the grounds that it had not been factually determined whether arm's length parties shared SBC costs in similar arrangements, the IRS conceded the case.

The IRS took the issue up again in *Xilinx v. Commissioner.*[9] At issue in *Xilinx* was the 1995 replacement to the 1968 regulation, which was generally similar, stating that 'a controlled participant's costs of developing intangibles for a taxable year mean *all of the costs* incurred by that participant related to the intangible development area', without expressly calling out SBC.[10] Like *Altera*, *Xilinx* took a tortuous path – after an initial tax court victory for the taxpayer, the Ninth Circuit reversed only to withdraw its own opinion and affirm the tax court outcome after one of the panellists changed his view. The Ninth Circuit's opinion in *Xilinx* concluded that the inconsistency between the 'all costs' rule in Treasury Regulation § 1.482-7 and the arm's length standard enshrined in Treasury Regulation § 1.482-1 must be resolved in favour of the latter[11] – and because the court found no evidence that unrelated parties share SBC costs in similar arrangements, the arm's length standard prevented the IRS from requiring their inclusion in CSAs between related parties.

5. *Altera Corp. v. Comm'r*, 926 F.3d 1061 (9th Cir. 2019), *rev'ing* 145 T.C. 91 (2015).
6. Treas. Reg. § 1.482-7A(d)(2). The present counterpart to this regulation is Treas. Reg. § 1.482-7(d)(3).
7. Treas. Reg. § 1.482-2(d)(4) (1968) (emphasis added).
8. *Seagate Tech., Inc. v. Comm'r*, T.C. Memo. 2000-388.
9. *Xilinx v. Comm'r*, 598 F.3d 1191 (9th Cir. 2010), *superseding* 567 F.3d 482 (9th Cir. 2009), *aff'ing* 125 T.C. 37 (2005).
10. Treas. Reg. § 1.482-7(d)(1) (1995) (emphasis added).
11. Note that the concurrence by Judge Fisher indicated that the provisions may be reconcilable but that the Treasury's interpretation must be rejected because taxpayers were not given fair notice.

Seagate and *Xilinx* indicate the IRS's decade-spanning commitment to pursuing its position on the inclusion of SBC costs in CSAs, which may have important implications for post-*Altera* enforcement.

1.2.2 The *Altera* Decision

The CSA regulation promulgated in 2003 expressly included SBC for the first time, and it is this regulation that was challenged in *Altera*: 'all stock-based compensation that is ... related ... to the development of intangibles covered by the arrangement is included as an intangible development cost'.[12] A 2011 update left the rule materially the same: 'all stock-based compensation that is ... directly identified with, or reasonably allocable to, the [intangible development activity] is included as an [intangible development cost]'.[13] This is the regulation that is currently in effect.

In the preamble to the 2003 regulations, the Treasury acknowledged comments asserting that unrelated parties did not, in fact, share SBC costs in CSAs but expressed the view that '[t]he uncontrolled transactions cited by commentators do not share enough characteristics of [qualified] CSAs involving the development of high-profit intangibles to establish that parties at arm's length would not take stock options into account in the context of an arrangement similar to a [qualified] CSA'.[14] Though little remarked upon at the time, the preamble also contained a brief but significant reference to the commensurate with income (CWI) standard, noting that the legislative history indicated that Congress intended to respect CSAs 'as consistent with the commensurate with income standard, and therefore consistent with the arm's length standard, if and to the extent that the participants' shares of income 'reasonably reflect the actual economic activity undertaken by each'.[15]

The taxpayer in *Altera* challenged the validity of the 2003 regulation. In 2015, the tax court held for the taxpayer with a unanimous opinion agreed to by fifteen judges. The tax court held that the regulation was arbitrary and capricious under the Administrative Procedure Act and that the Treasury had failed to engage in reasoned decision-making as required by applicable precedents because it lacked a factual basis for the rule and failed to respond to significant comments on the issue of whether unrelated parties share SBC costs.[16]

In July 2018, the Ninth Circuit released an opinion from a divided three-judge panel reversing the tax court decision but subsequently withdrew the opinion because of concerns relating to the death of Judge Reinhardt, who had joined the majority opinion but passed away before it was issued.[17] Judge Reinhardt was subsequently replaced on the panel by Judge Graber, and additional oral arguments were held during October 2018.

12. Treas. Reg. § 1.482-7A(d)(2) (2003).
13. Treas. Reg. § 1.482-7(d)(3).
14. T.D. 9088, 68 Fed. Reg. 51171 (26 August 2003).
15. *Id.* (quoting H.R. Conf. Rep. No. 99-841, at II-638 (1986)).
16. *Altera Corp. v. Comm'r*, 145 T.C. 91 (2015).
17. The original opinion, 2018 WL 3542989 (Nos 16-70496, 16-70497) (9th Cir. 24 July 2018), was withdrawn in August 2018. *Altera Corp. v. Comm'r*, 898 F.3d 1266 (9th Cir. 2018).

In June 2019, the Ninth Circuit again reversed the tax court,[18] agreeing with the government and taking a broad interpretation of the arm's length standard that allowed the IRS to dispense with an analysis based on comparable transactions. Judge Graber joined the majority opinion authored by Chief Judge Thomas while Judge O'Malley dissented.

The majority opinion reviewed the development of the arm's length standard and the 1986 introduction of the CWI standard under section 482. It rejected the taxpayer's argument that the arm's length standard required a comparability analysis and that the Treasury could therefore not require the inclusion of SBC costs unless it could show that unrelated parties share those costs. The majority noted that both the Treasury's 1988 White Paper and the regulations issued in 1994 and 1995 conceived of 'the arm's length standard as result-oriented, meaning that the goal is parity in taxable income rather than parity in the method of allocation itself'. In keeping with this understanding, the majority noted that the CWI standard is consistent with the arm's length standard.

Based on this analysis, which focused on developments prior to the promulgation of the challenged regulations, the majority concluded that the issuance of regulations requiring the sharing of SBC, despite the lack of evidence of unrelated parties sharing it, did not represent a departure from a long-standing policy of requiring an analysis of unrelated parties' behaviour.[19]

The majority concluded that the challenged regulations were entitled to deference under *Chevron, U.S.A., Inc. v. Natural Resources Defense Council, Inc.*[20] Under *Chevron*, courts will defer to an agency's interpretation of a statute if: (1) Congress has not spoken to the precise question at issue; and (2) the agency's interpretation is a reasonable construction of that statute. Neither section 482 nor its legislative history directly addresses the inclusion of SBC costs in intangible development costs (IDCs), and the court found that the 'Treasury reasonably understood § 482 as an authorization to require internal allocation methods [rather than comparability-based methods] in the [qualified] CSA context, provided that the costs and income allocated are proportionate to the economic activity of the related parties.'

Lastly, the majority determined that the regulations were valid under the Administrative Procedure Act because the Treasury engaged in a reasoned decision-making process as required by the Supreme Court's decision in *Motor Vehicle Manufacturers Association of the United States, Inc. v. State Farm Mutual Automobile Insurance*.[21] While *Chevron* generally addresses whether a regulation is a permissible interpretation of the statute passed by Congress, the *State Farm* standard focuses on the procedural correctness of the regulation's promulgation without regard to its substantive merits. Even if a regulation is reasonable, it may be invalid if the agency failed to follow the requisite procedures or failed to give consideration to significant comments.

18. *Altera Corp. v. Comm'r*, 926 F.3d 1061 (9th Cir. 2019).
19. This permitted the court to dispense with the heightened review that would have been required for such a departure. *Id.*, at 1085-1086 (discussing *FCC v. Fox Television Stations, Inc.*, 556 U.S. 502 (2009), and related cases).
20. 467 U.S. 837 (1984).
21. 463 U.S. 29 (1983).

The Ninth Circuit majority found that the Treasury had appropriately noted and responded to significant comments and had adequately supported its decision to require inclusion of SBC costs in IDCs. The majority noted that the preamble to the challenged regulations provided that the Treasury was relying on the CWI standard and concluded that the CWI – which only applies to transfers or licenses of intangibles – applies to qualified CSAs because they involve a transfer of rights in the intangibles to be developed. While noting that the Treasury's rulemaking process could have been improved, the court held that it was sufficient: 'Though it could have been more specific, Treasury "articulated a rational connection" between its decision' and the relevant facts.[22]

Judge O'Malley's dissent argued that the regulations were both procedurally invalid under *State Farm* and the Administrative Procedure Act as well as unreasonable under *Chevron*. The dissent asserted that, even if the Treasury's arguments before the Ninth Circuit could have sufficed as a reasonable basis for the regulation, the regulations were invalid because those arguments were not the ones that the Treasury made when promulgating the regulations.[23] The dissent disputed that the CWI standard applied to qualified CSAs because they involve the development of new intangibles and not the transfer of existing intangibles between the parties. The dissent concluded that section 482 does not authorize dispensing with a comparability analysis that is tied to the behaviour of third parties except in a limited set of cases in which the CWI applies.

A petition for rehearing *en banc* was denied over the dissent of an additional three judges.[24] Altera then requested that the Supreme Court grant certiorari. However, on 22 June 2020, the Supreme Court declined to issue a writ of certiorari in *Altera v. Commissioner*,[25] thus leaving intact the Ninth Circuit's 2019 decision upholding the validity of the Treasury regulations that require related parties to share the costs of the SBC as a component of their IDCs in CSAs.

The Supreme Court's denial of certiorari in *Altera* leaves taxpayers without any prospect that, in the near future, the SBC regulations will be successfully reversed. However, it is likely that future challenges will be made as these issues arise in other courts. For now, this means different things for different taxpayers, i.e., for taxpayers within and not within the jurisdiction of the Ninth Circuit. Taxpayers within the Ninth Circuit are generally bound by the Ninth Circuit opinion upholding the 2003 regulation. Taxpayers outside the jurisdiction of the Ninth Circuit can still rely on the unanimous 2015 tax court decision invalidating the 2003 regulation. Therefore, taxpayers should fully consider their tax return filing positions and, to the extent that they chose not to share the costs of SBC under their CSAs, should have a well-documented file supporting their position. Other issues arising from this decision include how to address CSA contractual provisions anticipating the regulatory litigation, Accounting Standards Codification 740, and the ability to use a nonqualified CSA in lieu of a qualified CSA

22. 926 F.3d at 1085 (quoting *County of Amador v. U.S. Dep't of Interior*, 872 F.3d 1012, 1027 (9th Cir. 2017)).
23. *Id.*, at 1093 (O'Malley, J., dissenting) (discussing the case through the lens of *SEC v. Chenery Corp.*, 332 U.S. 194 (1947)).
24. *Altera Corp. v. Comm'r*, 941 F.3d 1200 (denying petition for rehearing *en banc*).
25. *Altera Corp. v. Comm'r*, 141 S.Ct. 131 (2020) (denying petition for writ of certiorari).

depending on the taxpayer's specific facts. All of these issues can be very intricate, and all should be considered as taxpayers work through the implications of the *Altera* decision.

1.3 *Eaton v. Commissioner* (2013, 2017, 2019)

Eaton challenged the IRS's decision to set aside two advance pricing agreements (APAs) on the basis of Eaton's inadvertent failure to disclose certain information and the commission of computational errors that affected its compliance with the APAs.[26] During the APA period, Eaton discovered that it had committed several errors, all of which it corrected and reported to the IRS in its APA annual reports, including in amended APA annual reports and amended tax returns for certain years. In response, the IRS cancelled both APAs, citing misrepresentation, mistakes as to material facts, the failure of APA critical assumptions, and lack of good faith compliance with the APAs. The IRS then proceeded to make transfer pricing adjustments for the APA years.

The initial salvo came in 2013 when the tax court determined that the cancellation of the APAs should be reviewed using the abuse of discretion standard rather than the stricter contract law principles urged by the taxpayer.[27] This setback notwithstanding, the taxpayer went on to prevail in the tax court, which concluded in 2017 that the taxpayer's inadvertent errors were not 'material' and that the taxpayer's presentation of data based on its own viewpoint was not false or misleading and thus not a 'misrepresentation' under the applicable revenue procedure. Accordingly, the court held that the IRS had abused its discretion in cancelling the APAs.

The IRS advanced an alternative argument under section 367(d). If the court did not agree with the cancellation of the APAs and the transfer pricing adjustments, the IRS asserted that it had to conclude that intangibles had been transferred to the foreign affiliates as they could not have earned the returns that they did absent such a transfer. The court made short shrift of this argument, noting the IRS's failure to specify any intangible that had been transferred. However, given the expanded definition of intangibles now found in section 367(d)(4), it is possible that the IRS will continue to make broad, unspecific claims in future cases that value is transferred subject to section 367(d).

Eaton resurfaced at the end of 2019 with a supplemental opinion on the issue of penalties.[28] The IRS tried to assert penalties and. in particular. a heightened 40% net transfer pricing adjustment penalty. The tax court disagreed, holding that the APAs remained in effect for the years at issue and, therefore, the increase in the taxpayer's income did not result from a section 482 adjustment. As a result, there could be no net transfer pricing adjustment penalty. The opinion is still pending under Tax Court Rule 155, awaiting the parties' computation of the amounts of the APA adjustments related to the errors reported by the taxpayer.

26. *Eaton Corp. v. Comm'r*, T.C. Memo. 2017-147.
27. *Eaton Corp. v. Comm'r*, 140 T.C. 410 (2013).
28. *Eaton Corp. v. Comm'r*, 153 T.C. No. 6 (2019).

1.4 *3M Co. v. Commissioner*[29]

The *3M* case began in 2013 when the taxpayer filed a petition in the tax court. The case was submitted fully stipulated, meaning that no fact-finding trial was required. Oral arguments were subsequently held in November 2016. Since then, there have been no material developments, although the discussion of the blocked income issue in *Coke* suggests that an opinion in *3M* may be imminent.

Like *Coke*, *3M* concerns the validity of Treasury Regulation § 1.482-1(h)(2) blocked income rules to royalties that cannot be paid by a Brazilian subsidiary due to Brazilian legal restrictions. The IRS determined that 3M's Brazilian subsidiary should have paid USD 23.7 million in 2006 after factoring in a set-off for non-reimbursed research and development expenses. However, Brazilian law would not have permitted it to pay more than USD 9.4 million.

The Brazilian restrictions do not prevent payment of the income in any form; hence, they apparently do not satisfy the criterion of Treasury Regulation § 1.482-1(h)(2)(ii)(C), and the case, therefore, turns not on whether 3M complied with the regulation but on whether the regulation is valid. 3M challenges it under three theories: failure to comply with the Administrative Procedure Act by responding to material comments, failure to reasonably interpret section 482 under the *Chevron* framework, and inconsistency with prior judicial precedents.

The *Coke* case was largely a win for the IRS, but, as noted above, it failed to comment on the blocked-income issue that is at issue in the *3M* case. This issue will hopefully be decided in the near future.

1.5 *Whirlpool Financial Corp. v. Commissioner* (2020)[30]

From 2007-2009, Whirlpool Financial Corp. (Whirlpool) performed a restructuring of its Mexican manufacturing operations utilizing a CFC in Luxembourg (Whirlpool Luxembourg). As a result of the restructuring, Whirlpool used the Mexican maquiladora regime as part of a tax structure to have Whirlpool Luxembourg become the manufacturer of appliances in Mexico in conjunction with a disregarded Mexican subsidiary that benefited from Mexican tax incentives.

Appliances manufactured in Mexico and owned by Whirlpool Luxembourg were sold to Whirlpool for distribution to its end customers. This resulted in Whirlpool Luxembourg earning large amounts of income that, due to the circumstances, were exempt from tax from both a Mexican and Luxembourg perspective. Upon review, the IRS determined the income related to this arrangement qualified as foreign base company sales income (FBCSI) and therefore must be included in Whirlpool's income as subpart F income under section 951(a), increasing Whirlpool's taxable income by approximately USD 50 million. Subpart F is the US-CFC regime that currently taxes certain CFC income.

29. *3M Co. v. Comm'r*, Tax Court docket no. 5816-13.
30. *Whirlpool Fin. Corp. v. Comm'r*, 154 T.C. No. 9 (2020).

FBCSI generally results when an entity in a jurisdiction (i) purchases products manufactured outside that jurisdiction and (ii) sells them to customers outside that jurisdiction if either the seller or the buyer is a related party (or the sale or purchase is on behalf of a related party). Whirlpool's subpart F planning was intended to avoid the creation of FBCSI – specifically because the Mexican manufacturer was a disregarded entity; from a US tax perspective, Whirlpool Luxembourg produced the products itself. Section 954(d)(2) and the regulations thereunder include a so-called branch rule: if a CFC carries on activities outside its home country via a branch, and the tax effect of doing so is substantially the same as if the branch were a separate CFC, income from those activities may be treated as income from a separate CFC (and thus may be FBCSI), provided a tax rate disparity test is satisfied.

Whirlpool petitioned the tax court and then filed a motion for partial summary judgment arguing that the appliances sold by Whirlpool Luxembourg were 'substantially transformed by its Mexican branch from the component parts and raw materials it had purchased' and was therefore not considered FBCSI. The government argued that a genuine dispute of material fact existed as to whether Whirlpool Luxembourg actually manufactured the products. Further, the parties filed cross-motions for partial summary judgment as to whether the sales income was FBCSI under the branch rule.

The tax court ruled in favour of the government with respect to the application of the branch rule. The tax court agreed with the government that there was a genuine dispute of material fact. However, the court further analysed both the statutory language of section 954(d)(2) and the extensive regulations that have been issued implementing those rules. It concluded that whether or not Whirlpool Luxembourg is regarded as having manufactured the products, under section 954(d)(2), its Mexican branch is treated as a subsidiary of Whirlpool Luxembourg. Therefore, the court held that the sales income Whirlpool Luxembourg earned constitutes FBCSI taxable to the taxpayer as subpart F income.

Whirlpool argued that Whirlpool Luxembourg had no substance. Whirlpool Luxembourg (i.e., the remainder, as distinct from its Mexican branch) employed only one individual on a part-time basis, and therefore Whirlpool 'urge[d] that "the remainder performs no sales or purchasing activities" and hence that "the manufacturing branch rule is inapplicable."' However, the tax court rejected this contention, noting the following:

> This argument strikes us as facetious. The essence of petitioners' position under section 954(d)(1) is that Whirlpool Luxembourg was a real company engaged in real business activities. It owned all of the manufacturing equipment and purchased the raw materials used to manufacture the Products. It took title to the finished Products, as it was required to do in order to comply with Mexico's maquiladora decree. A transfer pricing study commissioned by [Whirlpool Luxembourg's Mexico branch] represented to the Mexican Government that 'no sales effort is made' by [Whirlpool Luxembourg's Mexico branch] and that 'all responsibility for the distribution, marketing, and sale of [the] products' fell to Whirlpool Luxembourg. In seeking partial summary judgment under section 954(d)(1), petitioners asserted that Whirlpool Luxembourg's operations 'without question were substantial' and that Whirlpool Luxembourg must be treated 'as having sold a manufactured product.' Asserting that Whirlpool Luxembourg's activities were

> insubstantial for purposes of seeking partial summary judgment under section 954(d)(2) is a classic example of an attempt to have one's cake and eat it too.

In addressing and dismissing Whirlpool's arguments that the manufacturing branch rule is inapplicable, the tax court also looked past the regulations, focusing instead on the statute and congressional intent in its reasoning. The tax court found that this situation was very clearly contemplated by the statute and that it could easily read the regulation to conform with statutory intent:

> By carrying on its activities 'through a branch or similar establishment' in Mexico, Whirlpool Luxembourg avoided any current taxation of its sales income. It thus achieved 'substantially the same effect' – deferral of tax on its sales income – that it would have achieved under U.S. tax rules if its Mexican branch were a wholly owned subsidiary deriving such income. That is precisely the situation that the statute covers.
>
> The statute's preconditions having been met, the second part of section 954(d)(2) specifies the prescribed tax treatment. The sales income attributable to the carrying on of activities through Whirlpool Luxembourg's Mexican branch 'shall be treated as income derived by a wholly owned subsidiary' of Whirlpool Luxembourg. And the sales income thus derived 'shall constitute foreign base company sales income of the [CFC].' Sec. 954(d)(2). In short, even without the refinements supplied by the regulations implementing section 954(d)(2), the bare text of the statute, literally read, indicates that Whirlpool Luxembourg's sales income is FBCSI that must be included in petitioners' income under subpart F.

The tax court emphasized this point by focusing on Congress' intent to address the specific activities in which Whirlpool was engaging:

> This conclusion comports with the overall statutory structure and with Congress' purpose in enacting subpart F. The sales income with which Congress was concerned was 'income of a selling subsidiary which has been separated from manufacturing activities of a related corporation merely to obtain a lower rate of tax for the sales income.' H.R. Rept. No. 87-1447, supra at 62, 1962-3 C.B. at 466. That is precisely the objective that Whirlpool aimed to achieve here.

Based on the tax court's reasoning, if Whirlpool Luxembourg had conducted its manufacturing operations in Mexico through a separate entity, its sales income would plainly have been FBCSI under section 954(d)(1). Section 954(d)(2) prevents petitioners from avoiding this result by arranging to conduct those operations through a branch. This is interesting because the case departs from the typical analysis of nuances in the Treasury regulations and instead looks to the statute.

As a result of the *Whirlpool* decision, it is important that companies revisit their intercompany agreements and how they align with the facts of the transfer pricing arrangements. Taxpayers should consider how this ruling could affect their own tax structures globally, especially with regard to subpart F planning techniques that may no longer be accepted by the IRS. A transfer pricing analysis and documentation that supports the allocation of income in a Whirlpool-like structure to the Luxembourg principal company may be an important consideration for companies with this type of structure.

1.6 *Adams Challenge (UK) Limited v. Commissioner* (2020, 2021)[31]

Adams Challenge addresses the interaction of bilateral tax treaties with section 882(c)(2)'s limit on deductions for foreign corporations that do not file US income tax returns, an issue that has hitherto gone unaddressed by US courts. While the case does not directly implicate transfer pricing, the domestic procedures that need to be followed in order to ensure permanent establishments in the United States are entitled to deductions are important for transfer pricing practitioners.

Adams Challenge is a UK company that chartered a multipurpose support vessel to an unrelated oil and gas services company for use in decommissioning oil and gas wells on the US's outer continental shelf (OCS) in the Gulf of Mexico. The charter of the vessel included a crew that was comprised of employees of one of Adams' affiliates. The decommissioning work involved shuttered wells that had been damaged by hurricanes and were not producing oil or gas. Adams earned approximately USD 45 million from this charter from 2009 through 2011.

In October 2013, believing that the charter had expired and that Adams' vessel would leave US taxing jurisdiction, the IRS issued a notice of jeopardy assessment covering 2009-2011. Adams demonstrated that its charter had been renewed, and the jeopardy notice was abated; Adams then proceeded to file a US income tax return (Form 1120-F) for 2011 in December 2013.

As of that time, it had not filed returns for 2009 and 2010, and the IRS proceeded to prepare tax returns for Adams in 2014.[32] These returns are commonly referred to as substitutes for returns (SFRs). A notice of deficiency was sent later in 2014; a tax court petition was filed in 2015; and, in 2017, Adams filed protective Forms 1120-F for 2009 and 2010, reporting no US income. The case was litigated in two phases, each resulting in a tax court opinion granting summary judgment in favour of the IRS.

Foreign corporations are subject to US income tax on income that is effectively connected with the conduct of trade or business within the United States (effectively connected income). This includes income from labour performed within the United States and income from leasing property that is located in the United States. Ordinarily, the OCS is not considered part of the United States for tax purposes. However, Treasury Regulation § 1.638-1(c)(4) expands the definition of 'United States' to include the OCS in the case of activities 'related to the exploration for, or the exploitation of, mines, oil and gas wells, or other natural deposits'.

The tax court interpreted this provision expansively, concluding that decommissioning is an integral (and legally mandated) component of exploitation and that Adams' charter on the OCS, therefore, gave rise to US effectively connected income. The breadth of the court's reading of 'exploitation' may justifiably have surprised Adams – some wells subject to decommissioning here had never produced oil or gas. Other

31. *Adams Challenge (UK) Ltd. v. Comm'r*, 154 T.C. No. 3 (2020) (addressing effectively connected income and permanent establishment issues); *Adams Challenge (UK) Ltd. v. Comm'r*, 156 T.C. No. 2 (2021) (addressing deductibility issues).
32. *See* § 6020.

companies operating on the OCS will want to consider the implications of this holding with respect to their own businesses.

Of course, when a bilateral tax treaty is involved, the existence of effectively connected income is not the end of the inquiry; a US permanent establishment is also necessary to give the United States taxing rights over the income. In *Adams Challenge*, there was no permanent establishment under the general principles of Article 5 of the US-UK treaty, but a permanent establishment did exist under the specific rules of Article 21, Offshore Exploration and Exploitation Activities.

The second phase of the case raised the issue of Adams' ability to claim deductions against its effectively connected income. It is in this context that the complex procedural timeline outlined above becomes relevant. Section 882(c)(2) provides that a foreign corporation shall only receive the benefit of deductions and credits against its effectively connected income if the corporation files a true and accurate return in the manner prescribed by the procedural provisions of the Internal Revenue Code. On its face, the statute contains no mention of a timing requirement, but Treasury Regulation § 1.882-4(a)(3) supplies one requiring that the foreign corporation's return be filed within eighteen months following its due date. The regulation also provides that the filing requirement can be satisfied by the filing of a protective return, i.e., a return indicating that the foreign corporation does not believe it has effectively connected income.

The validity of the Treasury Regulation § 1.882-4(a)(3) timing requirement was previously litigated in *Swallows Holding, Ltd. v. Commissioner*,[33] which involved a Barbados corporation but did not address treaty issues, perhaps because the corporation's ultimate owner was prevented by the limitations on benefits clause from claiming the benefits of the treaty. In *Swallows*, the tax court held that, under the standard set forth in *National Muffler Dealers Association v. United States*,[34] the timing requirement in the regulation was invalid. The Third Circuit reversed, holding that the *Chevron*[35] standard applied in lieu of *National Muffler* and that, under *Chevron*, the regulation was a reasonable interpretation of the statute.

The Third Circuit's holding in *Swallows* foreshadowed the Supreme Court's embrace of the *Chevron* standard for tax cases in *Mayo Foundation for Medical Education and Research v. United States* two years later.[36] *Mayo* largely brought about an end to tax exceptionalism, bringing tax into the mainstream of administrative law where *Chevron* had long been the accepted standard for judicial deference to agency regulations. Thus, *Mayo* settled the disagreement between the tax court and the Third Circuit over the appropriate framework for review squarely in favour of the latter – the tax court now applies *Chevron* deference to transfer pricing regulations, as seen in *Altera*.

However, that does not mean that the tax court would necessarily agree with the Third Circuit that Treasury Regulation § 1.882-4(a)(3) is valid if another case were to

33. *Swallows Holding, Ltd. v. Comm'r*, 126 T.C. 96 (2006).
34. *National Muffler Dealers Ass'n v. United States*, 440 US 472, 477 (1979).
35. *Chevron U.S.A., Inc. v. Natural Res. Defense Counsel, Inc.*, 467 US 837 (1984).
36. *Mayo Found. for Med. Educ. & Research v. United States*, 562 U.S. 44 (2011).

arise on the issue. Under the *Golsen*[37] rule, the tax court would follow the Third Circuit opinion in *Swallows* in cases appealable to that circuit but would remain free to exercise its own judgment in other cases. The parties' briefing in *Adams Challenge* suggested that this case would present the tax court with the opportunity to revisit *Swallows* and the validity of the regulation. Interestingly, it did not do so. The tax court held that section 882(c)(2) itself contains an implicit timing requirement and that it, therefore, did not need to reach the regulatory issue, leaving it for another day. This holding was based on a line of older cases that predate the regulation, which the opinion referred to as the 'terminal date' cases: *Taylor Securities, Inc. v. Commissioner*,[38] *Ardbern Co. v. Commissioner*,[39] *Blenheim Co. v. Commissioner*,[40] and *Georday Enterprises, Ltd. v. Commissioner*.[41]

From these cases, the court extracted the principle that, while section 882(c)(2) does not require the foreign corporation to file a timely return, it does require the taxpayer to file a return before the IRS prepares an SFR for it. This rule is premised on the policy grounds underlying section 882(c)(2). The IRS does not have the same level of visibility into the activities of foreign corporations as it has for domestic corporations, and it is accordingly difficult for it to determine whether a foreign corporation has effectively connected income unless it files a return. Section 882(c)(2) incentivizes filing by providing a stick that discourages foreign corporations from seeking to glide under the radar – non-filers will lose their deductions and credits. In the court's view, this objective would be frustrated if a foreign corporation could avoid filing, wait to see if the IRS prepares an SFR, and only then file a return ensuring its eligibility for deductions and credits. Thus, the preparation of an SFR acts as the 'terminal date' by which a foreign corporation must file its return.

In this case, Adams filed its 2011 return within the period provided by the regulation; the IRS subsequently issued SFRs for 2009 and 2010, and only after that did Adams file returns for the latter two years. Under the tax court's reading of section 882(c)(2), Adams was accordingly barred from claiming deductions for those years.

Again, there was also a treaty aspect to consider. Article 7 (Business Profits) of the US-UK treaty provides that 'there shall be allowed as deductions expenses that are incurred for the purposes of the permanent establishment', and Article 25 provides non-discrimination rules. The tax court held that neither article overrode the application of section 882(c)(2) to deny deductions. With respect to the business profits article, the court – stressing its duty to harmonize the treaty and the statute when it is possible to do so – interpreted 'shall be allowed' as meaning 'shall be allowed so long as certain conditions are met' rather than 'must be allowed no matter what'. In support of this reading, the court pointed to evidence that the treaty was not intended to disturb the countries' existing administrative practices.

37. *Golsen v. Comm'r*, 54 T.C. 742 (1970), *aff'd on other grounds*, 445 F.2d 985 (10th Cir. 1971), *cert. denied*, 404 U.S. 940 (1971).
38. *Taylor Securities, Inc. v. Comm'r*, 40 B.T.A. 696 (1939).
39. *Ardbern Co. v. Comm'r*, 41 B.T.A. 910 (1940), *modified and remanded*, 120 F.2d 424 (4th Cir. 1941).
40. *Blenheim Co. v. Comm'r*, 42 B.T.A. 1248 (1940), *aff'd*, 125 F.2d 906 (4th Cir. 1942).
41. *Georday Enterprises, Ltd. v. Comm'r*, 126 F.2d 384 (4th Cir. 1942).

With respect to non-discrimination, the court held that the section 882(c)(2) regime did not subject Adams to treatment that is more burdensome than would apply to a US corporation in the same circumstances. For one thing, the court took the view that foreign and domestic corporations are not similarly situated with respect to return filing obligations because it is more difficult for the IRS to glean information regarding foreign corporations if they do not file. For another, the court held that section 882(c)(2) does not impose obligations that are more burdensome on foreign corporations because they have an extended timeframe for filing a return in order to receive the benefit of deductions and credits and because they can discharge this obligation by simply filing a protective return reporting no income.

Ultimately, that is the key for similarly situated taxpayers. Filing protective Forms 1120-F is relatively easy and yields significant benefits by protecting against gross basis taxation. *Adams Challenge* serves as a reminder for foreign corporations of the importance of this prophylactic step.

2 DEVELOPMENTS IN IRS TRANSFER PRICING ENFORCEMENT

2.1 BEPS 2.0 and Treasury Secretary Mnuchin's Letter to the OECD

On 3 December 2019, US Treasury Secretary Steve Mnuchin wrote a letter to the OECD offering the United States government's views on the OECD BEPS 2.0 Project as well as the growing interest and appetite for unilateral measures by foreign taxing authorities. While the United States 'supports the discussion at the OECD to address the issues faced by the international tax system[,]' the United States remains 'firmly' opposed to digital services taxes (DSTs) and related unilateral measures. Secretary Mnuchin acknowledged general support from US taxpayers on the advertised BEPS 2.0 benefits of 'greater tax certainty and administrability'; however, US taxpayers are concerned about adopting new taxes that would stray from the traditional arm's length transfer pricing standard.

With respect to the BEPS Pillar 1 and Pillar 2 initiatives, Secretary Mnuchin advocated for making Pillar 1 a safe harbour regime – a non-starter for many OECD Inclusive Framework members – as well as general support for a 'GILTI-like Pillar 2 solution'. The effect of the latter statement would be to largely exempt US multinationals from Pillar 2. In the meantime, Secretary Mnuchin asked that all countries halt the implementation of DSTs in order for the OECD to come to a multilateral arrangement.

While Secretary Mnuchin's letter offers some context on the United States government's views on BEPS 2.0 and DSTs, the US's position is subject to change, especially in light of the new Biden Administration. Indeed, new Treasury Secretary Janet Yellen has already signalled that the United States is no longer advocating for a Pillar 1 safe harbour, a view that was generally welcomed by supporters of the BEPS 2.0 Project.

2.2 APMA: Telescoping for Competent Authority Resolutions

On 28 October 2020, the IRS's Advance Pricing and Mutual Agreement program (APMA) announced policy changes regarding the use of telescoping adjustments in multi-year mutual agreement procedure (MAP) cases.

Telescoping is the practice of implementing adjustments for earlier years in a later year. Historically, the APMA has generally allowed taxpayers to petition for telescoping, which can produce similar tax effects and eliminate the need for multiple years of amended returns. However, in late 2017, the Tax Cuts and Jobs Act (TCJA) was enacted, creating difficulties for effective telescoping. This was caused by the reduction of the US corporate income tax rate and the introduction of a host of new provisions generally effective for taxable years beginning after 31 December 2017. These new provisions included items such as § 965 repatriation and the global intangible low-taxed income (GILTI) rules. As a result of these changes, telescoping across the TCJA divide (i.e., telescoping covering years beginning before and after 1 January 2018) may have consequences that the IRS perceives to be inconsistent with the TCJA. The most obvious example of this is that income prior to 1 January 2018 may be taxed at a 35% rate, while income taxed after 1 January 2018 would be taxed at the post-TCJA tax rate of 21%.

To mitigate these issues, the APMA announcement calls for taxpayers who have MAP cases on both sides of the TCJA divide to generally file amended returns for each year. Telescoping across the TCJA divide may be permitted at the APMA's discretion for small cases involving adjustments of USD 10 million. Additionally, the announcement states that telescoping may be available for the years before the TCJA if the year that the adjustments are telescoped into is also pre-TCJA. The announcement does not directly address telescoping for post-TCJA years nor whether this concern about the TCJA divide will impact APA term tests, i.e., APAs that test compliance by considering the average results over all years covered by the APA.

2.3 APA Annual Report: Economic Environment and COVID-19

In March 2019, the APMA published a new model APA annual report template for APA agreements. In it, the APMA expanded the standard critical assumption to include a broad reference to the economic environment. This new language makes clear that a change in the 'economic environment' of the taxpayer will trigger a failure of the APA critical assumptions and lead to renegotiation or cancellation of the APA. Informally, the APMA has indicated that the older version of the standard critical assumption should be interpreted as consistent with this changing economic environment language. In addition, again informally, the APMA has indicated that the COVID-19 pandemic may well trigger this critical assumption on particular facts, but it remains unclear how the APMA will address the pandemic in any renegotiation of the APA terms. For bilateral APAs, any change would also require the agreement of the treaty partner.

2.4 Improving Documentation: IRS FAQs

In April 2020, the IRS' Large Business & International Division (LB&I) released six Frequently Asked Questions (FAQs) related to transfer pricing documentation.[42] The objective of these FAQs was to stress the significance of the penalties directive previously issued in January of 2018, which provided that documentation will not suffice to defend against penalties unless it is adequate and reasonable. The FAQs expressed the intent of incentivizing 'taxpayers to improve the quality of their transfer pricing documentation'.[43] The FAQs provide context on the LB&I's risk-focused enforcement strategy and guidance related to transfer pricing documentation. The FAQs emphasize the role that high-quality transfer pricing documentation may play in determining the course of an audit.

As a part of the FAQs, the LB&I included commentary on how to document the effects of economic downturns on a tested party. It states that the best practice is not to make extraordinary adjustments to fit the tested party results into the interquartile range. Rather, the LB&I recommends that taxpayers clearly document the external economic circumstances and how such circumstances factored into the tested party not falling within the interquartile range. This FAQ is especially important given the COVID-19 pandemic and should be considered as a best practice for documenting the effects of COVID-19 on the tested party transactions.

In reading the FAQs, it is worth noting that the majority of these FAQs serve more as suggestions for the best practices and are not explicitly required to be included in transfer pricing documentation for penalty protection under the § 6662 regulations.

2.5 COVID-19 Changes to Electronic Signature Requirements and Forms of Electronic Communication

In response to COVID-19 and the pandemic-induced remote working environment, the IRS announced a number of new initiatives directed at easing some of the administrative burdens on the IRS and taxpayers during the global pandemic. Among the temporary relief measures, the IRS issued important modifications to the electronic signature requirements on 27 March 2020 (the March Memorandum), which enabled IRS employees to accept scanned, photographed, and/or digital signatures on documents related to the determination or collection of tax liability.[44]

While the categories of documents falling under the umbrella of the new electronic signature policy were fairly prescriptive at first, the IRS has since expanded the scope to include additional documentation (on multiple occasions).[45] Moreover, the IRS has

42. Documentation FAQs.
43. *Id.* (introductory section).
44. US Department of the Treasury, Internal Revenue Service Memorandum (Control Number: NHQ-01-0320-0001), 27 March 2020.
45. US Department of the Treasury, Internal Revenue Service Memorandum (Control Number: NHQ-01-0620-0002), 12 June 2020; US Department of the Treasury, Internal Revenue Service Memorandum (No Control Number), 28 August 2020; US Department of the Treasury, Internal Revenue Service Memorandum (Control Number: NHQ-10-1220-0006), 28 December 2020.

taken an expansive view of acceptable digital formats (e.g., tiff, jpg, pdf, etc.), noting that permissible digital signatures may be created using many different technologies. The IRS has also made clear, in the form of interim guidance, that the new policy applies to IRS Appeals employees and procedures as well.[46]

In addition to expanding the scope of eligible documentation, the IRS also extended the effective date for the new electronic signature policy, which now runs through 30 June 2021.[47] Importantly for practitioners and taxpayers alike, the IRS has indicated that, while the new electronic signature policy remains a temporary solution, they are currently evaluating the potential for permanent changes to the handwritten signature requirements, balancing the benefits and flexibility of electronic signatures with the risks associated with confidentiality, inadvertent disclosure, and general tax administration.

Responding to specific requests for guidance on the impact of the new electronic signature policy on MAP requests and APAs, APMA announced in May 2020 that the electronic signature policy would apply to documents submitted under Revenue Procedure 2015-40, 2015-35 IRB 236 (Rev. Proc. 2015-40) or Revenue Procedure 2015-41, 2015-35 IRB 263 (Rev. Proc. 2015-41) addressing MAP and APAs, respectively. Moreover, all submissions required under Rev. Proc. 2015-40 and Rev. Proc. 2015-41 may be filed electronically in lieu of the traditional paper filing requirements.[48]

Accompanying the new policy on electronic signatures, the IRS announced guidance on expanded forms of permissible electronic communication between the IRS and taxpayers during the pandemic. While the new guidance encourages IRS employees and taxpayers to use traditional approved methods of receiving and transmitting documentation when possible (e.g., eFax or established secured messaging systems), the new electronic communication permissions provide taxpayers with additional options when traditional approved methods or formats are not available or unrealistic.

Under the new temporary policy, IRS employees are permitted to accept documents from taxpayers via email, which includes both encrypted and unencrypted email communication originating from the taxpayer. Of course, taxpayers electing to send documentation via unsecured or unencrypted methods are encouraged to remove or minimize the amount of sensitive and/or identifying information in the email. In contrast to the generally permissive policy associated with communication *from the taxpayer*, communication originating from the IRS remains subject to additional security protocols and requirements. Among the requirements listed, the March Memorandum notes that IRS employees are authorized to send documents electronically (with taxpayer consent) provided that SecureZip or other IRS established secured messaging system is used. Taxpayers interested in taking advantage of the alternative

46. US Department of the Treasury, Internal Revenue Service Memorandum (Control Number: AP-08-1220-0023), 8 December 2020.
47. US Department of the Treasury, Internal Revenue Service Memorandum (Control Number: NHQ-10-1220-0006), 28 December 2020.
48. 'Competent Authority Filing Modifications and APMA APA Consultations', US Department of the Treasury, Internal Revenue Service Announcement, 11 May 2020.

electronic communication options during the pandemic should review the list of requirements and instructions provided in the March Memorandum.[49]

3 CONCLUSION

In the past year, we have seen major legal developments in the United States related to transfer pricing, and there are several major cases worth noting for the future. The government won major decisions in *Coca-Cola, Whirlpool,* and *Altera,* thus making 2020 a year of several wins for the IRS. Additionally, several key court decisions are likely to be published in 2021, including on the blocked-income issue in the *3M* case, which will control the outcome of that issue in *Coca-Cola*, as noted above.

Lastly, BEPS 2.0, telescoping, and changes to the standard APA critical assumption are some additional developments to consider moving forward. In a letter to the OECD, Treasury Secretary Mnuchin stated that the United States supports an optional Pillar 1 alternative to DSTs and a GILTI exemption from Pillar 2; however, these perspectives are subject to change under the Biden Administration as highlighted by Secretary Yellen's most recent comments. Telescoping MAP settlements will be very limited when applied to years crossing the TCJA divide of 2017/2018, although it is still available for pre-TCJA years. APMA has informally indicated that the COVID-19 pandemic may trigger its standard critical assumption, but exactly how the pandemic would be incorporated into an APA remains unclear. Finally, taxpayers should take note of the relaxed procedures and expanded permissions associated with electronic signatures, which are applicable through 30 June 2021 under the current policy.

49. US Department of the Treasury, Internal Revenue Service Memorandum (Control Number: NHQ-01-0320-0001), 27 March 2020.

CHAPTER 4

Transfer Pricing: Recent Developments in Developing Countries and Emerging Economies

Mukesh Butani & Seema Kejriwal[*]

* The authors would like to thank Ms Divyasha Mathur (BMR Legal) for her assistance while writing this chapter.

This chapter focuses on transfer pricing developments in developing countries and emerging economies in the calendar year 2020. It discusses changes in transfer pricing legislation and practices together with landmark court decisions in select jurisdictions. The chapter also addresses developments in transfer pricing guidance for developing countries and emerging economies by the Organisation for Economic Co-operation and Development (OECD) and the United Nations (UN). It also seeks to provide insights into the interplay of key global developments with transfer pricing policies of developing countries and emerging economies. Finally, the paper attempts to provide an outlook for transfer pricing in developing countries and emerging economies in light of the combined developments in 2020.

For the purposes of this chapter, countries have been classified as developing countries or emerging economies based on the International Monetary Fund's (IMF's) Fiscal Monitor Database.[1] The database lists forty countries as emerging market and middle-income economies[2] and another forty as low-income developing countries.[3] Notably, thirty-one of the forty emerging market and middle economies but only fourteen of the forty low-income developing countries were members of the OECD/G20 BEPS Inclusive Framework.[4]

1. http://www.imf.org/external/datamapper/FMEconGroup.xlsx.
2. Emerging markets and middle-income economies – Algeria, Angola, Argentina, Azerbaijan, Belarus, Brazil, Chile, China, Colombia, Croatia, Dominican Republic, Ecuador, Egypt, Hungary, India, Indonesia, Iran, Kazakhstan, Kuwait, Libya, Malaysia, Mexico, Morocco, Oman, Pakistan, Peru, Philippines, Poland, Qatar, Romania, Russia, Saudi Arabia, South Africa, Sri Lanka, Thailand, Turkey, Ukraine, United Arab Emirates, Uruguay, Venezuela.
3. Low-income developing countries – Bangladesh, Benin, Burkina Faso, Cambodia, Cameroon, Chad, Congo, Dem. Rep. of, Congo, Rep. of, Côte d'Ivoire, Ethiopia, Ghana, Guinea, Haiti, Honduras, Kenya, Kyrgyz Republic, Lao P.D.R., Madagascar, Mali, Moldova, Mozambique, Myanmar, Nepal, Nicaragua, Niger, Nigeria, Papua New Guinea, Rwanda, Senegal, Somalia, Sudan, Tajikistan, Tanzania, Timor-Leste, Uganda, Uzbekistan, Vietnam, Yemen, Zambia, Zimbabwe.
4. https://www.oecd.org/tax/beps/inclusive-framework-on-beps-composition.pdf.

1 KEY TRANSFER PRICING DEVELOPMENTS

1.1 India

India's government implemented a notable expansion of its transfer pricing regime that was introduced in the government's annual budget for 2020. India extended its Advance Pricing Agreement (APA) program and safe harbour regime to cases of profit attribution for permanent establishments (PEs). These were earlier available only for transfer pricing issues. India also expanded the accessibility of its dispute resolution panel[5] to all non-residents. This was also earlier available only for transfer pricing disputes.

A little background is provided in order to understand the far-reaching ramifications of these amendments. With respect to non-residents, Indian tax laws provide that whichever of the provisions of the applicable tax treaty (if any) or the domestic tax law are more beneficial to the taxpayer shall apply. This right is available to the taxpayer even when he chooses to not exercise it, meaning it is the duty of the tax officer to give the taxpayer the benefit of the more beneficial provision even if the taxpayer has not claimed it while filing his return of income.

In India, when a non-resident has a PE either under a tax treaty or (business connection)[6] under Indian domestic law (in a case of no treaty or if the same is more beneficial to the taxpayer), the next step is to compute the taxable income attributable to such a PE.

The computation can be in accordance with domestic law or Article 7 of the tax treaty. As per Article 7 of most Indian tax treaties, profits are to be attributed to the PE as if it were a distinct and separate entity on the basis of the accounts of the PE. When detailed and accurate accounts are not available to enable the determination of profits attributable to the PE, they can be calculated by an indirect apportionment under Indian domestic laws. For the application of this method, the assessing officer in India can resort to domestic law through paragraph 4 of Article 7 of Indian DTAAs (in most cases), which, in the case of India, is provided in rule 10 of Income Tax Rules 1962.

At present, there are at least three commonly adopted versions of Article 7 that feature in tax treaties around the world: Article 7 recommended by the OECD model convention prior to 2010, revised Article 7 introduced in 2010, and Article 7 of the UN Model Convention. Several countries, including India, have made strong reservations (that are documented in the OECD Model Tax Convention) in the section on 'Position of Non-OECD Economies'. Accordingly, India does not accept or agree with the

5. The dispute resolution panel (DRP) is a collegium of Indian revenue officials who the taxpayer can approach before the first audit order is finalized by the officer. Prior to the 2020 budget, the accessibility to the DRP was restricted to foreign companies.
6. Though the concept of a business connection has existed since the 1922 act and continued in the present 1961 Act, it has been among the most interpreted part of the law with regard to taxation of non-residents, particularly in situations when the treaty provisions do not apply. In the past decade, several repairs and amendments to the business connection rule have been legislated with an intent to sharpen the focus on source-based taxation, introduce new concepts such as the SEP and, more importantly, the famous (or rather infamous) retrospective taxation of offshore transfer of shares and other interests also forms a part of business connection.

Authorized OECD Approach (AOA) to attribute profits to the PE on the basis of functions, assets, and risks (FAR).[7] Article 7 in the Indian treaties corresponds to the UN Model Tax Convention, which has certain similarities with the pre-2010 OECD Model Tax Convention.[8]

It is also noteworthy here that Articles 7 and 9 of Indian tax treaties operate in different spheres. Article 9, dealing with transfer pricing, cannot arguably be extended to cover cases of profit attribution under Article 7 since Article 9 is applicable only when the enterprises are residents of two different states. The update to the Indian laws also does not seek to extend the applicability of Article 9 to cases of profit attribution under Article 7.

Rule 10 of the Indian Income Tax Rules 1962 provides for-profit attribution as under:

(1) at such percentage of the turnover so accruing or arising as the tax officer may consider to be reasonable, or
(2) on any amount that bears the same proportion to the total profits and gains of the business of such person (such profits and gains being computed in accordance with the provisions of the Indian Income Tax Act (ITA)), as the receipts so accruing or arising bear to the total receipts of the business, or
(3) in such other manner as the assessing officer may deem suitable.

The Indian tax office released a stakeholder consultation document on 18 April 2019[9] wherein amendments were proposed to Rule 10 (draft rules). This is yet to be implemented. The proposed attribution rules under the same are:

(1) A formulary apportionment using intensity models by assigning weights to three factors (revenue, manpower (number of employees and wages), and assets employed).[10] The weight so assigned is to be multiplied by the business profits.

---

7. The AOA was a major deviation from the generally applicable accounting standards for determining business profits in which business profits cannot be determined without taking sales into account. (Refer para. 48 of India's stakeholder consultation document for Attribution of Profits to PE, released on 18 April 2019).
8. The first OECD draft double taxation convention was published in 1963. The first UN model tax convention was published much later in 1980. Thus, many Indian treaties during the 1960s and 1970s were based largely on the draft OECD model tax convention with specific variations to it as were preferred by India.
9. https://www.incometaxindia.gov.in/Lists/Press%20Releases/Attachments/757/CBDT_stakeholder_comments_Permanent_Establishment_18_4_19.pdf.
10. Profits attributable to operations in India = 'Profits derived from India' 92 $\times$ $[SI/3 \times ST + (NI/6 \times NT) + (WI/6 \times WT) + (AI/3 \times AT)]$
Where,
SI = sales revenue derived by Indian operations from sales in India
ST = total sales revenue derived by Indian operations from sales in India and outside India
NI = number of employees employed with respect to Indian operations and located in India
NT = total number of personnel employed with respect to Indian operations and located in India and outside India
WI = wages paid to personnel employed with respect to Indian operations and located in India

(2) For digital businesses, a fourth factor, i.e., number of users to be added and a proposed weight to be assigned to it.
(3) Business profits to be defined as a proportion of global profits to Indian sales or 2% of Indian sales in the case of global losses.
(4) In the event the taxpayer does not make any sales (or has total sales up to INR 1 million) to Indian customers but has a PE by virtue of some activities in India, attribution to such PE can be determined using the arm's length method prescribed for transfer pricing purposes.

With the amendment in the 2020 budget, the options available to non-residents for computation of profits attributable to PEs increased. The options now available are:

(1) Books of accounts maintained by the taxpayer.
(2) Safe harbour provisions.
(3) Rule 10 of the Indian Income Tax Rules.
(4) Attribution agreed under advanced pricing agreements.
(5) Reliance on methods proposed in draft rules (as guidance approach under Rule 10(iii)).

The manner in which the amendment has been introduced seeks to suggest that an arm's length price may not suffice for determination of profits attributable to a PE. This issue of transfer pricing sufficing for allocation of profits to PEs has been a subject matter of debate in Indian courts.

Indian income tax authorities also introduced and implemented a faceless audit and appeals scheme that is expected to extend to transfer pricing audits from the year 2021. India also adopted a taxpayers' charter during 2020.[11] Listed, *inter alia*, in the twenty-point charter is the Indian income tax department's commitment to respect the privacy of the taxpayer, maintain confidentiality, provide timely decisions, provide a fair and just system, and reduce the cost of compliance. A mechanism has been provided for taxpayers to seek compliance with this charter.

WT = total wages paid to personnel employed with respect to Indian operations and located in India and outside India
AI = assets deployed for Indian operations and located in India
AT = total assets deployed for Indian operations and located in India and outside India

Profits attributable to operations in India in cases of low and medium user intensity business models = 'Profits derived from India' [0.3 × SI/ST + (0.15 × NI/NT) + (0.15 × WI/WT) + (0.3 × AI/3 × AT)] + 0.1]

In the case of digital models with high user intensity, the users should be assigned a weight of 20% while the share of assets and employees should be reduced to 25% each after keeping the weight of sales as 30%, as under:

Profits attributable to operations in India in cases of high user intensity business models = 'Profits derived from India' [0.3 × SI/ST + (0.125 × NI/NT) + (0.125 × WI/WT) + (0.25 AI/3 × AT)] + 0.2].

11. https://incometaxindia.gov.in/Documents/taxpayer-charter.pdf.

With the introduction of the faceless assessment and appeals scheme and the taxpayer's charter, the Indian Government has tried to address the international community's concern regarding the high-handedness of the Indian income tax department and their lack of confidence in the protection of privacy of taxpayer's data, especially with respect to data submitted under bilateral APAs.[12]

Like every year, India saw a spate of transfer pricing rulings. More than 675 rulings on transfer pricing were reported across tribunals, high courts and the Supreme Court of India. The key issues spanned advertising, marketing and promotion (AMP) expenses, loans and guarantees, choice of comparables, and taxpayer rights. Two leading cases on AMP are pending before the Supreme Court – once resolved by the Supreme Court, significant clarity is expected on the treatment of AMP expenses.

1.2 Brazil

In 2017, Brazil expressed interest in joining the OECD. It followed up in May 2019 with a formal request with the OECD to initiate the accession process. Between 2017 and 2019, Brazil recognized that the discrepancies between the Brazilian TP Regs and OECD Guidelines could inhibit its accession to the OECD. The Brazilian tax administration, *Recieta Federal do Brasil* (RFB), began working with the OECD to evaluate the similarities and differences between the two TP systems. This effort, known as the 'Transfer Pricing in Brazil Project', was launched in February 2018 and entailed an in-depth analysis of Brazil's TP framework in comparison to the OECD Guidelines. This study represented the first comprehensive review of Brazil's TP Regs in decades. In July 2019, after a fifteen-month work program, the OECD and RFB jointly announced their conclusion that the Brazil TP Regs are not compatible with OECD Guidelines and suggested that Brazil will need to make changes to its system to align it with the OECD Guidelines in order to join the organization.[13] A formal, detailed report, 'Transfer Pricing in Brazil', was released in December 2019, documenting the findings of this project.

Briefly, the divergences include:

- the prevalence of fixed profit margins to set a benchmark price (ignoring the reality of each industry sector);
- the complexity of 'product-by-product' calculations;
- the taxpayers' freedom to select a TP method;
- the focus on goods at the expense of the so-called intangibles;
- the absence of express mention of the arm's length principle;

12. With respect to confidentiality of data provided under country-by-country reporting under Action Plan 13 of the OECD/G20 BEPS Inclusive Framework, which was a key concern of taxpayers across jurisdictions, CBDT had prescribed guidelines for the same vide instruction No. 2 of 2018 released in July 2018.
13. OECD, *Joint Statement on the OECD-Brazil Transfer Pricing Project* dt. 11 July 2019 available at http://www.oecd.org/tax/transfer-pricing/joint-statement-oecd-brazil-transfer-pricing-project-july-2019.pdf (accessed 29 November 2020).

- the misalignment with international methods such as the absence of the transactional net margin method and the profit split method (PSM);
- the absence of specific considerations regarding the treatment of financial transactions;
- the scope extended to exclusive distributors and tax havens;
- limiting the safe harbour rules to exports;
- the absence of rules for PEs;
- the absence of advanced price arrangements;
- undeveloped mutual agreement procedures (MAPs); and
- the absence of rules for secondary adjustments.

Considering the importance and use of safe harbours, the OECD and Brazil also launched a joint survey for stakeholder consultation on the development of transfer pricing safe harbours and other simplification measures, including the use of APAs.[14] One of the merits of a well-designed safe harbour is that, for eligible taxpayers, it can reduce the need to find uncontrolled comparables data and perform benchmarking studies in each case. They also prove useful in situations when comparables data is limited by eliminating the difficulties arising from the absence of comparables data, especially as they can be designed by relying on information available to the tax administration in internal databases, which may not be available in the public domain. Hence, the Brazilian safe harbour rules are intended to extend beyond exports.

It is known that the work on the new TP system is underway, and OECD representatives are in regular contact with the RFB. As for the timing of the alignment, even though the RFB has not proposed any dates, it is expected the same should happen before the end of President Bolsonaro's term, i.e., by year-end 2022.

Even though the alignment deadline has not been set, the alignment method was discussed in previous meetings between the OECD and Brazil. Two possibilities were suggested:

(1) Immediately: new rules consistent with the OECD standard and the arm's length principle applicable to all taxpayers as from a given date; or
(2) Gradually: new rules would progressively apply to different groups of taxpayers.

While the Brazilian authorities have shown resistance to giving up on the existing system altogether and emphasized its strengths (mainly its objectivity), defending a type of mix of local and international rules, the OECD has taken a firm stance requiring full compliance with OECD rules even if either gradually or immediately.[15]

14. https://www.oecd.org/ctp/transfer-pricing/oecd-and-brazil-federal-revenue-authority-invite-taxpayer-input-on-transfer-pricing-issues-relating-to-the-design-of-safe-harbour-provisions-and-other-comparability-considerations.htm.
15. https://www.internationaltaxreview.com/article/b1mm864qdjxlyl/brazil-advancing-towards-global-transfer-pricing-convergence.

1.3 Russia

The APA system works differently for domestic and foreign companies, for which there is a provision of 'unilateral' APAs for companies that are defined as the 'largest' taxpayers. For non-residents, an APA is only available for three years, after which extensions could be given subject to laws. Considering the growing importance of transfer pricing, a draft legislation was introduced by the Russian Legislature surrounding APAs, improving tax control over prices, and controlled transactions.[16] Hence, the domestic transfer pricing rules are continuously evolving to align with recommendations of the Action Plan 8-10 Report. For example, the said draft legislation proposes tweaking conditions for recognizing transactions as controlled and amending the process of concluding bilateral APAs to grant taxpayers higher transparency and predictability. Moreover, from 2020, the DEMPE analysis was formally introduced in the tax legislation with regard to transactions with intangible assets.

Russia has also revised its permissible range of limits for interest rates on controlled debt obligations for the period from 1 January 2020 to 31 December 2021.[17] The situations wherein transfer pricing analysis is not required is effectively broadened, thereby providing relief to small and medium taxpayers not indulging in cross-border business activities. However, if the loan interest rate is beyond the fixed range, transfer pricing analysis, as well as justification of adhering to arm's length price, may be required.

Specific audit guidance has been released for the tax administration on verifying expenses or service charges claimed for the provision of intra-group services with the help of economic justification and sufficient TP documentation furnished by the taxpayers.[18]

1.4 Vietnam

The government released new transfer pricing regulations *vide* Decree No. 132/2020/NĐ-CP dt. 5 November 2020, which is retrospectively applicable from 1 January 2020. Some of the notable changes include explicit reference to usage of commercial databases for benchmarking by taxpayers and tax authorities; revision of the tax deductibility cap from 20% to 30% of EBITDA, excluding certain types of financing; increase the minimum threshold of acceptable arm's length range from the 25th percentile to the 35th percentile; reduction in TP compliance and documentation by broadening the exemption category; expansion of the definition of 'related parties' to include situations of capital transfers and loans between enterprises and individuals

16. https://home.kpmg/us/en/home/insights/2020/12/tnf-russia-changes-apa-process-measures-related-controlled-transactions.html.
17. Federal Law No. 374-FZ (passed on 23 November 2020) that amended section 269 of the Russian Tax Code https://home.kpmg/us/en/home/insights/2020/12/tnf-russia-interest-rates-on-controlled-debt-obligations-transfer-pricing-analysis-not-always-required.html.
18. https://home.kpmg/us/en/home/insights/2020/08/tnf-russia-tax-audit-guidelines-verifying-reasonableness-of-expenses-for-intra-group-services.html.

that manage or control such enterprises or individuals satisfying prescribed thresholds; and enhancing country-by-country reporting (CbCR) requirements.[19]

1.5 Thailand

Earlier, the overall tax regime in Thailand was less burdensome for TP since there were many non-binding obligations to the benefit of companies operating in automotive and auto-ancillary, consumer electronics, rubber, gems, and jewellery industries. Owing to a budgetary crisis, several tax reforms have been made in the country, and the overall tax administration task force has been increased. With the increasing international tax scrutiny, Thailand's transfer pricing laws, although at a nascent stage,[20] have been witnessing regular developments and amendments. In November 2020, Thailand introduced new transfer pricing regulations[21] that prescribe guidance for tax officers for undertaking transfer pricing assessments and making subsequent adjustments in the taxpayer's income and expenses. The regulations provide for commercial or financial conditions that may affect the transfer price between related parties and guidance on when to use the internal and external CUP methods.

1.6 Malaysia

Malaysia has reformed its legislation[22] on related party transactions and effectively made transfer pricing more stringent. Further, it has also proposed to impose penalties on the failure to timely furnish contemporaneous TP documentation.

The following measures are proposed to be effective 1 January 2021:[23]

- Penalties for failure to furnish transfer pricing documentation (new section 113B): Currently, there is no specific provision in the tax law that penalizes a taxpayer that fails to furnish contemporaneous transfer pricing documentation in a timely manner (typically within thirty days of a written notice of request from the inland revenue board). The proposed measure would impose penalties for failure to timely furnish transfer pricing documentation.
- Authority to disregard structures in a controlled transaction (section 140A): Rule 8 of the Income Tax (Transfer Pricing) Rules 2012 would be inserted into

19. https://home.kpmg/us/en/home/insights/2020/12/tnf-vietnam-transfer-pricing-rules-are-updated.html; https://www.pwc.com/vn/en/publications/2020/201106-pwc-vietnam-newsbrief-decree-123-en.pdf.
20. In 2002, the Thai Revenue Department (TRD) released Guideline No. Paw. 113/2545 (2002) (PAW 113) which is non-binding transfer pricing guidance that parallels the OECD's Arm's Length Principle. In November 2018, the TRD released the Transfer Pricing Law (Revenue Code Amendment Act No. 47) that adds three separate sections on transfer pricing into the tax revenue code of Thailand. The law is effective for accounting periods commencing on or after 1 January 2019.
21. Ministerial Regulation No. 369 dated 6 November 2020 under the Thai Revenue Code.
22. Proposed amendments of Finance Bill 2020 shall come into effect from 1 January 2021.
23. https://home.kpmg/us/en/home/insights/2020/12/tnf-malaysia-transfer-pricing-measures-finance-bill-2020.html.

the tax law under new subsections that would grant authority to the director-general of inland revenue to disregard and recharacterize any structure adopted by a person in a controlled transaction. It is noteworthy that the Malaysian ITA has had an anti-avoidance provision since 1967. The law provides that, if a transaction directly or indirectly alters the incidence of a tax payable, relieves the tax liability of any person, evades or avoids any duty or liability, or hinders the operation of the tax law, such transaction shall be countered by tax authorities. The provision is wide and is not based on the modern main-purpose logic that India and other countries have adopted.[24]

- Surcharge for transfer pricing adjustment (section 140A): Currently, a penalty is imposed when a transfer pricing adjustment made during a tax audit results in additional tax payable. The penalty is to be applied to the amount of additional tax payable. However, in cases when a transfer pricing adjustment does not result in additional tax payable, penalties cannot be imposed. It is now proposed that new subsections be inserted in the tax law to allow the inland revenue board to impose a surcharge of not more than 5% on any transfer pricing adjustment made during all tax audit and investigation cases, whether the adjustment is taxable or not.

1.7 Nigeria

Nigeria's Tax Appeal Tribunal (TAT) issued its very first transfer pricing ruling on 19 February 2020,[25] whereby the transfer pricing methodology of TNMM was held applicable, and the appellant's reliance on the CUP method was disregarded due to lack of sufficient information. The case has evolved into a landmark case representing jurisprudence on transfer pricing methodology.

The facts of the case were such that the appellant was dealing in the business of trading imported plastics and petrochemicals. During 2013 and 2014, it submitted its transfer pricing report to the revenue authorities with the application of two different methods – the CUP for 2013 and the TNMM for 2014. The issues before the TAT were whether: (a) appropriate information was being shared by the appellant to the revenue authorities evidencing that the CUP was not possible in 2014; and (b) whether the revenue was correct in using gross profits/total revenue instead of net profits/total revenue to measure the PLI of the controlled transaction.

On the first issue, the TAT ruled in favour of the revenue authorities, holding that the CUP method was the most appropriate method for transfer pricing. The underlying rationale was that the comparable company was still functioning in the earlier manner, which meant that not only were the comparables available with the appellant, but they would remain unchanged for the controlled transaction analysis. This reasoning adopted by the TAT justified the position of the revenue authorities that the change in

24. https://www.lexology.com/library/detail.aspx?g=06d323e7-cce4-4e00-af80-03bdabeaccb2.
25. *Prime Platsichem Nigeria Limited v. Federal Inland Revenue Service [Appeal No. TAT/LZ/CIT/015/2017.*

transfer pricing analysis from the CUP to the TNMM was not necessary. On the second issue, the TAT held that the analysis done by revenue authorities to calculate additional penalties based on gross profits was correct given the nature of the business and relevant direct trading elements that required cost margins which would include sales revenues and the cost of importing to the country. This not only reduces the distortions but also focuses on the main item of controlled transaction, i.e., 'trading'. The TAT further held that using gross profits was not only good in law but was also in line with OECD guidelines and that the method of gross profits/total revenue was the most appropriate PLI option.

Separately, with the intent of easing transfer pricing compliance, an e-filing platform called 'E-TP PLAT 2.0' was launched,[26] which enables taxpayers to file annual transfer pricing returns and undertake CbCR electronically.

1.8 Zimbabwe

Zimbabwe has also made progress in transfer pricing regulation and has recently issued Transfer Pricing Practice Notes that are to be used by taxpayers and tax authorities in conjunction with the transfer pricing legislation. The aim of such practice notes was alignment with OECD's arm's length principle (ALP) under Article 9 of the OECD Model Tax Convention. It has also released transfer pricing documentation regulations and a transfer pricing return consisting of declaration details of controlled transactions.[27]

1.9 Ghana

Ghana has recently made progress by introducing new transfer pricing guidelines that transpose recommendations under BEPS Action Plans 4, 8-10, and 13.[28] The new regulations, *inter alia,* include rules on controlled transactions, value creation of intangible assets, and cost contribution arrangements and, more importantly, introduce safe harbour rules that exempt related parties to report certain transactions in contemporaneous transfer pricing documentation.[29]

1.10 Zambia

The Zambian Government, as part of the 2021 budget, announced in September 2020 that it has amended its laws to provide for the exchange of CbCRs even though there is still no requirement to prepare CbCRs for large MNEs operating in the country. Further, the annual revenue threshold for companies to prepare transfer pricing documentation

26. Launched on 17 March 2020 https://research.ibfd.org/#/doc?url = /linkresolver/static/tp_ng_s_19.
27. https://www.orbitax.com/news/archive.php/Zimbabwe-Issues-Public-Notice--41907.
28. Transfer Pricing Regulations, 2020 (L.I. 2412).
29. https://assets.kpmg/content/dam/kpmg/us/pdf/2020/12/tnf-tp-ghana-dec2-2020.pdf.

has been increased from ZMW 20 million to ZMW 50 million; however, this amendment is for local taxpayers and not multinational enterprises (MNEs).

The Zambian judiciary received global appreciation from the OECD[30] for a large transfer pricing case whereby the Zambian tax authority had to establish a case of tax avoidance against a mining company. The case[31] pertained to underpricing the sale of copper by the Zambian mining company to its Swiss shareholder company. The Zambian Supreme Court ordered the taxpayer company to pay the demand of USD 13 million as transfer pricing adjustment for the reason that the prices of copper sold to the Swiss entity were significantly lower than those of similar sales to third parties. In doing so, the court did not consider the impact of the hedging agreement entered into by the Swiss parent, which was relied on by the taxpayer.[32] The OECD noted that Zambia sent a message to all tax administrations to build confidence in handling complex and high-stake transfer pricing matters using technical capacity building.

1.11 South Africa

During the 2020 supplementary budget review, the South African Ministry of Finance (MOF) suggested focusing on aggressive tax planning using transfer pricing as a way of raising additional tax revenue considering the post-pandemic economic recovery of the nation.

Transfer pricing laws have accordingly been amended to refine the definition of 'affected transaction' to accommodate a situation where a transaction is between a controlled foreign company and a non-resident connected person. Further, the budget also proposed that transfer pricing rules shall apply before the application of the interest limitation rules. The net interest expense deductions shall be limited to 30% of EBITDA from the erstwhile 43%.[33]

1.12 United Arab Emirates

On 30 April 2019, the UAE MOF published tax rules governing CbCR requirements. All qualifying MNE groups are obligated to ensure compliance with CbC reporting rules from the financial year 1 January 2019. The implementation of CbC reporting rules shows the UAE commitment to achieving compliance with the OECD Convention on Mutual Administrative Assistance, which entered into force on 1 September 2018, and the OECD Multilateral Competent Authority Agreement on the automatic exchange of CbC reports joined on 24 June 2018. The UAE CbC reporting regulations largely follow the OECD's guidance issued under BEPS Action 13 that requires the MNE groups to:

30. http://www.oecd.org/tax/tax-global/building-capacity-to-prevent-profit-shifting-by-large-companies-in-zambia.pdf.
31. *Mopani Copper Mines Plc v. Zambia Revenue Authority*, Appeal No. 24 of 2017 http://www.judiciaryzambia.com/wp-content/uploads/2020/05/App-024-2017-Mopani-Copper-Mines-Plc-Vs-Zambia-Revenue-Authority-20th-May-2020-Mambilima-Cj-Malila-And-Mutuna-JJS.pdf.
32. https://tpguidelines.com/zambia-vs-mopani-copper-mines-plc-may-2020-supreme-court-of-zambia-case-no-2017-24/.
33. https://home.kpmg/content/dam/kpmg/za/pdf/pdf2020/budget-summary-2020.pdf.

- prepare CbC reports with aggregate data on the global allocation of income, profits, taxes, and economic activity among the tax jurisdictions of their operations; and
- file CbC reports that provide a breakdown of the MNE group's global revenue, profit before tax, income tax accrued, and some other indicators of economic activities for each jurisdiction in which they operate.

Prior to the introduction of the CbC regulations, the European Union (EU) Council included the United Arab Emirates in the list of non-cooperative jurisdictions, published on 5 December 2017 and again on the EU blacklist on 23 January 2019 for non-compliance with minimum requirements. The council later removed the United Arab Emirates from the blacklist on 10 October 2019 after it enacted some regulations concerning CbC reporting and economic substance, which shows the significance of such implementation.[34]

1.13 Conclusion

As can be seen, the spectrum of transfer pricing developments across developing countries and emerging markets is vast and ranges from the introduction of transfer pricing laws to amendments to existing laws and alignment with OECD to issuing landmark rulings. It is evident that emerging markets and developing economies have increased focus towards transfer pricing and are trying to align with global standards.

2 IMPACT OF COVID-19 ON TRANSFER PRICING IN DEVELOPING COUNTRIES & EMERGING ECONOMIES

The COVID-19 pandemic is construed to be yet another historical turning point akin to the world wars or the Great Depression.[35] Owing to the COVID-19 pandemic and The Great Lockdown,[36] the global economy is projected to dwindle by (-4.9)% in 2020, much worse than during the 2008-2009 financial crisis.[37] The world is yet to witness the aftermath of reviving and normalizing the economy that all national governments need to achieve by setting out effective policy goals. Tax policy is one of the key policy areas through which countries can rise from the recession caused by COVID-19 either by implementing effective enforcement or by raising taxes. From the viewpoint of MNEs, transfer pricing remains a concern that demands explicit policy advisories from governments all over the world. This is due to it being the global methodology to compute the income to be taxed by various jurisdictions as per their geographical

34. https://research.ibfd.org/#/doc?url=/collections/itpj/html/itpj_2020_02_ae_1.html.
35. *COVID-19 and US Tax Policy: What Needs to Change?*, by Reuven S. Avi-Yonah (Intertax Volume 48 Issue 8 & 9, p. 790).
36. G. Gopinath, *The Great Lockdown: Worst Economic Downturn since the Great Depression* (IMF 2020).
37. International Monetary Fund (IMF), *World Economic Outlook Update, June 2020: A Crisis Like No Other, An Uncertain Recovery* (June 2020), available at https://www.imf.org/en/Publications/WEO/Issues/2020/06/24/WEOUpdateJune2020 (accessed 25 November 2020).

operations by way of application of the ALP. Complex economic forecasts, revenue dips, increased losses, and changes in profit allocation across jurisdictions are expected outcomes.

On 18 December 2020, the OECD released 'Guidance on the transfer pricing implications of the COVID-19 pandemic' (OECD TP-COVID Guidance). This guidance represents the consensus view of the 137 member countries of the inclusive framework on transfer pricing considerations during COVID-19.[38]

2.1 Impact of COVID-19 on Growth

For emerging markets and developing economies, the IMF had projected a negative growth rate of (-1.0) % in 2020. Developing economies have the comparative demerits of coping with weaker health systems, currency pressures, limited capacity to provide fiscal support to a large population, and reversal in Foreign direct investment (FDI) flows.[39] They have had an experience of withdrawal of overall investment at a faster rate during the global financial crisis.[40] As compared to developed countries, developing economies have relied on smaller fiscal packages and limited guidance in specific areas of international tax like transfer pricing. Moreover, such countries are more reliant on more corporate taxes as a revenue source.[41] Hence, transfer pricing is an increased area of concern for these countries.

2.2 TP Guidance Issued by Developing and Emerging Economies with Respect to COVID-19

A number of developing countries have introduced extensions of timelines for tax payment as well as transfer pricing documentation and filing before tax authorities,[42] while some have reduced fines for late submission of transfer pricing documentation.[43] In fact, Argentina's Federal Tax Authority suspended its inspection, assessment, and appeal procedures in light of the pandemic.[44]

However, there are other developing countries like Russia that neither established a new submission deadline for transfer pricing documents nor relaxed CbC Reporting

38. https://research.ibfd.org/#/doc?url = /data/tns/docs/html/tns_2020-05-07_o2_1.html.
39. G. Gopinath, *The Great Lockdown: Worst Economic Downturn since the Great Depression* (IMF 2020).
40. OECD, *Tax and Fiscal Policy in response to the Coronavirus Crisis: Strengthening Confidence and Resilience* dt. 19 May 2020; p. 20.
41. OECD, *Tax and Fiscal Policy in response to the Coronavirus Crisis: Strengthening Confidence and Resilience* dt. 19 May 2020; p. 38.
42. Argentina https://research.ibfd.org/#/doc?url = /linkresolver/static/tns_2020-07-15_ar_2#tns_2020-07-15_ar_2; Sri Lanka https://research.ibfd.org/#/doc?url = /data/tns/docs/html/tns_2020-04-23_lk_1.html; India: Notification S.O. 3906(E) [NO. 88/2020/ F. NO. 370142/35/2020-TPL], dated 29.10.2020.
43. Thailand https://research.ibfd.org/#/doc?url = /data/tns/docs/html/tns_2020-09-11_th_1.html.
44. Argentina https://research.ibfd.org/#/doc?url = /data/tns/docs/html/tns_2020-11-12_ar_1.html.

obligations. Other countries like Oman[45]extended their deadline in light of the impact of the pandemic on businesses. Transfer pricing stimulus measures like safe harbours or additional guidance on new and existing APAs are also absent.

The Indian Government provided a slew of tax and regulatory relaxations to businesses taking COVID-19 into account. Transfer pricing reporting and documentation requirements have been extended repeatedly after taking stock of the situation. Benefits of existing safe harbour rules can be availed by taxpayers for the assessment year 2020-2021.[46] However, with respect to transfer pricing, the tolerance range or variance between the ALP determined under section 92C of the ITA 1961, and the price at which the impugned international transaction has actually been undertaken remained unchanged despite the COVID-19 pandemic.

Colombia is the only Latin American country that issued a press release on 18 June 2020 as guidance for taxpayers to comply with transfer pricing documentation filing obligations through its digital platform. The guidance focused on the inclusion of transfer pricing adjustments within the income tax return. However, the deadlines for compliance were not extended by the Colombian Government.[47]

The OECD TP-COVID Guidance that was released states that it represents the consensus view of 137 countries in transfer pricing considerations during COVID-19. It would be helpful if national governments of developing countries take a cue from some developed countries and introduce transfer pricing guidance that is tailored to individual crisis situations and transfer pricing practices. Some key issues to consider while introducing such specific guidance, *inter alia*, are a balanced approach to the problem of enhanced transfer pricing audits owing to increasing pressure on tax collection, revision, and extension of APAs, measures to ease compliance and reduce penalties to discourage litigation and, lastly, the need for closer cooperation between jurisdictions and treaty partners pertaining to documentation. This will not only boost resilience but also capacitate the developing countries to fight the pandemic. More so, it shall play an important role in tax certainty for the taxpayers.

2.3 Policy Shifts by Countries and Companies in Light of COVID-19 and Its Impact on TP Law

Vietnam is home to various contract manufacturers or service providers as well as low-risk distributors placed within a supply chain. Further, many MNEs are reported to reorganize their business operations to Vietnam as being an optimal alternative to China. The government's increased focus on transfer pricing can be seen from the amendments to Vietnam's transfer pricing vide decree issued on 5 November 2020.

45. https://home.kpmg/om/en/home/insights/2020/12/tax-flash-due-date-for-filing-country-by-country-notification-extended.html.
46. CBDT, Notification No. 25/2020 dated 20 May 2020.
47. https://home.kpmg/xx/en/home/insights/2020/04/colombia-tax-developments-in-response-to-covid-19.html; https://www.dian.gov.co/normatividad/Normatividad/Resoluci%C3%B3n%20000065%20de%2018-06-2020.pdf.

Bangladesh is another viable option for shifting manufacturing units, especially in the textile sector, owing to relatively inexpensive labour. Recently, the Transfer Pricing Cell has been enquiring information from all MNEs operating in Bangladesh about business activities and relevant tax compliance to generate a basic profile of the MNE taxpayer.[48]

The Government of India has also implemented several schemes, such as Make-in-India (launched in 2014), Digital India, and Start-up India. These have led to significant FDIs in services, telecom auto components, and construction development sectors. FDIs in India have witnessed a positive trend since the launch of the Make-in-India campaign in 2014. FDI inflow from April 2014 to March 2020 (USD 357.35 billion) has been 52.5% of the overall FDI received in the country since April 2000 (USD 680.91 billion). For the first time, India crossed the USD 70 billion mark in FY 2019-2020 and recorded a total FDI inflow of USD 73.45 billion.[49]

Further, Thailand may be another expected centre for relocating supply chains, and it is necessary for companies to ensure transfer pricing compliance. It is imperative for all companies to align customs documentation and transfer pricing and align with one another since tax authorities of both departments seek such information.

2.4 Way Forward for Taxpayers in Developing and Emerging Economies

The ongoing COVID-19 crisis poses some significant challenges pertaining to the current income allocation system and transfer pricing rules. With respect to an MNE's transfer pricing policy, the aim is to compute the ALP such that it ensures certainty and leaves room for deviation in the case of unprecedented events. Adherence to the substance over form principle is of utmost importance. For developing and emerging economies, country-specific guidance on the impact of COVID-19 on transfer pricing may be helpful for taxpayers.

In the absence of specific guidance issued by developing and emerging economies, the legal jurisprudence on transfer pricing that has developed during a series of prior economic crises can also be used and applied in the current scenario. For instance, in an Argentine case,[50] the Supreme Court of Argentina had to answer a question under

48. https://home.kpmg/xx/en/home/insights/2020/04/mesa-tax-update-april-2020.html.
49. https://www.makeinindia.com/sectors-attracting-significant-fdi-in-india-in-2019-20.
50. https://research.ibfd.org/#/doc?url=/collections/itpj/html/itpj_2021_01_ar_1.html#itpj_2021_01_ar_1_s_3 In December 2019, the Argentinian Supreme Court issued a tax ruling in the case of Transportadora de Energía S.A. The Supreme Court overturned the ruling of the lower courts to hold that interest paid by the Argentinian subsidiary to its parent was deductible even though the loan was subsequently converted into equity. The lower courts had ruled that a loan arrangement between associated parties cannot be recharacterized into equity by application of the principle of economic reality set out in Articles 1 and 2 of the Tax Procedural Law, known as the Argentinian GAAR. This was for the years 2001 and 2002. The ruling sets an interesting judicial precedent that serves for future cases involving intercompany loans in times of economic downturns and reaches beyond the circumstances of Argentina. The Argentinian economic and financial crisis of 2001 has many parallels with the problems that the world is facing today with the COVID-19 pandemic. The increased pressure on cashflow has affected the ability of businesses to fulfil contractual obligations. Many will find themselves in a position where either they or the counterparty will be unable to perform their obligations and will be in

appeal on the issue of the true nature of controlled transactions in light of the ensuing economic crisis in the country in 2001-2002. The taxpayer was a wholly owned subsidiary of a Brazilian company and dealt with the power transmission sector. Two loans were secured in 2001 for power projects but, due to the economic crisis and change in regulations of power companies, the taxpayer defaulted on its loans. The loans were restructured several times with the eventuality of the parent company converting the loan into equity.

The revenue authorities argued that both companies were related parties, and the true nature of the transactions was not a loan but rather an equity deal. The Supreme Court observed that the ensuing economic crisis has to be taken into consideration which would mean that not only would the economic meltdown have an impact on legal relations but also an equal impact on the reading of the principles of economic reality during a transfer pricing analysis. The Supreme Court, having considered the substance over form doctrine and principle of economic reality, overturned the lower court's decisions and held that the loan cannot be recharacterized into equity merely because the terms have been breached. The original intentions of the contracting parties remain to be the driving force in such cases.

There are several factors during the course of an economic crisis that may adversely impact the agreed transfer price for repayment of borrowing, like market conditions, currency fluctuations, government interventions, increase in taxes, etc. Therefore, taxpayers must possess robust documentation to justify their inability to abide by any contractual agreements and also invoke force majeure clauses in the case of delays or non-performance.

2.5 Conclusion

Developed countries have adopted a proactive approach in providing certainty on transfer pricing matters to taxpayers. However, clear emphasis on the need to document the economic impact on the business is something that very much applies to taxpayers in developing countries. Affected taxpayers must demonstrate and justify the allocation of losses to particular jurisdictions. Further, supply chain disruption through contract frustration and remote working of employees form important aspects in a FAR analysis of any business that must be reflected in reported documents.

breach of contract. Yet the mere breach of a loan agreement without carefully considering the background circumstances cannot lead to a recharacterization, i.e., loan into equity, otherwise, this would imply not recognizing the legal substance of a contractual arrangement. Accordingly, analysing what happened to a legal contract after the outbreak of an economic crisis serves to determine, to some extent, whether the original nature of the agreement truly reflected the intentions of the parties. When looking at the intention of the parties with respect to the nature of the legal agreement to determine whether there is an abusive situation that deserves the application of a GAAR or a specific anti-avoidance rule, i.e., transfer pricing rules, it is necessary to determine whether the external circumstances were the main driver for a change into the conditions of the agreement.

3 DEVELOPMENTS IN OECD ENGAGEMENT WITH DEVELOPING COUNTRIES AND EMERGING ECONOMIES

The OECD's commitment to supporting developing countries was recognized by the African Tax Administration Forum, which, in 2019, named the OECD as its best international partner. Other partners such as the General Authority of Zakat and Tax in Saudi Arabia and the Asian Development Bank are looking to the OECD to establish hubs or platforms to intensify capacity building support on a regional basis.

3.1 Overall Engagement

The OECD engages with developing countries on several fronts, and notable developments in 2020 are:

> The OECD/G20 Inclusive Framework, established in 2016, currently has 137 members, including 66 developing countries. Developing countries are also well represented in the steering group of the OECD/G20 Inclusive Framework, which includes deputy chairs from the People's Republic of China and Nigeria and other members from Brazil, Côte d'Ivoire, Georgia, India, Jamaica, Senegal, and South Africa.[51]

The OECD is also producing toolkits focused on the particular needs and priorities of developing countries in relation to profit shifting and base erosion issues, notably through the Platform for Collaboration on Tax (PCT). These toolkits aim at assisting developing countries in translating international tax norms so that they can be effectively implemented in their circumstances, bearing in mind capacity limitations and the practical realities faced by tax administrations in developing countries. A toolkit on offshore indirect transfers of interests was released on 4 June 2020, and another toolkit on implementing effective transfer pricing documentation is in the course of being developed – a draft version was released in 2019.

The Tax Inspectors without Borders (TIWB) initiative for developing countries released its annual report for 2020. This is a joint initiative of the OECD and United Nations Development Programme (UNDP) and is a unique approach to capacity building that embeds expert tax auditors in developing country tax administrations to provide practical hands-on assistance on actual tax audits of MNEs and related international tax issues. As of the end of June 2020, TIWB had forty completed, thirty-nine current, and nineteen upcoming programmes in forty-four different tax jurisdictions. The UNDP-managed roster of tax audit experts includes specialists from Australia, Canada, Ghana, India, Kenya, Nigeria, Peru, South Africa, and the United States. As of 30 June 2020, additional tax revenues raised by developing countries in connection with TIWB programmes amounted to USD 537 million, and overall tax

51. http://www.oecd.org/tax/beps/oecd-g20-inclusive-framework-on-beps-progress-report-july-2019-july-2020.pdf.

assessments were in excess of USD 1.84 billion.[52] The landmark tax ruling of the Court of Zambia discussed earlier in this paper was an outcome of this initiative.[53] In February 2020, the Georgia Revenue Service requested a new TIWB programme that will start in 2021. Through this new programme, the Georgia Revenue Service is aiming to conduct audits in the extractives sector to address profit shifting by large companies.[54]

3.2 Developments under the OECD/G20 BEPS Inclusive Framework

Under the OECD/G20 BEPS Inclusive Framework, the following are the notable developments with respect to developing countries and emerging economies:

> Multilateral Instruments (MLI) – By way of mutual consensus, many developing countries signed the MLI to incorporate the proposals agreed to within the BEPS framework. Bahrain recently became the 95th jurisdiction to sign the MLI. Algeria, Eswatini, Lebanon, and Thailand have also expressed their intent to sign the legislation.[55]

MAP – Emerging economies such as Pakistan, Nigeria, Zimbabwe, Kenya, Mauritius, Vietnam, Thailand, and Kazakhstan have witnessed a surge in MAP cases. Countries such as Indonesia, Mexico, Malaysia, and Qatar are running the MAP programme quite successfully, with an average of forty-five cases by the end of 2019. Nonetheless, this number still remains low compared to economies such as Germany, the United States, and India, where 2019 cases have been averaging around a thousand cases.[56]

This not only shows a commitment to undertake measures to adopt the MAP system but also a commitment to move towards resolving all MAP disputes that arise in their respective countries. Since MAP cases include transfer pricing as well other international tax-related disputes, a trend could be seen in larger economies of the developed world such as the United States, Germany, South Korea, and the United Kingdom, where non-transfer pricing cases constitute a majority of the MAP caseload. On the other hand, in developing and emerging economies such as India, whose transfer pricing case statistics were higher than 700 in 2019, transfer pricing cases constitute a majority of the total MAP caseload.[57] Similarly, for countries that are emerging

52. http://tiwb.org/resources/reports-case-studies/tax-inspectors-without-borders-annual-report-2020.htm.
53. http://www.oecd.org/tax/tax-global/building-capacity-to-prevent-profit-shifting-by-large-companies-in-zambia.pdf.
54. http://www.oecd.org/tax/tax-global/learning-by-doing-in-georgia.pdf.
55. http://www.oecd.org/tax/beps/beps-mli-signatories-and-parties.pdf.
56. *See* (a) Compare your country MAP statistics https://www1.compareyourcountry.org/map-statistics/en/0/all/default; and (b) Mutual Agreement Procedure Statistics 2019 per jurisdiction – Inventory https://www.oecd.org/tax/dispute/mutual-agreement-procedure-statistics-2019-per-jurisdiction-inventory.htm.
57. https://www.oecd.org/tax/dispute/mutual-agreement-procedure-statistics-2019-per-jurisdiction-transfer-pricing.htm.

economies, transfer pricing cases are more than other cases – for countries such as Kenya and Thailand, whose transfer pricing cases stand at four and one, respectively.[58]

Tax certainty is also one of the fundamental goals of the OECD/G20 BEPS Project and is a key element of the ongoing work on the tax challenges arising from the digitalization of the economy. In order to ensure tax certainty, reliable and efficient dispute resolution mechanisms are a crucial tool. In that respect, Action Plan 14 has set a minimum standard for MAPs. Members have to undergo a peer review process for monitoring the effective implementation of the action plan. Notably, as of July 2020, fifty-five jurisdictions have applied for or obtained a deferral for the peer review process; most of them are developing countries and emerging economies.[59]

CbC Reporting is part of the three-tiered approach to transfer pricing documentation foreseen in Action 13. It comprises a master file with an overview of an MNE group's business and transfer pricing policies, local files with more detailed information on specific transactions with a particular jurisdiction, and a CbC report containing information on the global spread of an MNE's activities, results, and where it pays tax. Over 105 jurisdictions, including several developing countries and emerging economies, have introduced CbC reporting and filing obligations into law.

The OECD continues to develop practical tools to support the use of CbC reports, including ICAP 2.0, CoRA and the release of the TREAT and the TRAQ. A brief discussion on the same is provided below:

> *International Compliance Assurance Programme (ICAP)*: ICAP is a multilateral risk assessment and assurance process that uses CbC reports and other risk assessment information to provide MNEs and tax administrations with increased tax certainty. A second pilot for ICAP, including 19 participating tax administrations, was launched in 2019 and is currently underway.
>
> *Comparative Risk Assessment initiative (CoRA)*: Building on the increasingly common information available to tax administrations for tax risk assessment, CoRA is an initiative to drive greater convergence in the perception of risk by tax administrations and in understanding how key risk indicators can be detected, including through an MNE's CbC report. It was expected that the outcomes of this work will be made available to tax administrations by the end of 2020.
>
> *Tax Risk Evaluation and Assurance Tool (TREAT) and Tax Risk Assessment Questionnaire (TRAQ)*: The TREAT is a tool to support tax administrations, in particular those in developing countries, in interpreting an MNE's CbC report to identify where further enquiries may or may not be needed. The TREAT incorporates training materials drawing on experience in ICAP and CoRA to assist tax

58. https://www1.compareyourcountry.org/map-statistics/en/1/all/default.
59. In total, forty-eight jurisdictions have obtained a deferral (Angola, Anguilla, Armenia, Belize, Benin, Bosnia and Herzegovina, Botswana, Burkina Faso, Cabo Verde, Cameroon, Congo, Cook Islands, Costa Rica, Côte d'Ivoire, Democratic Republic of Congo, Djibouti, Dominica, Dominican Republic, Egypt, Gabon, Georgia, Grenada, Haiti, Jamaica, Kenya, Liberia, Malaysia, Maldives, Mauritius, Mongolia, Montserrat, Republic of North Macedonia, Nigeria, Pakistan, Panama, Papua New Guinea, Paraguay, Peru, Saint Lucia, Saint Vincent and the Grenadines, Senegal, Seychelles, Sierra Leone, Sri Lanka, Turks & Caicos Islands, Ukraine, Uruguay, Zambia) whereas a decision on a deferral is currently pending for seven jurisdictions: (Albania, Antigua and Barbuda, Eswatini, Honduras, Jordan, Montenegro and Namibia) http://www.oecd.org/tax/beps/oecd-g20-inclusive-framework-on-beps-progress-report-july-2019-july-2020.pdf.

administrations in the risk assessment of MNEs. This is supported by the TRAQ, which may be provided by a tax administration to an MNE group, inviting it to provide additional information where possible indicators of potential tax risk appear to be present in the group's CbC report. It was expected that the outcomes of this work will be made available to tax administrations by the end of 2020.

3.3 Conclusion

It is widely known that the OECD/G20 BEPS Inclusive Framework has significantly changed the international tax landscape. The continuing engagement of the OECD with developing countries, especially in providing assistance towards audits and documentation as well as the formation of the PCT and the work it undertakes, all indicate the intent of the OECD to provide a level playing field to developing countries in the field of transfer pricing. With respect to providing certainty to taxpayers for international dispute resolution, while commendable efforts have been initiated, the resolution of MAP cases seems to be abysmally low. India and China reported closure rates at the rate of 10%. Russia did not close any cases. While Brazil and Saudi Arabia reported closures at 30% and 70%, respectively, the number of cases closed were in single digits (eight for Brazil and five for Saudi Arabia). Against these, developed countries have reported much higher numbers both in terms of percentages of closure as well as absolute numbers. Developed countries comprise fourteen out of the top fifteen nations for MAP inventory. India has the third-highest number of MAP cases. Germany and the United States, which have the top two number of cases, were able to achieve closure rates of 40% and 30%, respectively. Overall, developed countries in the top fifteen MAP jurisdictions comprised 85% of the total MAP closures reported, while their opening inventory was 70% of the total reported MAP inventory. This demonstrates the need for the OECD to engage more with developing countries on the MAP front.[60]

4 UPDATE OF UN PRACTICE MANUAL ON TP FOR DEVELOPING COUNTRIES

Almost all emerging economies and developing countries are members of the UN. The United Nations Practical Manual on Transfer Pricing for Developing Countries (UN TP Manual) forms an important guiding toolkit for developing and least developed countries. The manual was prepared in response to the need often expressed by developing countries for clearer guidance on the policy and administrative aspects of applying a transfer pricing analysis to some of the transactions of MNEs in particular.[61] The guidance has become even more relevant due to the complexity in business operations and the increase in disputes that demand relevant examples and simplifications for developing countries to embrace compliance with transfer pricing in a

60. Mutual Agreement Procedure Statistics for 2019, available at https://www.oecd.org/tax/dispute/mutual-agreement-procedure-statistics.htm.
61. https://www.un.org/development/desa/financing/sites/www.un.org.development.desa.financing/files/2020-03/UN_Manual_TransferPricing.pdf Please refer note at para. 3.

global environment. The inputs are practical and are gathered from useful capacity building exercises with tax administrations from developing and emerging economies.

The UN Committee of Experts on International Cooperation in Tax Matters (the Committee) formed a new Subcommittee on Article 9 (Associated Enterprises) in 2017: Transfer Pricing (the Subcommittee).[62] The Subcommittee is mandated to review and update the United Nations Practical Manual on Transfer Pricing for Developing Countries based on the following principles:[63]

(1) consistently reflects the text and commentaries on Article 9 of the UN Model Convention and the ALP embodied therein as well as the outcome of OECD/G20 Actions Plans of the BEPS Project that concern transfer pricing;
(2) reflects the realities and varying stages of capacity development of different developing economies;
(3) focusing on practically relevant issues and solutions pertaining to transfer pricing drawn from the experience of developing countries;
(4) draws from the updated work being undertaken in other forums.

The Subcommittee reports on its progress at the sessions of the committee and is expected to provide its final updated draft manual for discussion and adoption no later than the 22nd Session of the UN Committee meeting in 2021.

The Subcommittee currently comprises twenty-seven participants from tax administrations, academia, international organizations, and the private sector, including from MNEs and advisers. A Subcommittee of this size and diversity has been considered necessary because of the many issues and perspectives in this area, and it continues to operate very successfully.[64] Thus the updates to the UN Manual were set out after due deliberations and taking into account a variety of perspectives.

The updates to the 2017 manual are on the topics of comparability, transfer pricing, and customs valuations aligned with the guidance of the World Customs Organisation, profit split, additional guidance on centralized sales functions, group synergies and centralized procurement, financial transactions, establishing and updating transfer pricing regimes, and dispute avoidance and resolution. Country practices and experiences from several countries such as China, India, Kenya, Mexico, and South Africa have been incorporated.

The updates are comprehensive and explicitly recognize that all transfer pricing problems need a solution by taking cognizance of the need for a pragmatic approach. The revised guidelines also take into account the need for accurate delineation of transactions.

62. The term of the currently appointed Subcommittee on Article 9: Transfer Pricing shall come to an end in June 2021.
63. https://www.un.org/development/desa/financing/sites/www.un.org.development.desa.financing/files/2020-10/CRP40%20Transfer%20Pricing%20Manual%20Combined%20compressed.pdf.
64. https://www.un.org/development/desa/financing/sites/www.un.org.development.desa.financing/files/2020-05/CRP14%20-%20Transfer%20Pricing%20Manual%20Combined.pdf.

Notably, the guidance on the selection of companies under the TNMM has changed to a more conceptual guidance emphasizing the importance of the screening criteria and identifying the economically relevant characteristics of the accurately delineated transaction.[65]

With respect to commodity benchmarking, the guidance is updated to provide for the use of quoted prices; however, for less transparent markets, the guidance cautions on the contacts of the publisher to access the information and the ability of the publisher to make adjustments to raw data in a manner that may not be apparent.[66]

The guidance on the application of the PSM has been significantly amended. Against recognizing only two approaches for applying the PSM – the residual analysis and the contribution analysis – the amended guidance recognizes there may be several approaches to applying the PSM. The guidance emphasizes the need for a delineation of transactions.

The manual has also provided additional guidance for centralized procurement functions and has also introduced a new chapter on intra-group financial transactions, especially debt and equity financing, delving into the nature of loans and guarantees. The newly added practical examples pertaining to intra-group financial transactions are meant not only to usefully guide developing and emerging countries but also to supplement the new OECD Transfer Pricing Guidance on Financial Transactions 2020. In similar lines as the OECD, the UN rules also focus on the CUP being the best method of the ALP for loan contracts.[67] In addition, they also provide some additional CUP based alternatives to new and emerging economies by suggesting that unavailable benchmarking data could be effectively created (the Sixth Transfer Pricing Method) by looking at similar industries and their practices.[68] An updated, detailed, and dynamic UN Manual scheduled for release in 2021 is expected to largely align with OECD Guidelines in accordance with the PCT initiative.

5 DEVELOPMENTS IN TAXATION OF DIGITAL ECONOMIES

The current treaty rules of allocating taxing rights favour capital-exporting countries or developed countries based on the residence principle rather than capital importing countries or developing countries based on source principle. Hence, they are not well-equipped to tax the digital economy and enable MNEs to pay a fair share of taxes.

65. *See* paras 33 and 36 of https://www.un.org/development/desa/financing/sites/www.un.org.development.desa.financing/files/2020-10/CRP40%20Transfer%20Pricing%20Manual%20Combined%20compressed.pdf.
66. Paragraph 2.3.4.42 https://www.un.org/development/desa/financing/sites/www.un.org.development.desa.financing/files/2020-10/CRP40%20Transfer%20Pricing%20Manual%20Combined%20compressed.pdf.
67. https://www.un.org/development/desa/financing/sites/www.un.org.development.desa.financing/files/2020-05/CRP14%20-%20Transfer%20Pricing%20Manual%20Combined.pdf at para. B.2.3.1.9.
68. Paragraph B.9.3.2.8 https://www.un.org/development/desa/financing/sites/www.un.org.development.desa.financing/files/2020-05/CRP14%20-%20Transfer%20Pricing%20Manual%20Combined.pdf.

Tax policymakers are facing amalgamated challenges to fill the fiscal gap and raise revenue through taxing the digital economy, which has been thriving and witnessed a peak in business performance even during the pandemic. Developing countries form a part of two international collaborative mechanisms – the PCT and the Inclusive Framework on BEPS. The new design of the international tax framework must uphold the notion of 'global justice' in terms of distributing taxing rights.

Emerging economies and developing countries, especially populated nations with a high number of digital users, foresee an increasing number of economic justifications to broaden the scope to tax the digital economy. There have been several developing countries that either proposed or adopted new tax measures seeking a larger allocation of taxing rights in the absence of a global consensus-based solution. Countries like India, Indonesia, Israel, and Nigeria have introduced their own versions of 'significant economic presence' (SEP), whereby the foreign entity's taxable presence in a market jurisdiction is evidenced by a purposeful and sustained interaction with the users in that jurisdiction through the means of technology and other prescribed thresholds. The SEP follows the principle of allocating taxing rights where value is created and is based on the assumption that demand creates considerable value, especially in the context of digitalized business models. Resultantly, part of the income should be allocated to the marketplace or where the customers are based.[69] It is obvious that income can only be created if there is a market or demand for the supply. The aim is to prevent profit diversion by ensuring that the significant global MNEs reflect the economic substance of their activities in market jurisdictions. The biggest issue in implementing the SEP is its unilateral nature resulting in juridical double taxation for which residence countries may deny granting tax relief. Moreover, if strictly implemented, countries may foresee other retaliatory international trade measures.

Interestingly, the SEP was proposed by the G-24 that includes India and other developing countries as a virtual PE to be incorporated in Article 5 of the tax treaties.[70] In 2018, India incorporated the SEP concept, which is established by the application of revenue and user thresholds in exclusion to one another.[71] As per the statement of intent and taking support from the Action 1 Final Report, the SEP shall only apply when a purposeful and sustained interaction with the economy exists with the aid of technology and other automated tools.[72] Although this phrase is not included in the main provision, the intent of introducing this provision was only to establish a virtual business connection. Therefore, it aims to create a business connection between India and a fully dematerialized business that was not being taxed prior to the introduction of the SEP. However, in a plain reading of the SEP provision,[73] besides digital

---

69. Eric C.C.M Kemmeren, *If we need a destination-based corporate income tax, do we also need a production-based consumption tax?* International Taxation in a Changing Landscape – Liber Amicorum in Honour of Bertil Wiman, editors Jérôme Monsenego and Jan Bjuvberg, Alphen aan den Rijn: Kluwer Law International (2019), p. 148.
70. Proposal for Addressing Tax Challenges Arising from Digitization by G-24 Working Group on tax policy and international tax cooperation dt. 17 January 2019.
71. Memorandum explaining provisions of the Finance Bill, 2018.
72. Memorandum explaining provisions of the Finance Bill, 2018; para. 277.
73. Section 9(1) of Income Tax Act, 1961: The following incomes shall be deemed to accrue or arise in India:

transactions, all other residual transactions may also be covered under the SEP definition. To this end, it becomes all the more important to issue guidance and clarifications restricting the scope of such a broad definition. Moreover, the rules on profit attribution are awaited on the SEP. Since the discussions on addressing the tax challenges of digitalization remain ongoing with Pillar One, the implementation of the SEP provisions has been deferred to 1 April 2022. Hence, the SEP concept shall remain a proposed provision in its domestic law until suitable amendments are not made to India's tax treaties.[74]

Awaiting the global consensus, there are a number of nations that have been levying equalization levy or digital service taxes (DSTs) in different forms to suit their respective requirements. Kenya introduced Digital Tax Regulations in August 2020 that levies a DST of 1.5% on supplies procured through a digital marketplace.[75] Similarly, Brazil proposed a DST of 3% on income obtained in Brazil. Indonesia, to make up for the fiscal loss caused by the pandemic, issued regulations that levy corporate income tax by deemed PEs of overseas e-commerce companies that have a SEP in Indonesia based on the consolidated gross turnover of the business group, sales, and a number of active users on digital media.[76] These interim measures, if not handled properly, may result being detrimental to end consumers as well as foreign investors. Such unilateral action may qualify as a quick fix in the spirit of national tax sovereignty but could potentially damage inter-nation economic relationships. There are a number of risks and adverse consequences that might follow.[77]

Coming to DSTs, India was one of the first nations to introduce an equalization levy (in 2016) that targeted non-resident companies operating in the digital advertisement

---

(i) all income accruing or arising, whether directly or indirectly, through or from any business connection in India, or through or from any property in India, or through or from any asset or source of income in India, or through the transfer of a capital asset situate in India.

Explanation 2A – For the removal of doubts, it is hereby declared that the significant economic presence of a non-resident in India shall constitute 'business connection' in India and 'significant economic presence' for this purpose, shall mean –

(a) transaction in respect of any goods, services or property carried out by a non-resident with any person in India including provision of download of data or software in India, if the aggregate of payments arising from such transaction or transactions during the previous year exceeds such amount as may be prescribed; or

(b) systematic and continuous soliciting of business activities or engaging in interaction with such number of users in India, as may be prescribed:

Provided that the transactions or activities shall constitute significant economic presence in India, whether or not, –

(i) the agreement for such transactions or activities is entered in India; or

(ii) the non-resident has a residence or place of business in India; or

(iii) the non-resident renders services in India:

Provided further that only so much of income as is attributable to the transactions or activities referred to in clause (a) or clause (b) shall be deemed to accrue or arise in India.

74. Section 90(2) of the Income Tax Act, 1961.
75. https://home.kpmg/us/en/home/insights/2020/12/tnf-kenya-digital-services-tax-regulations-effective-date-2021.html.
76. Regulation No. 1 for 2020 (PERPPU-1) – effective 31 March 2020.
77. Interim Report, OECD 2018; pp. 178-179.

space. However, with Finance Act 2020, the said scope was substantially expanded to broadly cover income arising from the sale or use of data of Indian customers. Moreover, it mandates foreign suppliers to register with Indian tax authorities and fulfil compliance-related obligations. Unlike DSTs imposed in European countries that provide for a global revenue threshold, the expanded equalization levy of 2020 merely stipulates a *de minimis* threshold below which consideration of a particular transaction is not subject to tax that only factors the revenue derived from activities subject to the said levy.[78] In fact, the United States released its investigative findings on the discriminatory nature of the Indian equalization levy of 2020. The report has strongly disapproved of the levy, holding it to be discriminatory, unreasonable, and restricting US commerce.[79] The broad scope of India's equalization levy has been specifically pointed out, thereby observing it to tax a broader scope of services than other digital services taxes adopted around the world.[80]

Nigeria has been rather bold in taxing the digital space. The Nigerian Minister of Finance introduced the Companies Income Tax (Significant Economic Presence) (CIT (SEP)) Order 2020 on 29 May 2020. Similar to India, the Nigerian SEP concept hinges on two-fold threshold criteria of revenue and digital access that is applicable to non-resident companies. While the former prescribes several digital activities falling under the scope of the SEP along with a gross turnover limit, the latter provides for the formation of the SEP when companies operate with Nigerian domain names like '.ng' or 'com.ng'. The provision separately provides that, when a non-resident company customizes features on its website or application to reflect domestic market needs like language, currency, local support, delivery, and payment, it shall form a SEP basis such as purposeful and sustained interaction with the Nigerian market. Importantly, the prescribed rate of tax ranges from 20%-30% of taxable profits attributable to the Nigerian SEP.[81]

Challenges relating to the taxation of the digital economy have been a part of the UN's agenda as well. It has been playing a proactive role alongside the OECD on the said issue. This is because developing countries, being UN members, have the most to gain from the introduction of tax policies based upon source-based taxation.[82] Drifting from the PE concept, the UN has proposed an alternative solution *vide* Article 12B by the UN Tax Committee released in the UN Model Double Taxation Convention between

78. Report by ASSOCHAM and BMR Legal Advocates on 'Equalization Levy 2.0: India's Digital Service Tax in the Making'; p. 29.
79. USTR, Section 301 Investigations: Report on India's Digital Services Tax dated 6 January 2021, available at https://ustr.gov/sites/default/files/enforcement/301Investigations/Report%20on%20India%E2%80%99s%20Digital%20Services%20Tax.pdf.
80. USTR, Section 301 Investigations: Report on India's Digital Services Tax, available at https://ustr.gov/sites/default/files/enforcement/301Investigations/Report%20on%20India%E2%80%99s%20Digital%20Services%20Tax.pdf, p. 24.
81. Nigeria's Significant Economic Presence Income Tax on Digital Economic Activities: Challenges and Opportunities by Chimezirim Echendu, Bulletin for International Taxation, 2020 (Volume 74), No. 9, Published online: 3 September 2020 https://research.ibfd.org/#/doc?url=/collections/bit/html/bit_2020_09_ng_1.html#bit_2020_09_ng_1_s_3_5.
82. *Tax Challenges in the Digitalized Economy: Selected Issues for Possible Committee Consideration*, Committee of Experts on International Cooperation in Tax Matters, United Nations dt. 11 October 2017.

Developed and Developing Countries on 'income from automated digital services'. The proposed new Article 12B requires foreign providers of automated digital services to pay income tax at source by means of either (i) a withholding on gross income (whereby the rate is to be agreed upon by the parties to the treaty) or (ii) an apportionment formula on qualified profits from automated digital services. The UN believes in ring-fencing the digital economy as it was tasked with the specific issue of this economy. Further, it places paramount importance on simplicity as many developing countries have limited administrative capacity and need a simple, reliable, and efficient method to enforce tax imposed on income from services derived by non-residents. It is pertinent to note that the UN drafting group has undertaken this work in their personal capacity as experts to create a solution for developing countries. Subject to Article 12B becoming a reality, one of the probable challenges that may be faced by developing and emerging economies as market jurisdictions is the choice presented to the taxpayers to either tax income on a gross or a net basis. In the absence of sophisticated tax systems when compared to developed nations, emerging economies currently choose to tax income on a gross basis. Hence, the mere option to choose between the gross and net basis of taxation may result in incongruity for emerging economies. Moreover, it must be kept in mind that, while reaching a satisfying outcome to tax the digital economy, taxpayers must not be subjected to excessive taxation.

It is safe to say that the OECD's work on addressing tax challenges of the digital companies vide Action Plan One of the OECD/G20 BEPS Inclusive Framework has been the most followed international tax development of 2020. The OECD has made significant progress in this area, as is evident from its Pillar One and Pillar Two Blueprints released in October 2020. Developing countries and emerging economies are largely 'market jurisdictions' with large user bases as envisaged in the blueprints. The United States alone is home to eight out of the top ten digital companies and, as such, may qualify as the jurisdiction that will have to reallocate the largest share of its taxing rights in favour of market jurisdictions. This can be seen from the table below that captures a list of the top ten largest tech companies in the world in 2019:[83]

Rank	*Company*	*Country*	*Market Value (USD Billion)*	*Assets (USD Billion)*
1	Apple	United States	961	374
2	Samsung Electronics	South Korea	272	304
3	Microsoft	United States	947	259
4	Alphabet	United States	863	233
5	Intel	United States	263	128
6	IBM	United States	125	131

83. https://www.forbes.com/sites/jonathanponciano/2019/05/15/worlds-largest-tech-companies-2019/?sh=6149c2f8734f.

Rank	*Company*	*Country*	*Market Value (USD Billion)*	*Assets (USD Billion)*
7	Facebook	United States	512	97
8	Cisco Systems	United States	248	102
9	Tencent Holdings	China	472	105
10	Oracle	United States	186	109

The value created by developed countries in terms of the number of users vis-à-vis purchasing power parity of these countries is also a factor to consider. Thus, countries are working with differing objectives in reaching a consensus while recognizing the need to reach one. This has led to the playing out of Action Plan 1 as an event gathering the most attention from the international tax community, followed by a series of developments. Taxpayers, in some cases, are responding to unilateral levies by passing the same on to consumers in those jurisdictions while they await the consensus on Action Plan 1 to unfold.

Conclusion: Developing countries must be cautious of the fact that protectionist and unilateral measures, as well as related compliances, have a bearing on inbound FDI. Hence, it is necessary to be mindful that such measures are viewed as temporary and against the international coordinated consensus. With respect to transfer pricing, determining the taxable income attributable to such virtual PEs shall be challenging. For example, it will be rather difficult for national tax authorities to allow or disallow certain deductible expenses claimed by such non-resident companies. Moreover, even though the ALP does not address remote taxable presence, it is not wise for emerging economies to completely discount the principle. Hence, it should either be re-examined or applied in tandem with other approaches to arrive at an outcome. The debate centres around moving from the traditional FAR based analysis to a FARM (functions, assets, risks and market) based analysis to cover market or demand-related factors. A renewed focus on 'value creation' post-BEPS is accompanied by even stronger consideration of demand-side factors in developing jurisdictions.

6 OUTLOOK FOR DEVELOPING COUNTRIES AND EMERGING ECONOMIES

Transfer pricing will continue to be an area of increased attention and scrutiny by tax authorities in developing and developed countries alike. Developing countries and emerging economies will continue to align themselves to global best practices and with support from various initiatives from the OECD and the UN (such as the UN Manual on transfer pricing, the transfer pricing documentation toolkit developed by the PCT, the TIWB initiative of the OECD, and the developments in the OECD/G20 BEPS Inclusive Framework) and will significantly augment their audit and dispute resolution capabilities. The event to watch out for will be the unfolding of Action Plan 1 with respect to transfer pricing and taxation for digital businesses. A reasonable, administrable, economically rational, certain, and sustainable outcome is awaited. Countries will also engage more proactively in MAPs and bilateral APAs in an effort to boost taxpayer confidence with respect to certainty of tax outcomes. Overall, the key focus should be on amplifying tax certainty for MNEs and taxpayer experience altogether by resolving the gap between legislative intent and implementation on the ground level. The measures towards such a goal include simplification and streamlining of transfer pricing documentation (assess Action Plan 13 on CbCr), improving dispute resolution programmes, mobilizing of resources and technical training for effective dispute resolutions, more practical solutions on the level of adherence to the ALP, etc. In this way, the progress and efforts made in the area of transfer pricing policies can be successfully translated into a practical reality.

CHAPTER 5

Recent Developments on the Tax Challenges of the Digitalization of the Economy

Mary C. Bennett

1 INTRODUCTION

For those of us in the international tax community, discussion of the tax challenges arising from the digitalization of the economy has been a constant drumbeat for nearly a decade, the intensity of which has seemed to grow with each passing year. While the road ahead remains somewhat shrouded in mist at this point, the message of the drums suggests the possibility that 2021 could be the year when governments decide to make fundamental changes to the international tax system as a result of the digitalization tax challenges. Those changes could have implications well beyond the digital sector and could significantly alter the familiar rhythms of transfer pricing as it has been practised for several decades.

This chapter will begin with a high-level overview of the current state of global developments relating to the tax challenges of digitalization. These will include the OECD's ongoing work on Pillars One and Two; the United Nations (UN) Committee of Experts' consideration of a new Article 12B on the taxation of income from automated digital services (ADS); various countries' unilateral enactment or consideration of digital service taxes (DSTs) and similar levies as well as the trade disputes arising from those; and the European Union's (EU's) anticipated proposal for a digital levy as part of the 'own resources' that the EU needs to repay its COVID recovery-related borrowings. The chapter will then focus on a selection of specific issues addressed by Pillar One, which proposes new nexus and profit allocation rules for businesses that fall within its scope. The specific issues to be considered will be several that have particular relevance to transfer pricing practice and principles. They will include the proposed marketing and distribution safe harbour for avoiding double counting in market jurisdictions, the approach to eliminating international double taxation, the Amount B mechanism for allocating profits from baseline marketing and distribution activities, the proposals for dispute prevention and resolution, and the approach to implementation and administration of the new regime.

2 HIGH-LEVEL OVERVIEW OF RECENT DEVELOPMENTS

2.1 Status of Pillar One

As early as 2012, when the OECD was first formulating its project to address Base Erosion and Profit Shifting (BEPS), the organization identified as a key pressure point 'the application of treaty concepts to profits derived from the delivery of digital goods and services'.[1] Few were surprised, therefore, when the OECD's BEPS Action Plan released in July 2013 included to 'address the tax challenges of the digital economy' as the goal of its Action 1.[2] Despite the BEPS Project's foundational focus on these challenges, however, the Action 1 Final Report issued in October 2015[3] did not include any specific recommendations for addressing the direct tax challenges of the digital economy. Instead, it stated the delegates' conclusion that 'it would be difficult, if not impossible, to ring-fence the digital economy from the rest of the economy for tax purposes'. It mentioned three options that countries could consider adopting, provided they respect their treaty obligations: (i) a new nexus in the form of a significant

1. 'BEPS - A Background Brief', OECD, 20 November 2012, available as Tax Analysts Doc 2012-25123.
2. 'Action Plan on Base Erosion and Profit Shifting', OECD, 19 July 2013, available at https://www.oecd.org/tax/beps/action-plan-on-base-erosion-and-profit-shifting-9789264202719-en.htm.
3. 'Addressing the Tax Challenges of the Digital Economy, Action 1 – 2015 Final Report', OECD, 5 October 2015, available at https://www.oecd.org/tax/beps/addressing-the-tax-challenges-of-the-digital-economy-action-1-2015-final-report-9789264241046-en.htm.

economic presence; (ii) a withholding tax on certain types of digital transactions; and (iii) an equalization levy. It committed to further work on the topics.

By January 2019, the further work led to a policy note[4] from the OECD's Inclusive Framework (IF),[5] which described the IF's agreement to pursue work on two 'pillars', one on the allocation of taxing rights and a second on a global minimum tax regime. The policy note acknowledged that the Pillar One work would lead to a solution that would go beyond the arm's length principle (ALP) and also that it could 'affect not only a small group of highly digitalised businesses but [also] a much wider group of enterprises with cross-border business operations, for instance, those with marketing intangible profits but limited risk distribution structures in market jurisdictions'.[6]

The OECD then published a 'Secretariat Proposal for a "Unified Approach" under Pillar One'[7] in October 2019, which introduced the idea of a new nexus and profit allocation in market jurisdictions for multinational entities (MNEs) engaged in 'large consumer-facing businesses (CFB), broadly defined, e.g., businesses that generate revenue from supplying consumer products or providing digital services that have a consumer-facing element.'[8] To achieve this, it proposed that in-scope MNE groups compute a formulaic Amount A, a share of deemed residual profit to be allocated among market jurisdictions based on sales revenues, without regard to the physical presence or traditional arm's length determinations. It also called for an Amount B that was designed to be a fixed remuneration based on the ALP for baseline marketing and distribution activities actually conducted by MNE groups in market jurisdictions and an Amount C described as the return for activities in the market jurisdiction falling outside the coverage of Amount B.

Negotiations on Pillar One grew more complicated in December 2019 when US Treasury Secretary Mnuchin wrote to the OECD expressing serious concerns about Pillar One's potential mandatory departures from long-standing arm's length transfer pricing and nexus standards and suggesting Pillar One instead be a safe harbour regime.[9] The IF nevertheless issued a statement in January 2020 confirming their intention to proceed with negotiations on the basis of the 'Unified Approach' while noting the critical need to resolve the issue raised by the United States in order to

4. 'Addressing the Tax Challenges of the Digitalisation of the Economy – Policy Note', OECD, 23 January 2019, available at https://www.oecd.org/tax/beps/policy-note-beps-inclusive-framework-addressing-tax-challenges-digitalisation.pdf.
5. The IF is a forum in which over 130 OECD members, G20 countries, and other interested jurisdictions work together on developing standards on BEPS-related issues and reviewing and monitoring the implementation of the whole BEPS Package, https://www.oecd.org/tax/beps/beps-about.htm/.
6. 'Addressing the Tax Challenges of the Digitalisation of the Economy – Policy Note', OECD, 23 January 2019, available at https://www.oecd.org/tax/beps/policy-note-beps-inclusive-framework-addressing-tax-challenges-digitalisation.pdf.
7. Available at https://www.oecd.org/tax/beps/oecd-invites-public-input-on-the-secretariat-proposal-for-a-unified-approach-under-pillar-one.htm.
8. *Ibid.*, at para. 20.
9. *See* Letter from Treasury Secretary Mnuchin to OECD Secretary-General Gurría, 3 December 2019, available as Tax Analysts Doc 2019-45731.

achieve consensus.[10] The January 2020 statement refined the described scope of Amount A to include ADS and CFB. The G20 Finance Ministers met in July 2020 and mandated the IF to produce a report on the Pillar One Blueprint by October 2020 with a view to reaching a consensus on the proposal by year-end.[11]

The latest release from the OECD on Pillar One is the 'Report on the Pillar One Blueprint' issued for public consultation on 12 October 2020.[12] The Pillar One Blueprint not only reflects substantial technical progress (e.g., including the elimination of Amount C, elaboration on issues of scope, elimination of double taxation, and dispute prevention and resolution) but also acknowledges very significant political and technical issues that remain outstanding. At the same time, the OECD's Secretary-General informed the G20 Finance Ministers that the conditions for a political agreement had not yet been achieved but that the IF remained committed to reaching a future agreement based on the blueprint.[13] The G20 Finance Ministers urged the IF to address the remaining issues with a view to reaching a consensus agreement by mid-2021.[14]

Press reports at the beginning of 2021 indicated that the OECD believed positive signals from the new Biden Administration in the United States would be critical to reaching an agreement, and the recently departed senior negotiator on Pillar One for the Trump Administration's Treasury Department said that the United States would need to drop its safe harbour proposal if an agreement is to be reached.[15] The G20 Finance Ministers, therefore, welcomed the announcement by new US Treasury Secretary Janet Yellen at their meeting of 26 February 2021 that the United States was withdrawing the safe harbour proposal and was committed to 'engage robustly to address both Pillars of the OECD project'.[16] While this development prompted Pascal Saint-Amans, the director of the OECD's Centre for Tax Policy and Administration, to say on 4 March 2021 that 'the stars are aligned' for an agreement to be reached by mid-2021, he also rightly acknowledged that many other significant issues would need to be resolved for the mid-2021 target to be achievable.[17] As of this writing, the Biden Administration's exact position on a number of those issues, most particularly scope,

10. Statement by the OECD/G20 Inclusive Framework on BEPS on the Two-Pillar Approach to Address the Tax Challenges Arising from the Digitalisation of the Economy, OECD, 30 January 2020, available at https://www.oecd.org/tax/beps/statement-by-the-oecd-g20-inclusive-framework-on-beps-january-2020.pdf.
11. G20 Finance Ministers' Communiqué, 18 July 2020, available at http://www.g20.utoronto.ca/2020/2020-g20-finance-0718.html.
12. Available at http://www.oecd.org/tax/beps/tax-challenges-arising-from-digitalisation-report-on-pillar-one-blueprint-beba0634-en.htm ('Pillar One Blueprint').
13. OECD Secretary-General Tax Report to G20 Finance Ministers and Central Bank Governors, OECD, October 2020, available at http://www.oecd.org/tax/oecd-secretary-general-tax-report-g20-finance-ministers-october-2020.pdf.
14. G20 Finance Ministers' Communiqué, 14 October 2020, available at http://www.g20.utoronto.ca/2020/2020-g20-finance-1014.html.
15. *See*, e.g., 'U.S. Must Rethink Stance on Global Tax Reform Deal, Harter Says', Tax Analysts Doc 2021-1704, 15 January 2021.
16. 'U.S. drops "safe harbor" demand, raising hopes for global tax deal', reuters.com, 26 February 2021, available at https://www.reuters.com/article/us-g20-usa-oecd-idUSKBN2AQ2E6.
17. '"Stars Are Aligned" for Global Tax Reform Deal, Saint-Amans Says', Tax Analysts Doc 2021-8865, 5 March 2021.

remains unclear, and it remains to be seen whether the concerns of the United States and many other countries about various aspects of the Pillar One proposal can be addressed in time to meet the mid-year target.

2.2 Status of Pillar Two

Like Pillar One, the Pillar Two proposal for a global minimum tax was the subject of a blueprint report released by the IF in October 2020.[18] The IF has not yet reached an agreement on the Pillar Two Blueprint, but it, too, is said to provide a solid basis for further negotiation with a view to reaching a consensus agreement by mid-2021. Among the main features of the Pillar Two proposals are: (i) an 'income inclusion rule' by which the parent entity of an MNE group would include in its income the income of a controlled foreign entity that is taxed below an agreed minimum effective tax rate; (ii) an 'undertaxed payment rule' by which deductible intra-group payments that are taxed below the agreed minimum effective tax rate would be subject to a top-up tax in the source country; and (iii) a 'subject to tax rule' by which treaty benefits on intra-group payments would be scaled back when the nominal tax rate in the payee jurisdiction was below an agreed minimum rate. As with Pillar One, substantial political and technical issues remain to be resolved, including how the rules are to be coordinated, the minimum rates to be agreed, and interaction with the US regime on 'global intangible low-taxed income'.

2.3 UN's Article 12B

At its October 2020 meeting, the UN's Committee of Experts on International Cooperation in Tax Matters voted to include in the 2021 update to the UN Model Tax Convention a new Article 12B on ADS based upon a proposal developed by its Subcommittee on Tax Consequences of the Digitalized Economy.[19] Article 12B would allow a source state to impose a gross basis withholding tax (at an unspecified limited rate) on income from ADS defined as 'any payment in consideration for any service provided on the internet or an electronic network requiring minimal human involvement from the service provider'. The provision would allow the taxpayer to elect instead to be taxed by the source state at regular corporate income rates on its deemed profit allocable to that state from ADS; the deemed allocable profit would be equal to

18. Report on Pillar Two Blueprint, OECD, 12 October 2020, available at https://www.oecd.org/tax/beps/tax-challenges-arising-from-digitalisation-report-on-pillar-two-blueprint-abb4c3d1-en.htm (Pillar Two Blueprint).
19. *See* Draft Report on the 21st Session (20-29 October 2020), UN Committee of Experts, available at https://www.un.org/development/desa/financing/sites/www.un.org.development.desa.financing/files/2021-01/21st%20Session%20Report_advance%20unedited%20version.pdf and Co-Coordinators' Report on the Work of the Subcommittee on Tax Issues Related to the Digitalization of the Economy, Document E/C.18/2020/CRP.41, UN Committee of Experts, 11 October 2020, available at https://www.un.org/development/desa/financing/sites/www.un.org.development.desa.financing/files/2020-10/CITCM%2021%20CRP.41_Digitalization%20101020%20Final%20A.pdf.

30% of the amount determined by multiplying the relevant MNE group's overall profitability ratio from its relevant business segment times the gross annual ADS revenue from the source state. The Committee of Experts identified numerous technical concerns with the proposal, but the subcommittee has been directed to work on those with a view towards having a final draft ready for decision-making by the Committee at its April 2021 meeting. A UN official has recently suggested that the proposal reflects developing country concerns with the OECD's Pillar One proposal, including its complexity, the limitations on its scope, the requirement of mandatory dispute settlement, and the low revenue impact.[20]

2.4 Unilateral Measures and Trade Disputes

One of the acknowledged objectives of Pillar One is to prevent the proliferation of uncoordinated unilateral measures by individual governments and to achieve the elimination of the 'relevant' unilateral measures adopted to date.[21] The existence of the discussions around Pillar One has not been particularly successful in preventing the consideration, proposal, and/or adoption of DSTs by a significant and growing number of countries around the world. After a DST proposal put forward by the European Commission in 2018 failed to achieve unanimous approval by the EU Member States, the first national DST to go into effect (in 2019) was that enacted by France.[22] Other countries followed suit, including Austria, India, Italy, Kenya, Spain, Turkey, and the United Kingdom. Numerous others have similar laws under consideration.

The enactment of the French DST quickly led to the initiation of a so-called Section 301 investigation' by the US Trade Representative (USTR) on 10 July 2019 to determine whether the French DST was unreasonable or discriminatory and whether it burdened or restricted US commerce.[23] In December 2019, the USTR concluded that the French DST was actionable under section 301 and proposed tariffs on certain French goods.[24] In January 2020, France and the United States agreed to a truce through the end of the year under which France would hold off on collecting the DST, and the United States would suspend the imposition of tariffs in order to give the OECD's IF the opportunity to reach a global solution. Meanwhile, the USTR initiated section 301 investigations in June 2020 into the DSTs enacted or under consideration in ten other jurisdictions: Austria, Brazil, the Czech Republic, the EU, India, Indonesia, Italy, Spain, Turkey, and the United Kingdom.[25]

---

20. 'U.N. Digital Tax Plan Reflects Developing Nation Views: Official', *Bloomberg Daily Tax Report* (10 December 2020).
21. Pillar One Blueprint, para. 848.
22. India introduced a narrow equalization levy on digital advertising revenues in 2016 and then expanded it into a full-blown DST in 2020.
23. Section 301 of the US Trade Act of 1974, as amended (Pub. L. 93-618, 19 U.S.C. § 2411) authorizes the President to take actions, including the imposition of tariffs, in response to foreign acts that are unreasonable or discriminatory and that burden or restrict US commerce.
24. *See* https://ustr.gov/issue-areas/enforcement/section-301-investigations/section-301-frances-digital-services-tax and 84 FR 66956 (6 December 2019).
25. https://ustr.gov/about-us/policy-offices/press-office/press-releases/2020/june/ustr-initiates-section-301-investigations-digital-services-taxes.

Most recently, on 7 January 2021, the USTR announced an indefinite suspension in the tariffs against French products, citing the ongoing section 301 investigations in the ten other jurisdictions.[26] Within a few days of that announcement, it released its findings on the DSTs in India, Italy, and Turkey[27] as well as those in Austria, Spain, and the United Kingdom,[28] in each case finding that they discriminated against US companies. The USTR also released a status update outlining its preliminary concerns with the proposed DSTs in Brazil, the Czech Republic, the EU, and Indonesia.[29] The USTR deferred taking any action, clearly leaving the incoming Biden Administration the decision of how to take these trade disputes forward. The Biden Administration's new USTR, Katherine Tai, has not yet indicated what direction she will take, saying only at her 25 February 2021 confirmation hearing: 'I will review the status of those actions and will work with my colleagues at the Treasury Department to address digital services taxes as part of the multilateral effort to address base erosion and profit shifting through the OECD/G20 process.'[30]

At least to date, the US threats of retaliatory trade measures do not seem to have stemmed the tide of DSTs. The OECD's Secretary-General Angel Gurría told the IF on 27 January 2021 that, if they did not deliver a solution on the digital project by mid-2021, 'over 40 countries are considering, or will move ahead, with a DST'.[31] There are also numerous other taxes affecting digital activity that are not specifically styled as DSTs that will likely need to be considered as part of the IF's goal of eliminating 'relevant' unilateral measures.[32] As indicated in the Pillar One Blueprint, 'it is expected that any consensus-based agreement must include a commitment by members of the Inclusive Framework to implement this agreement and at the same time to withdraw relevant unilateral actions, and not adopt such unilateral actions in the future'.[33] Of course, even if a political agreement is achieved in 2021, the actual implementation of any Pillar One regime by countries around the world may be several years in the future,

26. https://ustr.gov/about-us/policy-offices/press-office/press-releases/2021/january/suspension-tariff-action-france-digital-services-tax-investigation.
27. https://ustr.gov/about-us/policy-offices/press-office/press-releases/2021/january/ustr-releases-findings-dst-investigations. In response to the USTR announcement on 7 January 2021, Benjamin Angel, Director for Direct Taxation, DG TAXUD, European Commission, tweeted 'The Commission will support all EU Member States targeted by the US procedure.'
28. https://ustr.gov/about-us/policy-offices/press-office/press-releases/2021/january/ustr-releases-findings-and-updates-dst-investigations.
29. https://ustr.gov/sites/default/files/files/Press/Releases/StatusUpdate301InvestigationsBEUIndCR.pdf.
30. 'Katherine Tai, USTR designate, on addressing WTO reform including dispute settlement if confirmed; the USTR 2021 Trade Policy Agenda', Terence P. Stewart, Current Thoughts on Trade blog, 2 March 2021, https://currentthoughtsontrade.com/tag/digital-services-taxes/.
31. http://www.oecd.org/about/secretary-general/oecd-sg-at-meeting-of-the-inclusive-framework-on-beps-27-january-2021.htm.
32. For an illustrative list of such taxes, including certain diverted profits taxes, anti-abuse laws, and offshore receipts taxes, see the comment letter of the Digital Economy Group to the OECD, 14 December 2020, available at http://www.oecd.org/tax/beps/public-comments-received-on-the-reports-on-pillar-one-and-pillar-two-blueprints.htm.
33. Pillar One Blueprint, para. 848.

so DSTs may well be a significant part of the international tax landscape for years to come.[34]

2.5 Anticipated EU Digital Tax Proposal

Further complicating the picture is the EU's proposed adoption of some form of EU-level 'digital levy' as part of its 'own resources' to finance a portion of its EUR 750 billion coronavirus recovery package. The European Commission has been saying for some time that it would put forward a digital tax proposal if the OECD was unable to achieve consensus on a solution.[35] By May 2020, the commission was suggesting a digital tax 'that would build on OECD work on corporate taxation of a significant digital presence' as part of the EU's recovery budget 'if no global agreement is reached'.[36] In July 2020, the European Council reached a political agreement on the recovery package which stated: 'As a basis for additional own resources, the Commission will put forward in the first semester of 2021 proposals on a carbon border adjustment mechanism and on a digital levy, with a view to their introduction at the latest by 1 January 2023.'[37] On 17 December 2020, the European Council adopted the EU Budget for 2021-2027, which included the mandate to the commission to propose a digital levy by June 2021 for the EU's 'own resources'.

The exact nature of the EU's anticipated digital tax proposal remains unclear. As noted above, commission officials in early 2020 were describing it as something that would build on the OECD work on a significant digital presence to be pursued if the OECD could not achieve a consensus. The commission told the European Parliament in July 2020 that the EU digital levy would not be a DST and would build on the OECD's Pillar One work.[38] More recently, in January 2021, the commission published an

34. Worth noting here are the proposed foreign tax credit regulations issued by the US Internal Revenue Service in September 2020 (REG-101657-20, 85 F.R. 72078 (12 November 2020), available at https://www.irs.gov/pub/irs-drop/reg-101657-20.pdf), which would deny US taxpayers a foreign tax credit for DST-type taxes, thereby heightening double taxation concerns many observers already felt existed.
35. *See*, e.g., 'EU Could Revisit Digital Tax if OECD Work Stalls, Official Says', *Bloomberg Law News* (17 July 2019); 'New EU Tax Commissioner Supports Digital Tax', *Tax Notes Today International* (17 September 2019), 2019 TNTI 180-1; 'Momentum Builds Toward EU Digital Tax, Vestager Says', *Law 360* (21 February 2020), 2020 Law360 52-23.
36. EU Budget Communication: 'The EU budget powering the recovery plan for Europe', European Commission (27 May 2020).
37. European Council Conclusions, 17-21 July 2020, available at https://www.consilium.europa.eu/en/press/press-releases/2020/07/21/european-council-conclusions-17-21-july-2020/.
38. 'European Commission Won't Pursue EU-Wide DST', *Tax Notes Today International* (14 July 2020), 2020 TNTI 134-3 (quoting then Acting Director of DG TAXUD Benjamin Angel as saying to the European Parliament's Committee on Economic and Monetary Affairs: 'In the event where the OECD discussion would fail, we will need to look for a permanent solution, not a temporary one, and in that respect, we will have to take another route than the one of the DST. This route would obviously build very much on the work which has been done in the last two years within the OECD.'; 'Angel said the commission does not have an official position on what such a tax would look like after OECD countries reach an agreement, but he offered some possibilities. One possibility, he said, is that some portion of a company's profit would be apportioned to EU member states, which could tax the profit given to them under domestic rules and rates and then send the tax to the EU budget as an own resource. Another possibility is for digital revenue to be

inception impact assessment on its potential digital levy[39] (and shortly thereafter launched a public consultation),[40] which mentioned three possible policy options: (i) a corporate income tax top-up to be applied to all companies conducting certain digital activities in the EU; (ii) a tax on revenues created by certain digital activities conducted in the EU; and (iii) a tax on digital transactions conducted business-to-business in the EU. The announcement for the consultation said, 'The levy will be designed in a way that is consistent with the ongoing work at the OECD, and in the G20, and will be compliant with WTO and other international obligations.'[41] That being said, it is not clear that the options mentioned are necessarily under serious consideration by the commission nor that any EU digital levy would be integrated with or in addition to any global solution that might be reached under Pillar One.[42]

3 PILLAR ONE SELECTED ISSUES

With that unsettled background landscape in mind, discussion can turn to Pillar One itself and several of its features that are of particular relevance to citizens of the transfer pricing practitioner community. This chapter will not dwell on the basic design of Amount A. As clearly stated in the original Unified Approach released in October 2019, 'the new profit allocation rules would go beyond the arm's length principle and beyond the limitations on taxing rights determined by reference to a physical presence, two principles generally accepted as cornerstones of the current rules'.[43] Amount A is a purely formulaic creation, and any effort to draw a connection between it and familiar notions of distinguishing residual from routine profit, identifying profit attributable to marketing intangibles, or determining profit that is allocable to a jurisdiction based on

---

taxed at the same rate in all member states, to be decided unanimously, he said. The average corporate tax rate in the EU is about 22.5 percent, he noted.').

39. https://ec.europa.eu/info/law/better-regulation/have-your-say/initiatives/12836-Digital-Levy.
40. https://ec.europa.eu/info/law/better-regulation/have-your-say/initiatives/12836-Digital-Levy/public-consultation.
41. https://ec.europa.eu/digital-single-market/en/news/fair-taxation-commission-launches-public-consultation-digital-levy.
42. *See*, e.g., 'EU Digital Tax Will Hew To OECD Proposal, Official Says', *Law360* (15 January 2021), 2021 Law360 15-19 ('The European Union-wide digital tax will reflect any proposal for global tax reform springing from the ongoing negotiations to remake the international tax system in light of digital business models, an EU official told Law360 Friday. ... The three options contained in a consultation document released Thursday by the European Commission – the EU's executive branch – do not represent the bloc's favored designs and are merely intended to be illustrative, the senior EU diplomat said, speaking on the condition of anonymity. ... The EU official said the commission was seeking to explore what the other policy options are for the tax in addition to the three identified, adding, "At this stage, there is no favored design or designs." In light of the OECD's work, which involves 137 countries and territories, the commission is keen to stress that any new initiative will be designed to be completely compatible with any proposal that emerges from the global process. "The new initiative will be designed in a way such that is [in sync] with the ongoing work at the OECD level on the reform of the international corporate tax framework," the official said.').
43. 'Secretariat Proposal for a "Unified Approach" under Pillar One', OECD (9 October 2019), para. 28, available at https://www.oecd.org/tax/beps/public-consultation-document-secretariat-proposal-unified-approach-pillar-one.pdf.

functions performed, assets used, or risks assumed there would leave one less than satisfied. At its core, Amount A reflects the dissatisfaction experienced by some governments and their populations when they realized that, without radical changes to the prevailing international tax norms, other aspects of the BEPS Action Plan (e.g., Action 7 on permanent establishment status and Actions 8-10 on transfer pricing) were not going to produce the revenue windfall to market jurisdiction fiscs some early rhetoric had led them to expect. Only by abandoning traditional arm's length, separate entity, and nexus principles and erecting a new structure could the desired political objective be achieved. It is no accident that the language of architecture has featured so prominently in this work (i.e., pillars, building blocks, blueprints, etc.) – the exercise is squarely designed to build a wholly new edifice. Whether the foundations being laid are sufficiently solid to allow the new structure to remain erect long enough for an official opening, let alone meet the current political objectives or survive for the century for which the prior structure has stood, remains to be seen. In the meantime, the remainder of this chapter will focus on some Pillar One issues that have something of a closer connection to familiar transfer pricing concepts and practices.

3.1 Marketing and Distribution Profits Safe Harbour

Commentators on the secretariat's 'Unified Approach' originally released in October 2019 expressed concern that the introduction of Amount A could result in double counting of profits in market jurisdictions where the MNE group already realizes residual profits under traditional transfer pricing principles. The Pillar One Blueprint responds to this concern with a tentative proposal for a marketing and distribution profits safe harbour.[44] In essence, the safe harbour would 'cap' the allocation of Amount A to market jurisdictions that already have taxing rights over a group's residual profits under existing rules.

Both the blueprint and commentators acknowledge that the kind of market jurisdiction double-counting at which the safe harbour is directed would be addressed, at least in part, through Pillar One's general mechanism for avoiding double taxation. The latter mechanism, discussed below, aims at identifying entities within the group (paying entities) with profits to be used to cover the Amount A allocations to market jurisdictions and to give those paying entities relief from taxation in their residence countries on that share of their profits. When a market jurisdiction entity earns residual profits that are viewed under the double taxation relief mechanism as profits of a 'paying entity' used to fund the Amount A pool that is allocable to market jurisdictions, that share of the entity's profits should, in principle, be 'netted off' against its taxable profits in its residence jurisdiction. However, the blueprint and commentators both expressed concern that the 'netting off' double tax relief mechanism would be very complex, particularly in decentralized business models where entities throughout the

44. Pillar One Blueprint, paras 501-504, 528-546.

group may, for example, own marketing intangibles relevant to their own jurisdictions.[45] Moreover, the concern was also expressed that, in light of the theory that Amount A is necessary to address the phenomenon of MNE groups deriving significant profits from market jurisdictions without having a taxable presence there or being subject to tax there on any of their residual profits under current rules, it would be counterintuitive to force Amount A allocations to market jurisdictions where the group was already being taxed on its residual profits.

As described in the Pillar One Blueprint, in order to apply the marketing and distribution profits safe harbour, a group with a taxable presence in a market jurisdiction (either through a resident entity or a permanent establishment) would need to make several determinations. It would first determine the amount of its profits allocated to that jurisdiction under current rules from its marketing and distribution activities conducted there that are 'connected to locally sourced in-scope revenue' (its 'existing marketing and distribution profit'). The MNE group would then compare that existing marketing and distribution profit to the 'safe harbour' return, defined as the sum of: (i) the Amount A that is allocable to that jurisdiction under the Amount A formula, and (ii) 'a fixed return for in-country routine marketing and distribution activities, which could include a regional, and industry uplift'. If the existing marketing and distribution profits are lower than the fixed return, the safe harbour does not apply, and the MNE group has a full Amount A allocation to that jurisdiction. If the existing marketing and distribution profit exceeds the fixed return but falls below the total safe harbour return, the Amount A allocation to that jurisdiction would be capped at the difference between the total safe harbour return and the existing marketing and distribution profit. If the existing marketing and distribution profits exceed the total safe harbour return, there would be no Amount A allocation to that jurisdiction.

The marketing and distribution profit safe harbour proposal received widespread support from the commentators on the Pillar One Blueprint. The proposal reflects a clear preference to allow the existing rules on the ALP to continue to operate to the greatest extent possible when there is no pressing need to introduce the new Amount A regime. Adoption of the proposal would thus signal some continuing level of tolerance for the use of existing transfer pricing rules, notwithstanding the general intention to have Amount A operate outside the ALP and to minimize implementation challenges for developing country tax administrations with limited capacity.

The proposal presents some obvious challenges from a design and administration standpoint. One such challenge is the need to determine under existing rules the profits derived by a market jurisdiction entity or a permanent establishment from its marketing and distribution activities conducted there that are 'connected to locally sourced in-scope revenue'. This clearly requires distinguishing activities connected to in-scope revenues from other activities, those connected to locally sourced revenues from non-locally sourced revenues, and profits attributable to marketing and distribution

45. Examples in Appendix C of the Pillar One Blueprint illustrate the potential application of the marketing and distribution profits safe harbour and the double taxation relief 'netting off' mechanism for groups with both centralized and decentralized business models (*see* Boxes C.3 and C.4).

activities connected to those revenues from those attributed to other activities or assets. This will require a fair amount of transfer pricing expertise and judgment and could be the source of potential disagreements between taxpayers and governments or among governments,[46] particularly when the local entity or permanent establishment is engaged in more than just marketing and distribution activities or has revenues from more than just local sources. Given this fact, it could certainly be argued that the application of the marketing and distribution profits safe harbour should be an election on the part of the MNE group.

Another aspect of the safe harbour requiring attention is the manner in which the 'fixed return for in-country routine marketing and distribution activities' will be calculated, including whether it might involve a regional or industry uplift. The Pillar One Blueprint does not explicitly indicate what relationship, if any, this fixed return might have with the fixed return provided to remunerate 'baseline marketing and distribution activities' under Amount B, but there seems to be at least a facial similarity with the blueprint's description of Amount B as applicable 'to a distribution entity that, according to the accurate delineation of the transaction, performs functions, owns assets and assumes risks that would characterise it as a routine distributor at arm's length'.[47] A number of commentators on the Pillar One Blueprint suggested that there should be a direct correlation between the Amount B fixed return on baseline marketing and distribution activities (discussed further below) and the proposed safe harbour's fixed return on 'in-country routine marketing and distribution activities', and that suggestion has a fair amount of appeal.

The Pillar One Blueprint correctly notes that another issue to be faced is how to deal with transfer pricing adjustments, lagged threshold permanent establishment claims, or denials of deductions for shared costs that are made after the safe harbour has been applied in the market jurisdiction.[48] Certainly, any such adjustments that reduced (or increased) the local taxpayer's 'existing marketing and distribution profit' in the relevant market jurisdiction could have implications for whether the marketing and distribution profits safe harbour applied at all and whether, if applicable, it affected the MNE group's Amount A allocation to that market. Consideration will likely need to be given to whether materiality thresholds for such adjustments should play a role in determining whether they require any adjustments, either retroactively or prospectively, to the group's Amount A allocations and related double taxation relief. It should be noted that the potential impact of such subsequent adjustments is not limited to cases in which the marketing and distribution profits safe harbour may be in play; the blueprint aptly notes that they may also affect the identification of 'paying entities' under the basic operation of Amount A.[49]

Finally, the Pillar One Blueprint also correctly notes that the marketing and distribution profits safe harbour are not necessarily adequate to prevent double

46. A determination that profits would be taxable in a market jurisdiction under existing transfer pricing rules rather than through an Amount A allocation could affect which other jurisdiction(s) where the MNE group operates may have the obligation to provide double taxation relief.
47. Pillar One Blueprint, para. 663.
48. *Ibid.*, para. 555.
49. *Ibid.*, paras 615-616.

counting of residual profits in market jurisdictions, particularly when the market jurisdictions have collected withholding taxes from members of the MNE group on payments (e.g., royalties) that may constitute part of the residual profits taken into account in determining Amount A allocations to market jurisdictions.[50] A failure to address that problem as part of the double counting risk could be a serious flaw in any final Pillar One regime.

3.2 Elimination of Double Taxation

The Pillar One Blueprint introduced a novel process of up to four steps for identifying the 'paying entities' within the MNE group that would bear the Amount A tax liability (and whose jurisdictions of residence would be required to relieve the double taxation arising from Amount A). The four steps are:

(1) Step 1 (Activities test): Identify the entities within an MNE group that perform activities that make a material and sustained contribution to the group's ability to generate residual profits.
(2) Step 2 (Profitability test): Apply a profitability test to ensure the entities identified have the capacity to bear the Amount A tax liability.
(3) Step 3 (Market connection priority test): Allocate, in order of priority, the Amount A tax liability to the entities that have a connection with the market(s) where Amount A is allocated.
(4) Step 4 (Pro-rata allocation): Allocate, on a pro-rata basis, where no sufficiently strong connection(s) is (or are) found or where those with a market connection lack the necessary amount of profit.

The activities test in Step 1 would require a qualitative functional analysis taking into account the relevant entity's functions, assets, and risks of the type familiar in conventional transfer pricing practice. Proponents of Step 1 argue that it appropriately tries to identify those entities within the group that should produce the residual profits that correspond to Amount A. A number of commentators, however, believe that it would introduce unwarranted subjectivity and potential for controversy into the critical step of identifying the 'paying entities'.

Similarly, the market connection priority test in Step 3 is favoured by those commentators who believe an entity should not bear an Amount A tax liability that relates to a market jurisdiction with which it does not have an identifiable connection. The blueprint contemplates the possibility that, under this test, the Amount A tax liability 'would first be allocated to the paying entity with a direct or otherwise the "strongest" connection'.[51] This test would require a highly factually nuanced and novel analysis of each group, its operating structure, and the nature and strength of connections between individual group members. The OECD has acknowledged that a

50. *Ibid.*, para. 528.
51. *Ibid.*, para. 605.

number of commentators (and some IF members) have expressed serious concern about the novelty, complexity, and subjectivity of the market connection priority test and about the possibility that it could lead to contentious disputes about which jurisdictions will have double taxation relief obligations with respect to Amount A.

The critical process of identifying 'paying entities' for purposes of avoiding double taxation with respect to Amount A well illustrates the uneasy coexistence of Amount A's formulaic, objective design with the desire to retain certain familiar but subjective features based on the ALP and notions of where 'value' is created. The public consultation on the Pillar One Blueprint revealed starkly differing opinions, even within the business community, on whether the market connection priority test should be retained as part of the process. In order to come up with a final process that meets the competing objectives of participants in the process, the members of the IF will have to weigh the complexity and dispute potential of this test against the benefits it might produce in the way of satisfying instinctual beliefs about which countries should bear the cost of the Amount A profit reallocations to market jurisdictions. They will also have to consider the extent to which the objectives of this test might be more easily approached by application of the Amount A rules on a regionally segmented basis when appropriate.

Once the paying entities are identified, the Pillar One Blueprint contemplates that their residence jurisdictions could choose to relieve the resulting juridical double taxation using either an exemption or credit method according to their choice. The business commentators on Pillar One expressed a strong preference for application of the exemption method, citing its greater simplicity and its freedom from the necessity of calculating limitations for relieving the Amount A tax payable to each separate market jurisdiction and from the need to make adjustments to tax liability in the paying jurisdictions in the event that adjustments had to be made to the allocation of Amount A among market jurisdictions (e.g., due to the resolution of any disputes concerning application of the revenue sourcing rules).

The Pillar One Blueprint acknowledges the challenge to the double taxation relief mechanism that could arise from transfer pricing adjustments to the profits of group entities that might (or might not) have been identified as paying entities with respect to Amount A prior to the transfer pricing adjustments.[52] Such adjustments, which might not be settled for several years after the taxable year in question, could raise questions about how much (if any) Amount A allocation should have been borne by the relevant entity, and thus how much should have been borne by other group entities identified as paying entities. The blueprint notes that further work needs to be done to develop an appropriate mechanism for dealing with this highly realistic scenario, at least in the case when the transfer pricing adjustments are sufficiently 'material', with the materiality threshold to be defined. It mentions an innovative option that could take into account the apportionment of the Amount A liability as part of the mutual agreement procedure (MAP) rather than having to make retroactive or prospective allocations to Amount A liability under the broader Amount A mechanism.

52. *Ibid.*, paras 615-616.

The Pillar One Blueprint wisely rejects an alternative approach to the Amount A profit reallocation that would have deemed the Amount A profit to arise in a group entity already taxable in the local market jurisdiction, if there is one.[53] Under that alternative approach, the imposition of the Amount A tax liability on a group entity that might not actually have earned the profits on which the Amount A calculation was based would lead to the potential for economic double taxation and to the need for transfer pricing-style corresponding adjustments to be made in the countries of residence of appropriately identified profitable group entities. As the blueprint notes, the alternative approach would likely have led to a series of complicated secondary adjustments, withholding taxes, etc., related to the mismatch between the location of and taxing rights over the relevant group profits. While the blueprint holds the possibility open that this alternative reallocation approach may be revisited in the future, it is difficult to imagine the scenario where this alternative, with all its complexities, would be found acceptable.

3.3 Amount B

From its inception, Amount B has been aimed at simplifying the administration of transfer pricing rules as applied to the pricing of distribution arrangements adopted by MNE groups by providing a standardized return consistent with the ALP on so-called 'baseline marketing and distribution activities' conducted in a market jurisdiction. Amount B would apply to all local subsidiaries or permanent establishments of MNE groups in a market jurisdiction that perform the baseline marketing and distribution activities without regard to the scope limitations of Amount A (i.e., not limited to the ADS or CFB sectors). As currently drafted, the description of in-scope 'baseline marketing and distribution activities' is based upon a 'positive list'[54] of 'typical functions performed, assets owned and risks assumed at arm's length by routine distributors (based on a narrow scope, akin to limited risk distributors)' as well as a 'negative list'[55] of functions, assets, and risks not performed, owned, or assumed at arm's length by 'routine' distributors.[56] While the current draft explicitly aims at a narrow definition of baseline marketing and distribution activities, it notes that some IF members would prefer a broader scope for Amount B and that some do not believe 'limited risk distributors' and 'routine distributors' are synonymous.[57] Quantitative factors may also be taken into account in determining whether an entity's activities exceed the 'baseline' category.[58]

The public consultation on the Pillar One Blueprint revealed that there is broad support for Amount B in principle; the main issue from the business side is whether it will be well-designed to produce the tax certainty and arm's length consistency that

53. *Ibid.*, para. 623.
54. *Ibid.*, paras 668, 670, and 672.
55. *Ibid.*, paras 669, 671, and 673.
56. *Ibid.*, para. 13.
57. *Ibid.*, para. 655 and footnote 135.
58. *Ibid.*, paras 674-678.

comprise its purpose. A number of commentators suggested that the scope of Amount B should be broad enough that it would not leave excessive opportunity for market jurisdiction tax authorities to argue that an entity's activities went beyond the baseline and required an additional return; otherwise, tax certainty would not be achieved. Others believed broadening the scope would increase the need for variations in the required return and increase the potential for disputes. Some commentators suggested that the baseline should be broad enough to cover any activities that were benchmarkable and to which the transactional net margin method (TNMM) could appropriately be applied. Clarifications are needed to confirm the application of Amount B to the resale of services as well as products.

The establishment of the fixed return for the Amount B baseline activities will also be critical to Amount B's success. The Pillar One Blueprint proposes that the return be determined by applying the TNMM using a return on sales as the profit level indicator, with further technical work to be done to determine the profit measurement (e.g., EBIT or EBT).[59] The blueprint notes that further work will be done to determine whether the return should vary by industry or region, and it posits that there is no need to differentiate the return by functional intensity as long as the definition of baseline activities retains its current narrow scope. A number of commentators suggested the complexity of varied returns for different regions and industries should be avoided. One economic study, prepared by KPMG and submitted as part of a comment letter from Microsoft to the OECD,[60] usefully revealed that 'arm's length returns to sales, marketing and distribution functions are very consistent across geographies and industries and do not increase as industry profitability increases', thereby calling into question the need for complex variations in the fixed returns to be prescribed under Amount B. The blueprint mentions the potential need for a multilateral instrument (MLI) to implement Amount B, and it further mentions the need to articulate the process by which benchmarks will be completed and periodically refreshed.

3.4 Dispute Prevention and Resolution

Achieving greater tax certainty is one of the central objectives of Pillar One and will be a prerequisite for obtaining the business community support that will likely be necessary to make it politically palatable in those jurisdictions that may be net losers (or at least not significant net winners) of tax revenue as a result of implementing Pillar One. The Pillar One Blueprint lays out a laudable effort to develop innovative approaches to preventing and resolving disputes under the rules that would apply once Pillar One is implemented. The proposals are divided into those relating to Amount A and those for issues that go beyond Amount A.

59. *Ibid.*, paras 686-687.
60. *See* Microsoft letter to OECD, 14 December 2020, available at http://www.oecd.org/tax/beps/public-comments-received-on-the-reports-on-pillar-one-and-pillar-two-blueprints.htm and KPMG, *Transfer Pricing Analysis of Arm's Length Returns to Sales, Marketing & Distribution Activities* (February 2020), available at https://www.wu.ac.at/fileadmin/wu/d/i/taxlaw/institute/WU_Global_Tax_Policy_Center/KPMG_-_Amount_B_Econ_Analysis_-_full_report.pdf.

The Amount A regime itself is obviously novel in a number of respects, including: the creation of new grounds for nexus; a determination of tax liability based on characteristics of a worldwide corporate group rather than only on a local taxpayer basis; taxing right allocation principles that are based at least in part on formulaic multilateral sharing of an MNE group's taxable base; double tax relief obligations that may also be shared, at least in part, among multiple countries; and reliance on a series of new concepts that are not currently reflected in any legal instruments and have no history of interpretation by governments. For all of these reasons, the Amount A regime creates new risks of double (or multiple) taxations and, in particular, the risk that adjustments initiated by any one jurisdiction in which a group has nexus could have implications for the group's liability in many or all of the other jurisdictions where it has nexus.

For Amount A issues, the Pillar One Blueprint puts forward a mandatory, binding dispute prevention mechanism to provide early certainty to the MNE group and governments, potentially involving the participation of successive 'panels' (i.e., a 'review panel' and a 'determination panel'). The blueprint contemplates that a group coordinating entity (likely the parent) will file a single self-assessment return and documentation package for the entire group with a lead tax administration (likely the parent country administration). After a high-level review by the lead tax administration, that administration would be expected to share the filing with all other affected tax administrations (i.e., those where the group has a local presence or nexus) within fifteen months after the close of the taxable year.

The blueprint provides that the MNE group would have the ability to file a request with the lead tax administration for early certainty on Amount A issues within six months after the close of the taxable year. The lead tax administration would have the option to conduct its own initial review of the group's return and suggest changes. It would subsequently share the return and documentation package with all other affected tax administrations, stating whether or not it believes a 'review panel' of representative tax administrations should be formed. Any of the affected tax administrations would have the ability to request a review panel if the lead tax administration had not. When there is no need to convene a review panel, the MNE's self-assessment (as possibly amended by agreement with the MNE based on discussions to that point) would be binding on the MNE group and in all IF jurisdictions. If a review panel is formed, it would typically have six to eight representatives from a variety of tax administrations and would typically have about nine months to decide whether to recommend changes to the self-assessment return. If the review panel agrees to changes with the MNE group, those would be communicated to all other affected tax administrations who could decide whether to object. If the review panel has not been able to reach an agreement with the MNE group or if another affected tax administration objects to the agreement and that objection cannot be resolved, the relevant questions would be referred to a 'determination panel' that is obligated to reach a decision. That decision would be binding on all parties unless the MNE group objects, in which case tax administrations could make adjustments on their own.

The blueprint suggests that most MNE groups will initiate early certainty requests, at least in the early years of implementation. It also suggests that MNE groups may not be guaranteed access to the tax certainty mechanism and would have to rely on domestic law remedies or a bilateral MAP in particular jurisdictions if they had not initiated a request for early certainty.[61]

The blueprint states that no solution has yet been finalized to address the situation when material transfer pricing adjustments are made by individual countries after the MNE group has gone through the early certainty process, and those adjustments affect the Amount A allocations or double tax relief obligations.[62] The lack of a clear process to deal with these inevitable situations is of concern. Different approaches may need to be considered for different situations (e.g., depending on whether the adjustment shifts profits between a market jurisdiction and a 'paying entity' jurisdiction or between two 'paying entity' jurisdictions with respect to Amount A allocable to one or more market jurisdictions, etc.). The reluctance to retroactively reopen allocations of tax liability and double taxation relief obligations under Amount A is understandable, but some reliable approach to preventing double taxation arising after the fact is needed.

Regarding the Amount A early certainty mechanism, business commentators were predictably pleased, in principle, with the proposals but also worried that the tax administration resources needed to make it work effectively for the thousands of MNE groups likely to be within the scope of Amount A may not be realistically available. Numerous commentators accordingly expressed support for a phase-in of the Amount A regime and for actions that might be taken to streamline the multi-step panels mechanism.

For issues beyond the application of Amount A, the Pillar One Blueprint refers to tax certainty work being done under three steps, all of which could significantly affect the practice of transfer pricing experts:

- improvements to dispute prevention processes (e.g., expansion of the International Compliance Assurance Programme, joint audits, improved Advance Pricing Agreement (APA) processes, use of standardized benchmarks in common transfer pricing situations, time limits to make transfer pricing and permanent establishment adjustments, and suspension of tax collection during disputes);
- improvements to the MAP (e.g., requiring APA programs in some cases, requiring competent authority training, providing criteria on access to a MAP and on the content of MAP requests, ensuring that penalties and interest charges are aligned in proportion to MAP outcomes, ensuring MAP agreements are implemented, and ensuring the possibility of multiyear MAP resolutions); and
- a binding dispute resolution beyond Amount A (e.g., a to-be-designed mandatory binding dispute resolution mechanism for all disputes related to transfer pricing or permanent establishment adjustments to any members of an MNE group that is within the scope of Amount A, mandatory binding or advisory dispute resolution mechanisms for other MNE groups' material

61. *Ibid.*, para. 788.
62. *Ibid.*, paras 790-791.

transfer pricing and permanent establishment adjustments that cannot be timely resolved through a MAP, mandatory binding dispute resolution as a last resort for all Amount B disputes, and elective binding dispute resolution commitments in over fifty developing countries with very limited MAP experience).

Much of this work is being done in the context of ongoing work under BEPS Action 14, for which a productive public consultation meeting was held on 1 February 2021.

3.5 Implementation and Administration

As noted above, recent remarks at the political level seem to be signalling rising hopes for reaching a political agreement on Pillars One and Two by mid-2021. If that were to happen, the focus of the international tax community would quickly shift to the details of implementing any such deal and administering the new regimes it might call for, as well as to the timeline for getting from here to there.

The Pillar One Blueprint gives an advance look at what would remain to be done after a high-level political agreement is reached. Even a casual skim of the Pillar One and Pillar Two Blueprints reveals references to dozens of technical issues that remain to be resolved to finalize each pillar. The Pillar One Blueprint explains that participating countries will have to make domestic law changes to accommodate many different aspects of the new regime, including Amount A taxing rights and double tax relief provisions, the procedural provisions for implementing, and the tax certainty provisions. It does not mention that the IF will draft model legislation to assist countries (once the technical issues are resolved), so the length and coherence of the process of preparing that legislation in each participating country remain uncertain.

A multilateral convention will also need to be drafted to implement Pillar One (and likely Pillar Two as well). This would be different from the MLI that was drafted for the BEPS Project in that the new convention will need to be a truly multilateral agreement and not an instrument aimed at modifying bilateral treaty relationships. The BEPS MLI was not opened for signature until more than a year and a half after the final BEPS Reports were issued, even though the core text of the relevant MLI Articles had already been agreed upon during the three-year BEPS Project. The Pillar One multilateral convention will have to be drafted from its very fundament once the political and technical details of Pillar One are resolved, and there is no obvious model on which to base such a novel and complex multilateral tax convention. The drafting of such a multilateral convention by the IF could reasonably be expected to be a several-year exercise by itself.

Once the relevant legislation and multilateral convention are prepared, they will have to go through the enactment/signature-ratification process in all of the participating countries, another step that could take some time.[63] The Pillar One Blueprint notes that the multilateral convention would come into effect only once a 'critical mass'

63. For context, the MLI was opened for signature by the 100 + IF members in June 2017. Three and a half years later (i.e., by 15 January 2021), only about 60 IF members had ratified the MLI.

of jurisdictions have fully implemented it, although the meaning of 'critical mass' is not yet determined.[64] The blueprint does not provide any guidance on how the Amount A would apply to an MNE group with operations in or revenues from many countries, some of which may have proceeded to implement Pillar One but others of which may not yet have done so. For many groups, this will likely be a realistic scenario for a number of years, so guidance will eventually need to be developed.

The blueprint does mention that guidance will need to be developed (and periodically refreshed) on many aspects of Pillar One in order to supplement domestic legislation and the multilateral convention. There is evidently an expectation that some body, perhaps the IF, will have continuing status to develop guidance under countries' domestic legislation and the multilateral convention. The parameters of such an arrangement remain to be articulated.

Finally, the blueprint notes that 'it is expected that any consensus-based agreement must include a commitment by members of the IF to implement this agreement and at the same time to withdraw relevant unilateral actions, and not adopt such unilateral actions in the future'.[65] As suggested above, however, the actual 'implementation' of the Pillar One regime by members of the IF could be several years in the future, even if a political consensus is reached by mid-2021. Thus, affected MNE groups might reasonably expect they will be living with DST and similar regimes for years to come regardless of the progress made on the political front this year.

4 CONCLUSION

The potential for a Pillar One agreement to effect radical changes in the international taxation of MNE groups and in the familiar rituals of transfer pricing practice is there for all to see. Practitioners accustomed to the rigorous application of the ALP on a separate entity basis would need to become familiar with a form of formulary apportionment at a global group level, fixed return approaches to determining the remuneration for some activities, novel double taxation relief concepts, innovative compliance and procedural requirements, and much more. That being said, huge amounts of work remain to be done to prepare the new regime for its final rollout even after a high-level political consensus is achieved, and there will likely be a significant opportunity to analyse the many technical and policy issues that will need to be resolved to launch a well-functioning regime.

64. Pillar One Blueprint, para. 851.
65. *Ibid.*, para. 848.

CHAPTER 6

Recent Developments in Transfer Pricing and COVID-19*

*Gianni De Robertis***

* The views and opinions expressed in this chapter are those of the author and do not necessarily reflect those of KPMG.

** I wish to thank Filippo Bertoletti and Federico Faccioli for their research assistance and Gillian Parker and Marina De Bartolo for their editorial assistance; likewise, all of those other colleagues and clients with whom I have had many interesting discussions on the topic covered in this chapter.

1 INTRODUCTION

Since 2020, as the health crisis has unfolded and hit the economy, multinational companies have been facing the many challenges that the new unprecedented economic conditions have created for the setting and testing of prices of intra-group transactions and the application of the arm's length principle. These challenges arise in both strategy and compliance.

On the strategy side, disruption to operations and to global supply chains in many sectors has required companies to refocus their strategy and take swift action to ensure business continuity by, for example, protecting their employees and stepping up health and safety measures, preserving liquidity, and ensuring sufficient funding. Other consequences will emerge in the medium term as the pandemic is likely to drive companies to rethink their structure and organization and to focus increasingly on achieving the right balance between national and international supply. As a result, in the medium term, there could be a wave of business restructuring.

On the compliance side, the economic downturn has challenged well-established compliance processes and mechanisms which need to be revised in order to reflect the current exceptional market conditions. Companies will have to be prepared to manage the accounting and tax implications of value chain restructuring but will also have to address the various issues arising in connection with day-to-day compliance with transfer pricing rules.

Application of the arm's length principle relies on the analysis of market prices and dynamics between independent parties. The pandemic-related supply and demand shocks have affected company behaviour and disrupted market prices in many sectors; as a result, identifying the correct prices of intra-group transactions has become particularly challenging. Companies have been asking themselves many questions:

- What sources of information will provide the best comparable data?
- Will the crisis be fully reflected in the margins of comparable sets?
- To what extent will price and margins need to be adjusted?
- Can a company change its terms of payment to help its subsidiaries?
- Should a routine entity bear some of the losses arising from the crisis?

- How should coronavirus-related exceptional costs be treated?
- What is the interaction between government support and transfer pricing?
- Will advance pricing arrangement (APA) commitments still need to be met?
- How will TP documentation have to change?

In addition to these specific questions, companies have also been considering whether, overall, their existing transfer pricing policies are suited to the times.

This chapter will examine the implications of the COVID-19 pandemic for intra-firm trade and intra-group pricing. Section 2 provides an overview of the unprecedented economic conditions caused by the outbreak of COVID-19; section 3 summarizes the guidance developed by national authorities and the Organisation for Economic Co-operation and Development (OECD) to address the intra-group pricing challenges that have arisen or been exacerbated by the pandemic; section 4 sets out a framework for transfer pricing analysis during a pandemic; section 5 puts emphasis on a framework for transactional net margin method (TNMM) analysis; section 6 focuses on issues related to financial transactions; section 7 aims to highlight long-term transfer pricing consequences of COVID-19; and section 8 draws some conclusions.

2 THE ECONOMY IN 2020

Impact of COVID-19 on the economy

The COVID-19 pandemic is blighting the global landscape: by 3 January 2021, the human cost was enormous, with a death toll of more than 1.8 million and more than 84.6 million recorded cases across the globe.[1] The effects of the pandemic span every dimension of human activity, creating unprecedented disruption to the global economy and to business organizations.

In 2020, government actions to combat and contain the pandemic often required extraordinary measures[2] such as lockdowns, school closures, travel bans, and restrictions on personal freedom with the closure of non-essential businesses, the suspension of social activities, and the shut-down of large parts of the economy. This generated an unprecedented supply shock throughout the economy with the stoppage of production of goods and services and, at the same time, a demand shock due to the fall in spending caused by the tight restrictions on social activities and by social distancing. Simultaneously, because of the interplay between supply and demand, the supply shock fuelled a further contraction in demand as workers in the sectors most affected by the pandemic lost spending power. This resulted in a largely unprecedented contraction in

1. *COVID-19 Dashboard by the Center for Systems Science and Engineering* (CSSE) at Johns Hopkins University (JHU).
2. Blavatnik School of Government, *Variation in government responses to COVID-19*, Oxford University (December 2020).

2020 of the world Gross Domestic Product (GDP) which the International Monetary Fund (IMF)[3] forecasts at minus 4.4% compared to the previous year.[4]

Although the pandemic is a global phenomenon, its effects are not evenly spread across territories, industries, and companies. Table 6.1 illustrates GDP growth estimates for 2020 (by country) and expected performance in 2021.

*Table 6.1 Figures Based on IMF Data, GDP by Country (% Change)**

	Actual	*Projections*	
	2019 (%)	*2020 (%)*	*2021(%)*
World Output	2.8	–4.4	5.2
United States	2.2	–4.3	3.1
Euro Area	1.3	–8.3	5.2
Germany	0.6	–6.0	4.2
France	1.5	–9.8	6.0
Italy	0.3	–10.6	5.2
Spain	2.0	–12.8	7.2
Japan	0.7	–5.3	2.3
United Kingdom	1.5	–9.8	5.9
Canada	1.7	–7.1	5.2
Emerging and developing Asia	5.5	–1.7	8.0
China	6.1	1.9	8.2
India	4.2	–10.3	8.8
Emerging and Developing Europe	2.1	–4.6	3.9
Latin America and the Caribbean	0.0	–8.1	3.6
Middle East and Central Asia	1.4	–4.1	3.0
Sub-Saharan Africa	3.2	–3.0	3.1

* IMF, 'World Economic Outlook: A Long and Difficult Ascent' (October 2020).

3. International Monetary Fund, *World Economic Outlook: A Long and Difficult Ascent* (October 2020).
4. V. Guerrieri, G. Lorenzoni, L. Straub, I. Werning *Macroeconomic implications of COVID-19: can negative supply stocks cause demand shortage?* (2 April 2020). University of Chicago, Becker Friedman Institute for Economics, Working Paper No. 2020-35; M. Maiello, *How COVID-19 shocked both supply and demand*, Chicago Booth Review (May 2020); J.E. Stiglitz, *Priorities for the COVID-19 economy* (1 July 2020); W.C. Shih, *Global supply chains in a post-pandemic world*, Harvard Business Review (September-October 2020).

Among the advanced economies, the euro area is expecting a contraction of 8.3% and the United States of 4.3%. This reflects a sharper downturn in the euro area economy in the first part of the year than in the United States.

Even within the same geographic areas, the impact is uneven: according to a study by the Joint Research Center (JRC) of the European Commission,[5] within the euro area, 'GDP losses are highly correlated with drops in employment rates, with regions that rely on tourism being the hardest hit.'

Various analyses of industrial sectors provide further insights into the uneven effects of the pandemic.[6] According to an analysis by Mediobanca,[7] for instance, the consequences of COVID-19 boosted certain industries while it penalized many others. Sectors revolving around software and the internet, online retail distribution, electronics, food, and pharmaceuticals benefitted from an increase in demand for home entertainment, online retailing, food products, and services, etc., these being fuelled by lockdown, travel restrictions, and social distancing measures. At the same time, the oil and gas, airline, fashion and hospitality industries, and also many others were forced to downsize because of the anti-coronavirus measures.

Company size also proved to be another relevant factor in the impact of the pandemic, with small- and medium-sized enterprises suffering more[8] than their larger counterparts due partially to greater difficulty in accessing credit. The unprecedented nature of the pandemic generated significant uncertainties in the economy that were reflected in the significantly higher volatility of the financial and economic markets.

Most governments reacted promptly and strongly to offset the economic consequences of the crisis through economic support plans such as the EUR 750 billion European Union pandemic recovery plan. These interventions were aimed at stabilizing the financial markets, ensuring liquidity, containing interest levels, and regaining market stability. They also aimed to support the economy via unemployment/wage subsidies, facilitate access to credit, freeze layoffs, and transfer cash to the households and companies most affected by the lockdowns.

While these measures helped mitigate the economic impact of the pandemic, their ultimate effectiveness will largely depend on the duration of the overall crisis.

Impacts of COVID-19 on businesses and international trade

At a company level, COVID-19 dramatically tested the capabilities of businesses to react quickly and effectively to transformed economic circumstances as the pandemic hit their business models in various ways across every spectrum of activity and, in

5. Joint Research Center, *JRC analyses COVID-19 impact on economy and labour markets to help guide EU response*, DG-JRC (3 August 2020).
6. *COVID-19 Heat Map: Updated Sector Views Show Diverging Recoveries*, S&P Global Ratings (29 September 2020).
7. *Briefing Note: Impacts of COVID-19 Pandemic On 9 Months 2020 (MNES and FTSE MIB)*, Area Studi Mediobanca, Milan (19 November 2020).
8. *World Economic Outlook: A Long and Difficult Ascent* International Monetary Fund (October 2020); P. Blake, D. Wadhwa, *2020 Year in review: the impact of COVID-19 in 12 charts*, World Bank Blogs (14 December 2020).

particular, supply chain management.[9] As noted above, the current crisis has strained the global supply chain since the virus has impacted most geographies, and this has been amplified by the highly interconnected economy. It is very common for companies to rely on specialized suppliers (often based in specific locations) and resort to just-in-time production techniques for which a component/product is manufactured only when requested. This limits the level of stocks and reduces the time-to-market. Accordingly, a shock in one of those locations (e.g., China) quickly propagates along the entire global supply chain with reverberations across markets and industries.[10]

In the short term, the significant constraints posed by COVID-19 and the havoc caused to supply chains has led to increased attention on the part of traders to force majeure clauses in commercial agreements or to the possibility of renegotiating the agreements due to the unforeseeable change in circumstances. However, the possibility of activating such clauses is often uncertain and prone to controversy. In the medium-term, businesses will be rethinking their supply chain organization so as to become less dependent on specific suppliers or have more flexibility in managing potentially recurring shocks of this type.[11]

International trade has also been significantly affected by the supply and demand shocks produced by the health crisis. The World Trade Organization estimates[12] that world merchandise trade volume will shrink by 9.2% in 2020 compared to the previous year due to the health crisis. Similar estimates are provided by the IMF.[13] The extraordinary measures introduced to contain and combat the pandemic have affected not only international and intra-firm trading of products but also trading of both business and personal services (e.g., hospitality).

Overall, for many companies, the adverse economic conditions have resulted in a sharp drop in turnover and in widespread losses. Table 6.2 provides a picture of the per cent change in revenues and EBIT in 2020 (nine months) compared to 2019 for a panel of publicly listed companies.[14]

9. Eric Sherman, *94% of the Fortune 1000 are seeing coronavirus supply chain disruptions: Report*, Fortune (21 February 2020).
10. International Labour Organization, *The effects of COVID-19 on trade and global supply chains* (June 2020).
11. *Ibid.*; Beata Javorcik, *Coronavirus will change the way the world does business for good*, Financial Times (2 April 2020).
12. World Trade Organization, *Trade shows signs of rebound from COVID-19, recovery still uncertain* (6 October 2020).
13. International Monetary Fund, *World Economic Outlook: A Long and Difficult Ascent* (October 2020).
14. Area Studi Mediobanca, *Briefing Note: Impacts of COVID-19 Pandemic on 9 Months 2020 (Mnes and Ftse Mib)*, Milan (19 November 2020).

Table 6.2 Area Studi Mediobanca, Net Sales & EBIT, 9M 2020/2019, % Change, MNE by Sector

Industry	*Net Sales (% Change)*	*EBIT (% Change)*
WebSoft	18.4	14.2
Large-scale distribution	8.8	25.7
Electronics	5.7	14.1
Food	3.7	6.0
Pharma	3.1	−1.4
PayTech	0.3	−16.7
Telco	−1.8	−2.6
Drinks	−5.4	−16.5
Media & Entertainment	−9.4	−31.1
Automotive	−17.4	−65.8
Fashion	−21.3	−98.8
Aircraft	−30.6	neg./pos.
Oil & energy	−32.3	−66.6

3 GUIDANCE FROM NATIONAL AUTHORITIES AND FROM THE OECD

During the initial months of the pandemic, it became clear that 2020 was going to be an exceptional year in many respects. Multinational companies and tax professionals were pondering the implications of the economic downturn and how to manage intra-group trade and intra-group transactions in a scenario of falling GDP, reduced international trade, widespread losses, and market uncertainty. They were looking to the OECD and national tax authorities for guidance on the various practical challenges they were encountering in determining correct transfer prices under such unusual market conditions.

The OECD's international response was to indicate in the first part of last year that it was working on developing guidance on transfer pricing but that the process of developing guidance and reaching a consensus among member countries of the Inclusive Framework would take time; hence, guidance would be published towards the end of 2020.

The national response of many countries was to publish guidance, clarifications, and special measures to tackle the general tax implications of COVID-19 and the particular implications for specific areas, such as customs duties or value-added tax (VAT); however, official guidance on transfer pricing has been very limited.

Considering the multilateral nature of transfer pricing and ensuring generally accepted solutions to the issues faced by companies, most countries have preferred to assist the OECD in its work rather than publish their own unilateral guidance. A few countries, however, such as Australia, New Zealand, Singapore and, to a more limited extent, the United States, not only participated in the OECD work but also published domestic clarifications during the year as the pandemic developed. These clarifications that mainly focused on transfer pricing documentation and compliance were generally aimed at anticipating and complementing the OECD guidance that was taking shape at the time, and that was finally published in December 2020.

3.1 Domestic Guidance on Transfer Pricing and COVID-19

Australia

In July 2020, the Australian Taxation Office (ATO) published useful information for companies that have been impacted by COVID-19 and intend to document the arm's length nature of their transactions.[15] In particular, the ATO lists the factors that would need to be examined and documented when assessing the impacts of COVID-19 on related-party transactions in the Australian economy:

- the economic circumstances in Australia and in the industry in question;
- the functions, assets and risks before and after COVID-19;
- the contractual agreements and any changes to them;
- how COVID-19 has affected the specific service/product and the financial results; and
- changes in business strategy.

The ATO acknowledges that a comparable analysis may not reliably substantiate arm's length transactions affected by COVID-19 and should also seek to understand the financial results that would have been achieved *but for* the impact of the virus. This would include focusing on:

- profit and loss and changes in revenue and expenses, including any change resulting from COVID-19 and the explanation for it;
- the reason behind any higher allocation of costs or reduction of sales to the Australian entity, taking into account its function, asset, and risk profile; and
- any government assistance received.

With respect to companies with an APA already in place, the ATO recognizes that the current economic conditions may result in the breach of a critical assumption; therefore, it recommends early engagement with the ATO to agree whether the APA can continue as it is, be amended, or be temporarily suspended. APA processes already underway can continue as normal unless COVID-19 has had a significant impact on the

15. Australian Government, Australian Taxation Office, *COVID-19 economic impacts om transfer pricing arrangements*, https://www.ato.gov.au/Business/International-tax-for-business/In-detail/Transfer-pricing/COVID-19-economic-impacts-on-transfer-pricing-arrangements/?page=1#How_we_assess_the_economic_impacts_of_COVID-19_on_transfer_pricing_arrangements (Last modified: 15 July 2020).

business, in which case the parties can agree whether to put the process on hold or terminate it.

The ATO has also expressed its view on the interaction between government assistance programs and transfer pricing (*Transfer pricing arrangements and JobKeeper payments – COVID-19*, July and November 2020). Generally, the ATO expects that government subsidies will not be shared between the parties to a transaction but will be retained by the entity that receives them.

New Zealand

During the course of 2020, the New Zealand Inland Revenue (IRD) published guidance on how to approach the impact of COVID-19 on businesses and the transfer pricing issues that may arise.[16] According to this guidance, during the COVID-19 pandemic, transactions should generally continue to follow the arm's length principle on the basis of the OECD's current transfer pricing guidelines (TPG). The IRD acknowledges that applying the arm's length principle may be difficult during the current period; hence, it emphasizes the importance of contemporaneous transfer pricing documentation and encourages businesses to document:

- the material impact of COVID-19 on the group and local business;
- responses to the pandemic such as changes in business strategy, products, or services;
- changes in business functions, assets, and risks and how they relate to the business' exposure to and mitigation of COVID-19;
- changes in intra-group transactions, contractual terms, and transfer prices; and
- the impact of COVID-19 on the profitability of the Multinational Enterprise (MNE) group and the local entity.

In the absence of reliable comparables because of the extraordinary economic environment, the approach suggested by the IRD is to analyse the variances (both positive and negative) between pre-pandemic budgets and actual results. This would involve an analysis of:

- change in local sales;
- changes in local expenses;
- unusual financial items;
- amendments to intra-group transactions;
- government assistance; and
- any transfer pricing adjustments.

With respect to 'limited-risk arrangements and losses', the IRD guidance states the importance of the 'accurate delineation of the transaction' and the quality of the comparability analysis. In particular, entities should bear losses only if they are related

16. New Zealand Inland Revenue, *COVID-19 Exceptional economic circumstance*, https://www.ird.govt.nz/international-tax/business/transfer-pricing/practice-issues/covid-19.

to risks that they assume, and the assumption of a specific risk should not emerge only during the current economic downturn.

The relationship between government assistance programs (wage subsidies) and transfer pricing is also discussed. Companies would generally be expected to retain the benefit of the subsidies received as they are linked to the employment-related risks borne by the entity and support the payment of wages and salaries without providing a market advantage. A recipient entity would not generally be expected to change its pricing of transactions with related parties because of the subsidies received unless specific independent comparable transactions provide evidence to the contrary.

In the early weeks of the pandemic, the IRD also issued guidance that simplified the decision-making processes of companies by permitting them to make crucial business decisions that may breach existing APAs without having to notify the authority. These breaches will be discussed during the review of the annual compliance report rather than at the time the decision is made.

Singapore

Guidance on transfer pricing and COVID-19 was published by the Inland Revenue Authority of Singapore (IRAS) in October 2020 in the form of a set of 'Frequently Asked Questions' (FAQs).[17] The guidance covers the options available to taxpayers in relation to transfer pricing documentation and to APAs.

If a business has been severely affected by the pandemic, the IRAS recommends substantiating the arm's length nature of company transactions by including the following information:

- an analysis of the impact of COVID-19 on the industry and on the company;
- documentation on the decision-making process as related to the pandemic;
- a functional analysis of the companies involved in the transaction before and after the pandemic;
- the contractual terms and whether any of them have been varied, amended, or terminated;
- a comparison of the budgeted and actual results of the profit and loss analysis;
- evidence of why profit has been negatively affected; and
- government assistance received.

The IRAS acknowledges that the impact of the pandemic may vary significantly, affecting different taxpayers in different ways; therefore, it allows companies to apply testing over a multiple-year period (generally over three years – 2018-2020) rather than annually. In general, this 'term-testing' in Singapore is only allowed under exceptional circumstances and after consultation with the IRAS. It is to be seen as a one-off concession to help companies manage the unusual volatility experienced during 2020.

17. Inland Revenue Authority of Singapore, *COVID-19 Support Measures and Tax Guidance, Transfer Pricing,* https://www.iras.gov.sg/irashome/COVID-19-Support-Measures-and-Tax-Guidance/Tax-Guidance/Transfer-Pricing/.

An APA application or an APA renewal request can be filed on the condition that COVID-19 has not significantly impacted the company's business. If impacted by COVID-19, APA applications under review should be discussed with the tax authority and, if necessary, put on hold. Potential breaches of current APAs would need to be discussed with the IRAS.

United States

In April 2020, the US Inland Revenue Service (IRS) also issued a list of 'FAQ' on best practices for transfer pricing documentation.[18] While not specifically covering the impact of the pandemic, the answer to question 1 contains an example that is relevant in the current economic environment. The example illustrates how a subsidiary that would generally expect to earn a routine profit margin on its intra-group transactions may legitimately incur losses due to an unexpected change in market conditions.

In the example, a US distribution entity purchases products from its foreign parent for resale in the US market. Based on intercompany agreements, transfer prices are set so that the distributor earns a return of x% of sales (i.e., using a TNMM/comparable profit method). In 2017, due to a sharp drop in demand, sales volume decreased, and the distributor incurred losses. Assuming the initial transfer pricing policy was consistent with the arm's length principle, the losses caused by the unexpected change in business circumstances are legitimate and not caused by mispricing. In this case, the IRS recommends that the company prepare detailed documentation to explain the unforeseen business circumstances that have generated the loss and to substantiate the correctness of the initial transfer pricing method.

While the example does not refer directly to COVID-19, it illustrates a fact pattern that will be very common during the pandemic.

3.2 OECD Guidance on the Transfer Pricing Implications of the COVID-19 Pandemic

The OECD guidance was published on 18 December 2020 under the title 'Guidance on the transfer pricing implications of the COVID-19 pandemic' (OECD Guidance).[19] As the OECD Guidance represents the view of the 137 member countries of the OECD Inclusive Framework on Base Erosion and Profit Shifting (BEPS) (in the meantime, already 139 member countries), it extends far beyond the 37 OECD member countries. It is worth noting that, unlike other recent OECD projects on transfer pricing, the OECD Guidance represents a consensus of opinion among the 137 (139) countries, a remarkable achievement in such a short period of time.

18. US Internal Revenue Service, *Transfer Pricing Documentation FAQs*, https://www.irs.gov/businesses/international-businesses/transfer-pricing-documentation-frequently-asked-questions-faqs (Page Last Reviewed or Updated: 14 April 2020).
19. OECD, *Guidance on the Transfer Pricing Implications of the COVID-19 Pandemic*, OECD Policy Responses to Coronavirus (COVID-19), OECD Publishing, Paris (18 December 2020).

The aim of the OECD Guidance is to clarify and illustrate the application of the arm's length principle and of the 2017 OECD TPG[20] to the practical pricing issues that have arisen during the pandemic; it is not to provide new specialized guidance beyond that already set out in the OECD TPG. Therefore, countries and taxpayers should continue to rely upon existing transfer pricing principles, regulations, and legislations and apply them to the unusual economic conditions triggered by the pandemic.

The OECD Guidance is composed of four chapters, each one dedicated to one of the main priority issues for the application of the arm's length principle during COVID-19. These issues are interrelated and need to be considered jointly in the framework of the OECD TPG:

- Chapter I: Transfer Pricing Guidance on Comparability Analysis.
- Chapter II: Transfer Pricing Guidance on Losses and the Allocation of COVID-19 Specific Costs.
- Chapter III: Transfer Pricing Guidance on Government Assistance Programmes.
- Chapter IV: Advance Pricing Arrangements (APAs).

The next sections will briefly summarize and comment on the OECD Guidance. After that, a framework will be set out for conducting transfer pricing analyses consistently with the OECD TPG and OECD Guidance.[21]

3.2.1 *Transfer Pricing Guidance on Comparability Analysis*[22]

The unprecedented economic conditions of 2020 generated by the COVID-19 outbreak are such that a comparability analysis presents unusual challenges. In particular, the use of historical data, which is very common in this type of analysis, becomes less reliable as prior-year data reflect very different economic conditions. The OECD Guidance invites tax administrations and taxpayers to consider practical approaches to address the lack of information, including the use of comparability adjustments and consideration of the possible behaviour of independent parties under similar circumstances. The main challenges of a comparability analysis are illustrated in a nine-point question and answer section.

Source of contemporaneous information

The OECD Guidance notes that any form of publicly available information may be useful in estimating arm's length conditions and provides a list of possible sources of information for comparability analyses and comparability adjustments. These include: an analysis of sales volumes, capacity utilization, incremental or exceptional costs, the

20. OECD, *OECD Transfer Pricing Guidelines for Multinationals Enterprises and Tax Administrations 2017*, OECD Publishing, Paris (2017).
21. *KPMG Report: OECD Guidance on the Transfer Pricing Implications of the COVID-19 Pandemic*. KPMG (23 December 2020).
22. OECD, *Guidance on the Transfer Pricing Implications of the COVID-19 Pandemic*, OECD Policy Responses to Coronavirus (COVID-19), OECD Publishing, Paris, Chapter I (18 December 2020).

extent of government assistance and interventions, interim financial statements of public companies, macroeconomic information, industry indicators, statistical methods such as regression or variance analysis, internal budget/forecasts, an analysis of profitability, and behaviour in previous recessions.

Use of budgeted financial information

Comparing budgets/forecasts with actual financial results could help in estimating the effect of the pandemic on revenues, costs, and profits. The impact would then need to be allocated to intercompany pricing in light of the contractual terms and risks assumed by the parties.

Most pronounced timing issues

While contemporaneous data are generally available for financial transactions and internal transactions, timing issues may be most pronounced in the application of the TNMM, as 2020 data would generally be available after mid-2021. In such cases, taxpayers would necessarily need to perform a comparability analysis based on prior-year data and use whatever contemporaneous data are available to substantiate the transfer prices.

Practical approaches to address information deficiencies

Due to the scarcity of real-time data on comparable transactions and the evolving economic scenario during the COVID-19 pandemic, the OECD Guidance recommends the use of pragmatic approaches to estimate arm's length pricing. These include:

- Using reasonable commercial judgments supplemented by contemporaneous information.
- Focusing on price testing (rather than *ex ante* price-setting) and allowing taxpayers to use information that becomes available after the closing of the financial year.
- Allowing *compensating adjustments* to be made before the filing of the tax return.
- Ensuring access to a Mutual Agreement Procedure or other procedures for which tax administrations could provide early certainty.
- Using more than one transfer pricing method to corroborate the arm's length prices.

On the use of data generated by another crisis

The OECD Guidance does not recommend performing a comparability analysis solely on the basis of the 2008/2009 financial crisis due to the unique nature of the current economic conditions. However, as indicated above, data from previous recessions may prove to be a useful source of information (e.g., to perform comparability adjustments).[23]

Period used to evaluate arm's length pricing

While the OECD TPG approach of using multiple-year data for testing arm's length conditions remains valid, numerous considerations may come into play in defining the most appropriate testing period (e.g., availability of information, choice of method and comparables). The OECD Guidance indicates that, in some cases, it may be more reliable to use a carefully circumscribed testing period to separate the years affected by the economic downturn from the others; in other cases, combining periods may produce better outcomes.

Price-adjustment mechanisms

The OECD Guidance notes that when permissible under domestic law, the use of *ex post* price-adjustment mechanisms (applied when a greater amount of information becomes available) may provide the flexibility needed to ensure that arm's length conditions are applied as this would address the lack of contemporaneous information. Caution needs to be used with regard to the potential consequences of this approach on VAT and customs duties.

Evaluation of the set of comparable companies or transactions used

Since the pandemic has altered economic conditions compared to previous years, existing comparable sets may need to be reviewed and possibly revised, also in light of the uneven impact of the crisis across geographies.

Use of loss-making comparables

The OECD TPG does not provide an overriding rule on the use of loss-making companies. When conducting a comparability analysis for 2020, it would be appropriate to include loss-making companies if they are consistent with the delineation of the transaction under review.

3.2.2 Transfer Pricing Guidance on Losses and Allocation of COVID-19 Specific Costs[24]

The economic conditions resulting from the pandemic have pushed many MNE groups into heavy loss due to factors such as falling demand or increasing exceptional costs. Three key issues emerge when analysing the allocation of losses between group companies:

- the allocation of risk between the parties affects the allocation of losses;

23. OECD, *Guidance on the Transfer Pricing Implications of the COVID-19 Pandemic*, OECD Policy Responses to Coronavirus (COVID-19), OECD Publishing, Paris, para. 11 (2020).
24. *Ibid.*, Chapter II.

- the allocation of exceptional costs between associated entities needs to be consistent with what independent parties would do; and
- the application of a force majeure clause impacts the allocation of losses or COVID-19 specific costs.

Like Chapter I, Chapter II of the OECD Guidance illustrates five additional points in a question and answer section.

Losses and companies operating under limited-risk arrangements

The OECD TPG do not rule out the possibility for companies with limited functions and risks (so-called *limited-risk* entities) to incur losses in the short term. Whether losses should be borne by a limited-risk entity depends on the specific facts and circumstances and, in particular, the risk assumed by the company. While a company that bears market risk may sustain losses due to a market downturn, companies insulated from market turbulence should not. On this point, the guidance in Chapter I of the OECD TPG is particularly useful as it refers to risk in commercial and financial transactions. Specific attention should be paid to the position of the company before and after the pandemic and to any differences that emerge, and purported changes in risk assumption should be analysed.

Modification of arrangements under COVID-19

Modification of existing arrangements needs to be analysed under Chapter 9 of the OECD TPG, and reference should be made to: the behaviour of independent companies operating under similar conditions; the options realistically available; long-run effects; profit potential; and possible indemnification. In the absence of clear third-party evidence, renegotiation should be treated with caution.

Allocation of exceptional costs

For many companies, exceptional and non-recurring activities and costs scaled up during 2020 while they tried to manage the disruption to supply and demand as well as to their operations created by COVID-19 and by countries' reactions to the pandemic. The allocation of these costs requires an accurate delineation of the transaction in order to identify the roles and responsibilities, and the risks assumed. The allocation of the costs needs to be consistent with what independent parties would do. Certain operating costs may not be considered exceptional or non-recurring if they relate to permanent or long-term changes to the company's operating model.

Exceptional costs and comparability analysis

The role of exceptional costs in a comparability analysis should be considered. In particular, the OECD Guidance focuses on three aspects:

- exceptional costs should be excluded from the net profit indicators (both from the comparables and from the tested party) unless they are specifically related to the delineated transaction;

- when exceptional costs are included in the cost basis, it is necessary to evaluate whether they are pass-through costs; and
- adjustments may be required to ensure accounting consistency in the treatment of costs.

Force majeure and allocation of losses

The OECD Guidance notes that 'force majeure clauses may be invoked in order to suspend, defer, or release an enterprise from its contractual duties without liability in certain situations'.[25] The starting point of the transfer pricing analysis should necessarily be the agreement and the legal framework.

There is no predefined answer to the applicability of a force majeure clause in related-party transactions. When a taxpayer seeks to invoke a force majeure clause or renegotiate contracts, tax administrations should analyse the position of the company under Chapter I and IX of the OECD TPG and also in light of the behaviour of independent parties.

3.2.3 Transfer Pricing Guidance on Government Assistance Programmes[26]

The reaction of most governments to the COVID-19 pandemic has been to focus on both the public health implications and the economic consequences. Governments have provided economic support in various ways through job retention schemes and the provision of financial aid and liquidity, including guarantees, tax reliefs, etc. From a transfer pricing perspective, the impact of these programmes needs to be taken into account in: (i) the delineation of the actual transactions, and (ii) the comparability analysis. Five aspects are discussed in Chapter III of the OECD Guidance, again in a question and answer section.

Is the receipt of government assistance an economically relevant characteristic?

Not all government interventions represent an economically relevant characteristic for a transfer pricing analysis: while wage subsidies, debt guarantees, or short-term liquidity may have a direct impact on the controlled transaction and on the comparable transactions, other types of interventions do not. Economically relevant government interventions should be documented and factored into the transfer pricing analysis.

Local market features and government assistance

The effect of government interventions is considered a condition of the market in which a company operates, and the OECD Guidance sets out the factors that should be considered in the analysis: whether the intervention confers a market advantage; the increase in revenue and decrease in costs compared to potential comparables; whether

25. *Ibid.*, para. 55.
26. *Ibid.*, Chapter III (18 December 2020).

the benefit is passed on to consumers or suppliers; how independent companies would split the benefit that is not passed on to customers or other suppliers.

Receipt of government assistance and pricing of controlled transactions

The OECD Guidance notes that the potential effect of government assistance on transfer prices will depend on: (i) the economically relevant characteristics of the transactions, (ii) the delineation of the controlled transaction, with a particular reference to risk, and (iii) the performance of a comparability analysis. It cannot be assumed that the mere intervention in itself will affect prices. The OECD Guidance concludes that 'in the absence of reliable comparables or other reliable information … regarding how independent parties would allocate government assistance, caution should be exercised in assessing whether a purported sharing of government assistance represents an arm's length outcome'.[27]

Receipt of government assistance and allocation of risk

The OECD Guidance highlights that the provision of government assistance does not change the allocation of risk between associated entities, as set out in Chapter I of the OECD TPG. While assistance reduces the negative impact of a risk that materializes and may allow a company to meet its obligations, this does not alter how the risk is allocated between the parties to a transaction. An example of this point is provided in the OECD Guidance.

Receipt of government assistance and comparability analysis

The receipt of government assistance may influence the terms of open market transactions; hence, it is an element that needs to be considered when conducting a comparability analysis. In particular, as public programmes vary significantly across countries, it would be preferable to select comparable transactions from the same geographical market. The OECD Guidance notes that, when applying one-sided transfer pricing methods, attention should be paid to how government assistance payments are treated for accounting purposes by both the tested party and the comparables.

3.2.4 Advance Pricing Arrangements[28]

Existing APAs were entered into when economic conditions differed significantly from those prevailing under the pandemic. It is therefore important to establish whether the change in economic conditions affects the application of existing agreements. In addition, tax authorities and taxpayers need to decide how to factor the current unprecedented economic conditions into APAs that are currently being negotiated. The OECD Guidance illustrates the possible impact of COVID-19 on both existing APAs and

27. *Ibid.*, para. 79.
28. *Ibid.*, Chapter IV (18 December 2020).

those being negotiated. Tax administrations and taxpayers are encouraged to take a constructive, collaborative, and transparent approach in the APA process.

Existing APAs

The OECD Guidance states that the terms of existing APAs should be respected unless there is a breach of one or more of the *critical assumptions* of the agreement. Whether the change in the economic conditions brought about by the pandemic should be considered a breach of critical assumptions should be analysed on a case by case basis as the pandemic has not had the same impact on all industries and companies. A mere change in business results should not generally be considered a breach of critical assumptions (unless otherwise stated in the agreement). If taxpayers believe that the terms of an APA are no longer appropriate, they should contact the relevant tax authority rather than unilaterally breaching the agreement.

The consequences of a breached critical assumption should be evaluated in accordance with Chapter IV of the OECD TPG and should consider: (i) the terms of the APA, (ii) any agreements between tax administrations, and (iii) applicable domestic law or provisions. A breach of a critical assumption of an APA could have three potential outcomes:

- revision of the agreement: for example, when there has been a material change in the conditions noted in the critical assumptions of the APA;
- cancellation of the agreement (termination): when there is a material breach as a result of a change in the economic circumstances or if the taxpayer fails to comply; and
- revocation of the agreement (rescission): when there is a misinterpretation, mistake, or omission attributable to neglect, carelessness, or wilful default on the part of the taxpayer or the taxpayer fails to materially comply with the fundamental terms of the agreement.

Early notification of a breach of a critical assumption is encouraged in order to give the parties more time to reach an agreement on revising or cancelling the APA. In terms of documentation, the OECD Guidance provides a list of useful documents which includes: a description of the business segment; copies of the proposed or actual modifications of pre-existing contracts; a narrative of the expected effects of the new economic conditions; a detailed P&L statement; and information about third-party behaviour.

APAs under negotiation

The OECD Guidance acknowledges the important role of APAs in preventing disputes and encourages the adoption of a flexible approach when negotiating an agreement under the current unusual economic conditions. Various options are available to the parties, including: agreeing to a short-period APA for the COVID-19 period followed by a separate APA for the subsequent period; allowing retrospective adjustments once the full impact of the pandemic is known; extending the period of the APA to mitigate the weight of the short-term effects of the pandemic; and using a cumulative test or term-test throughout the APA.

In order to continue current negotiations and ensure the benefits of APA programmes, the OECD Guidance also states the importance of overcoming the practical difficulties created by the pandemic by using technological solutions such as virtual meetings, electronically shared information, etc.

3.3 Comments on the OECD Guidance

The OECD Guidance represents a consensus of opinion among the 137 member countries of the OECD Inclusive Framework on BEPS regarding the application of the arm's length principle and the OECD TPG to issues and challenges raised by the pandemic. The agreement extends beyond the thirty-seven OECD member countries and has been achieved in a remarkably short time considering the complexities of the technical matters and of reaching a consensus among so many countries.

It is important to consider that, according to the OECD, the guidance 'focuses on how the arm's length principle and the OECD TPG apply to issues that may arise or be exacerbated in the context of the COVID-19 pandemic. Thus, it should be regarded as an application of existing guidance under the OECD TPG … and it should not be regarded as an expansion or revision of the OECD TPG …'.[29]

As could be expected – given the complexity of the task, the number of parties involved, and the limited time available – the OECD document merely provides some general principles and a few examples of how the arm's length principle can be applied to the practical pricing issues that have arisen during the pandemic. It does not necessarily prescribe specific solutions or providing firm answers to the many challenges and questions that companies and tax administrations are facing.

However, while many practical questions are not specifically addressed by the OECD Guidance, it does provide a *map* that can be used to steer towards the correct answers within the framework of the application of the arm's length principle and the OECD TPG.

The main coordinates provided by this OECD map to help companies navigate through the transfer pricing challenges raised by the pandemic can be summarized as follows:

- the *arm's length principle* and the OECD TPG apply to intra-group transactions in both good and bad economic conditions;
- in unusual economic conditions, it remains of paramount importance to understand the *behaviour of unrelated parties* engaged in comparable transactions (e.g., when analysing possible renegotiations of contractual terms and conditions);
- the approach of tax administrations and taxpayers should be *constructive, flexible, collaborative, and transparent*;

29. *Ibid.*, para. 5.

- *accurate delineation* of each transaction is a key part of the analysis;
- *consistency* in the pre- and post-pandemic position of the taxpayer is crucial (in particular with reference to the *allocation of risk*);
- any form of publicly available information could be of use in ascertaining the arm's length nature of a transaction;
- routine entities operating at arm's length may incur losses under certain circumstances;[30] and
- *documentation* is a key element of any solution.

If all of the answers to transfer pricing questions are to be found in the arm's length principle and in the OECD TPG, was there really a need for further guidance and clarification? The answer is yes because the OECD TPG has been drafted, debated, and applied over many decades, mostly with reference to normal economic conditions and profit-making business activities rather than to recessionary times and losses. For example, while the word *profit* appears in the OECD TPG more than eight hundred times, the word *loss* is mentioned only one hundred times. Therefore, in an economic environment such as the one created by the pandemic that is characterized by a deep recession and widespread losses, further guidance from the OECD and tax administrations on the right interpretation of the OECD TPG is certainly useful.

4 TRANSFER PRICING ANALYSIS

4.1 COVID-19 Challenges to Transfer Pricing Analysis

The COVID-19 pandemic has impacted all areas of intra-group transactions: product sales, provision of services, licensing of intangible assets, and financial flows. As indicated in section 2, products, industries, and geographies have been unevenly impacted. This is also the case for transfer pricing issues, with some transactions and some transfer pricing methods or policies being more affected by the fallout of the unprecedented economic circumstances than others. Although the impact of the pandemic will depend on the actual facts and circumstances of each taxpayer and each transaction, Figure 6.1 attempts to provide an indication of the extent to which different areas of transfer pricing have been affected.[31]

30. OECD, *OECD Transfer Pricing Guidelines for Multinationals Enterprises and Tax Administrations 2017*, OECD Publishing, Paris, paras 1.129 and 3.65 (2017), and OECD, *Guidance on the Transfer Pricing Implications of the COVID-19 Pandemic*, OECD Policy Responses to Coronavirus (COVID-19), OECD Publishing, Paris, paras 38-41 (18 December 2020).
31. M. Andrew, R. Collier, *COVID-19 challenges for the arm's length principle*, Tax Notes 1 (9 June 2020); S. Prasanna, G.C. Cardoso, *Developing a transfer pricing policy framework for the current economic crisis and beyond*, International Transfer Pricing Journal, Vol. 27, No. 5 (2020); R. Petruzzi, *Dealing at arm's length in times of social distance: a case study*, Tax Notes International (21 September 2020).

Figure 6.1 Aspects of Transfer Pricing Affected by the Pandemic

Less affected	More affected
– CUP method, GCP Method, RPM Method, Profit Split Method – Full – risk entities – Use of internal comparables – Profitable transaction – APAs under discussion	– Transactional Net Margin Method – Routine and limited – risk entities – Use of external comparables – Loss – making transactions – Existing APAs

Other areas

- Pandemic – related and crisis – management costs
- License agreements and royalty arrangements
- Management services fees
- Financial transactions (including probability of default)
- Government assistance
- Intangible assets (valuation and licences)
- Remote work

Of the five transfer pricing methods set out in the OECD TPG, the one most heavily impacted by the current economic downturn is clearly the TNMM, as this method is based on the determination of a stable profit margin for affiliated entities performing routine functions and bearing limited risks. In a time of very unstable economic and market conditions, the premises of the TNMM are necessarily affected as risks materialize and are likely to impact also limited-risk entities. Moreover, the application of a TNMM very often requires the use of external comparable data, which are generally not available in real-time and thus reflect historical rather than current market conditions. The other transfer pricing methods are relatively less affected either because they rely on internal comparables (hence, data directly available to the company) or on external data that are available in real-time (e.g., the comparable uncontrolled price method) or because they are more suited to pricing transactions with unstable economic results (e.g., the Profit Split Method). In general, in a period of significant market discontinuity, such as 2020, any transfer pricing analysis or evaluation that requires the use of external data presents more challenges than an analysis based on internal data.

Considering that application of the TNMM often incorporates an analysis of most of the challenging transfer pricing issues that arise during economic downturns (i.e., analysis of routine/limited-risk entities, the need for external comparables, loss-making transactions, APAs), the next section will focus on the TNMM. However, some of the issues discussed will be relevant also to the other OECD transfer pricing methods.[32]

4.2 COVID-19 Challenges to the TNMM and the Remuneration of Routine Entities

The TNMM is considered to be the most commonly used pricing method in intra-group transactions[33] as many MNEs have organizational structures based on a *principal* entity that performs most of the value-adding activities and owns most of the assets and *routine* or limited-risk entities that carry out manufacturing or commercial activities. Under this operational structure, MNEs set intra-group prices so that subsidiaries that perform routine manufacturing or commercial functions are remunerated with a target operating margin in line with the margins earned by independent companies engaged in similar transactions. The arm's length margin tends to be relatively stable over time to reflect the limited functions, risks, and assets of the routine entities.

Given its technical features, the TNMM has also been the method for which the application has presented the most practical challenges during the pandemic, as the widespread losses generated by the economic downturn make it difficult for MNEs to grant stable positive profit margins to affiliates performing routine activities, both from an economic and an operational point of view. Granting positive margins to affiliates would often result in significant price/margin adjustments and increased losses for the principal company.

Groups that adopt the TNMM must decide how to apply the method during the current economic difficulties, which often means deciding whether routine or limited-risk companies may incur losses in an arm's length situation. In many cases, the correct application of the arm's length principle will rely on analysis of third-party behaviour and of the profits and prices applied in transactions between independent parties (i.e., comparable companies and comparable transactions) to establish the remuneration of routine manufacturers or distribution entities and service providers. As acknowledged in the OECD Guidance, one of the main challenges faced by taxpayers is the lack of real-time comparable data.[34]

Obviously, arm's length pricing for transactions taking place in 2020 should be based on current market conditions.

32. C. Chi et al., *COVID-19 puts limited risk structure at risk: analysis from the chinese angle*, Bloomberg Tax, Bureau of National Affairs (March 2020); N. Mori, N. Mert-Beydilli, G. Poole, *Transfer pricing in troubled times*, Tax Management, Transfer Pricing Report, BNA, Vol. 18, No. 1, 5-14-09, 1-7 (2009).
33. *See* HMRC Internal Manual, April 2016 (updated January 2021).
34. OECD, *Guidance on the Transfer Pricing Implications of the COVID-19 Pandemic*, OECD Policy Responses to Coronavirus (COVID-19), OECD Publishing, Paris, Chapter I (18 December 2020).

4.3 Comparability Analysis

4.3.1 Lack of Real-Time Comparable Data

Some companies adjust their intra-group prices and margins during the year, while others adjust prices and margins only at the end of the year. In either case, comparable data are needed within the year to be able to make reliable price/margin adjustments. The reason for making adjustments within the fiscal/financial year is to ensure that the correct prices/margins are reflected in the company accounts.

In normal market conditions, companies often rely on comparable data of previous years to make such adjustments; for instance, if the current year is N, the adjustments are generally made using comparable data for the preceding three years (N-3 to N-1). Market conditions may vary from one year to the next but, under normal circumstances, the use of a three-year average N-3-N-1 provides a sufficiently reliable estimate of the result for year N.

When market conditions are very unusual, as, in 2020, this approach would not be correct as the use of prior-year data would not reflect current market conditions. Therefore, setting prices/margins or adjusting them based on comparable data of previous years is likely to distort the result and not meet the arm's length standard. This is also acknowledged by the OECD Guidance,[35] which states that one of the effects of the pandemic is the reduced possibility to rely on historical data as they do not reflect current economic conditions.

4.3.2 Comparables Screening Procedures

Another issue is the search procedure used to identify comparable companies. In many countries, tax authorities require comparable search procedures to screen out loss-making companies. The rationale for this is that, under normal circumstances, it is assumed that routine companies would not expect to make losses. Obviously, in a year of extraordinary economic turmoil, this assumption does not hold well: in very deep and sudden recessions, routine companies may, and often do, sustain significant losses as most businesses fight for survival. The current health crisis is so extraordinary that independent companies are renegotiating contracts. Therefore, many commentators say that screening out loss-making companies would not be correct when creating a comparable set for 2020. This is also confirmed by the OECD Guidance.[36] Search procedures need to be revised to ensure compliance with the arm's length principle.

4.3.3 A More Fundamental Issue with Comparables

There is an additional issue, however, which is often underestimated and greatly impacts the reliability of any transfer pricing analysis. Comparable sets, by their own

35. *Ibid.*, para. 9.
36. *Ibid.*, para. 33.

construction, understate the impact of deep recessions on company margins. Good comparable sets are composed of independent companies, and, very often, these companies are small and medium-sized. These independent companies will be affected to different degrees by a recession: a limited number of them may not be affected or may even benefit from the economic turmoil, while the majority are likely to be affected severely and some of them very severely.

While the companies that are less affected by the recession will survive and will appear in the comparable sets, some of the severely affected companies will not survive and will not appear. Therefore, comparable sets identified in years of deep recession have an intrinsic bias, often referred to as a *survival bias*, where only the relatively less affected companies will appear in the final set. As a result, such sets do not show the full impact of the recession on company margins. Arm's length margin ranges will decrease – but not as much as might be expected in such conditions.

This effect was evident in the previous economic crisis of 2008-2009. The 2009 comparable sets showed a reduction in margin ranges but to a more limited extent than the severity of the recession might have indicated. While the impact of the 2008-2009 crisis was such that many companies in the market seemed to make losses, these results did not fully show up in comparable ranges. A closer look at the companies included in the sets often showed that some of them did not make it through the recession and were closed or liquidated.

Subsidiaries of MNEs, which are just as heavily impacted by the crisis as independent companies, are more likely to survive during free-falling markets and absorb losses for one or more years. Independent companies, on the other hand, tend to close, reconvert, or go out of business much more quickly when facing heavy losses. The survival of subsidiaries is helped by the support they receive from their headquarters via capital injections. The headquarters may provide this support for various reasons, for example, because there are positive externalities for the group in having a wide geographical presence. In transfer pricing, comparability analyses must focus on the OECD comparability factors and the features of the shareholder, and its decision to support or not support a subsidiary via a capital injection would generally not play a role and should not affect the way arm's length margins are estimated.

When performing comparability analyses and comparable searches using 2020 data, this factor will need to be considered and adjusted to ensure that the comparable set fully reflects the impact of the crisis on all players in the market. Therefore, the next section will illustrate what adjustments can be made to comparable sets to ensure that they fully reflect current market conditions.

4.4 Comparability Adjustments

As was seen in the previous section, one of the main difficulties that companies face in complying with transfer pricing regulations during economic turmoil is the lack of reliable external market benchmarks: real-time data on comparable companies are often unavailable in most countries,[37] standard screening procedures tend to screen out those companies most affected by the recession, and multiple-year averages do not capture economic events that unleash their effect within one year.

In the middle of an economic downturn, after having reviewed their screening procedure and updated their comparable companies, most companies still end up with a benchmark that reflects pre-crisis conditions. Using the same comparables to set or test margins (and prices) would necessarily produce the wrong answer as it would not reflect the current market conditions.

Comparability adjustments become the main way forward. This is acknowledged by the OECD Guidance, which states that comparability adjustments may be required as a practical way of resolving the information deficiency.[38] While some tax authorities are reluctant to accept comparability adjustments under normal circumstances, under such abnormal circumstances as the current ones, there seem to be very few alternatives to trying to improve comparability through adjustments. Comparability adjustments can take many shapes and forms, from very simple to very complicated ones.[39]

4.4.1 Modification of Target Margins

One very simple form of adjustment is to modify the part of the profit range used as the target. Companies may decide to target the lower quartile instead of the median or may decide to calculate and use different percentiles in the range (e.g., 10th to 60th percentiles rather than the usual 25th and 75th percentiles). While this approach does not improve the degree of comparability of the overall set, it is an attempt to identify that part of the pre-crisis range that may be closer to the current market conditions.

4.4.2 Adjustments to Company Data

As the comparable set reflects pre-crisis conditions, tax managers may adjust the financial data of their own company to cancel out the effect of the crisis. Various items of a company's P&L and balance sheet may be affected by the economic turmoil. For example:

- turnover may decrease due to demand shocks;
- variable costs may increase due to supply shocks;
- capacity utilization may drop due to lower demand;
- the share of fixed cost to sale or to variable costs may rise due to the decrease in turnover; and

---

37. This is true, for example, in the European Union where private companies are used as comparables. In a limited number of jurisdictions, due to the lack of private company data, public companies are selected as comparables, and these provide financials that are more up-to-date.
38. OECD, *Guidance on the Transfer Pricing Implications of the COVID-19 Pandemic*, OECD Policy Responses to Coronavirus (COVID-19), OECD Publishing, Paris, para. 9 (18 December 2020).
39. S. Chroustovsky, M. Petutschnig, *Comparability adjustments: a literature review*, WU International Taxation Research Paper Series, No. 2018-08, 19 (2018).

- bad debts may rise due to liquidity problems in the market.

Adjusting company financial data to a pre-crisis level would allow comparison with a pre-crisis comparable set. Obviously, the comparability adjustments should focus on items that do not derive from intercompany transactions: for distributors buying from related parties, comparability could be improved by adjusting the level of SG&A, turnover, or bad debt but not the level of the cost of goods sold that comes from a related party. Conversely, for a manufacturer selling to related parties, comparability may be improved by adjusting the cost of raw materials but not turnover.

For example, a hypothetical manufacturing entity could be considered that sells products to related parties and that, in 2020, saw an increase both in costs of raw materials due to disruption in the international supply chain and in operating expenses due to the precautionary measures taken to protect its employees from COVID-19 (*see* Table 6.3).

At first sight, looking at the 2020 financial data, the price charged for the intra-group sales may seem inadequate as it does not allow the manufacturer to achieve a profit margin in line with the arm's length range. A comparison with prior-year data, however, indicates that the lack of profits does not depend on the sale price but on the excessive costs. If the 2020 data are adjusted to exclude the impact of the pandemic, it becomes evident that the transfer prices of the products sold are consistent not only with prior-year prices but also with the arm's length range.

Table 6.3 Aspects of Transfer Pricing Affected by the Pandemic

	2020	*Average 2017-2019*	*Difference*
Intra-group sales (i.e., transfer price)	100	100	-
Cost of raw material	50	40	+ 10
Other production costs	30	30	-
Operating expenses	22	20	+ 2
Operating profit	–2	10	-12
Net Cost Plus Margin (in %)	–2	10	-
Arm's length range (pre-2020 comparables) (in %)	7-12	7-12	-

The main weakness of this approach, however, is that it does not provide a full answer to the transfer pricing challenges faced by the MNE: while comparing/adjusting 2020 data to prior-year data allows using existing (pre-2020) comparable sets and, in this example, indicates that the price of the products is at arm's length, this approach does not suggest who needs to bear the extra costs generated by the pandemic. Should the extra costs be borne by the manufacturer, or should they be recharged to other group entities, i.e., the intra-group customers or the head office?

In some cases, therefore, a more complete answer may be obtained by making adjustments to the set of comparable companies rather than to the 'tested party'.

4.4.3 Adjustments to Comparable Companies[40]

More often, adjustments are made to the financial data of the comparable companies to ensure they reflect the current economic conditions. Depending on the actual facts and circumstances, several types of adjustments are possible according to the type of data and the type of statistical technique that is used.

- Adjustments based on macroeconomic data: e.g., change in GPD, level of unemployment, stock markets (*see* Figure 6.2).
- Adjustments based on microeconomic data: e.g., change in sales, SG&A, capacity utilization, fixed costs, extraordinary costs, bad debts (*see* Figure 6.3).

Data needed to make adjustments can be derived not only from the market, i.e., from 2020 interim financial statements, but also from the comparables themselves by looking at their performance in past recessions or their historic performance overall. The OECD Guidance does not support the use of a comparability analysis solely based on financial information from the global financial crisis.[41] However, an analysis of the effect of the economic crisis on profitability or on third-party behaviour observed in previous recessionary periods may prove useful,[42] in particular, to perform comparability adjustments to current comparable sets.

Most of the adjustments indicated above can be made using statistical tools, from the very basic ones such as medians and other measures of tendency and dispersion to more advanced ones such as regression analyses. Adjustments to the level of SG&A expenses can be made by reference to their average level over time, while the link between profits and changes in GDP or sales can be estimated via a regression analysis.

For example,[43] an empirical analysis shows a correlation between changes in GDP and in operating margins at the industry level in various industries and also a generally stronger correlation between changes in turnover and costs at the firm level. These correlations can be used to perform comparability adjustments on profit ranges of comparables.

40. S.D. Felgran et al., *Adjusting pricing methods for APAs in an economic downturn*, Tax Management, Transfer Pricing Report, BNA, 9-10-09, 1-7 (2009).
41. OECD, *Guidance on the Transfer Pricing Implications of the COVID-19 Pandemic*, OECD Policy Responses to Coronavirus (COVID-19), OECD Publishing, Paris, para. 25 (18 December 2020).
42. *Ibid.*, para. 11, last bullet point.
43. G. De Robertis, D. Kondi, *How to improve the estimation of intra-firm prices for financial and tax reporting during economic downturns*, Working Paper, 27 (2020).

Figure 6.2 Change in GDP and Change in Operating Margin – Industry 1

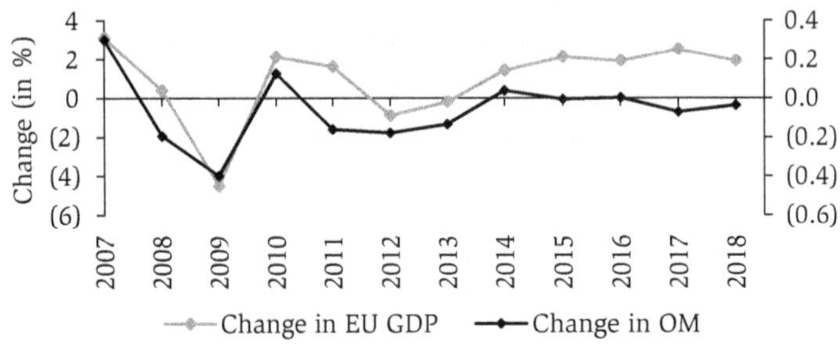

Figure 6.3 Change in Turnover and Change in Costs

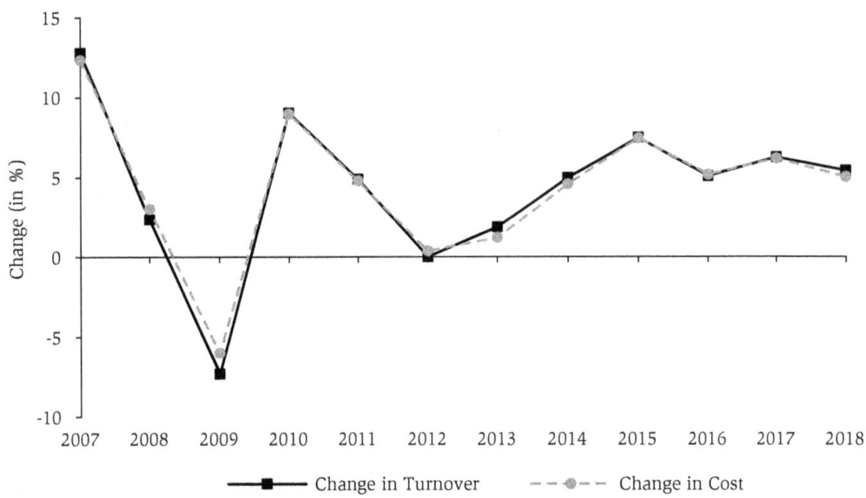

Which adjustment to make and which technique to use are decisions that depend on both the specific circumstances of the company (its sector, functional profile, and value chain, as well as how it has been affected by the downturn) and the characteristics of the identified comparable companies. There is also a trade-off between simplicity and accuracy which needs to be considered: tax authorities could be sceptical about complex comparability adjustments and generally prefer simpler adjustments which may be less subjective and easier to audit rather than more accurate but more complex ones that rely on many assumptions.

4.5 Additional Sources of Information

The use of data from independent comparable transactions and comparable companies is, under normal circumstances, the prevailing approach in the application of the TNMM. However, the OECD Guidance indicates that the determination of arm's length pricing can be supported by other sources of information (listed in section 3.2.1. above) through a comparability analysis. This information can be used, for example, to quantify the impact of the pandemic (e.g., 'a comparison of internal budgeted/forecasted data ... to actual results')[44] and to make comparability adjustments (e.g., 'macroeconomic information like country-specific GDP data or industry indicators', 'statistical methods').[45]

4.6 Routine Entities and Losses

One of the most common questions in the application of the TNMM during economic downturns is whether routine or low-risk entities can bear losses. As indicated in sections 3.22 and 3.3, the OECD TPG does not rule out the possibility for companies with limited functions and risks (so-called *limited-risk* entities) to incur losses in the short term. Whether losses should be borne by a limited-risk entity depends on the specific facts and circumstances.[46]

In the industries that have been heavily affected by the recession, many independent companies incurred losses in 2020. Therefore, it would not be unusual for comparable sets to present ranges that may (partially) show losses.

5 A FRAMEWORK FOR A TNMM ANALYSIS UNDER COVID-19

Many factors need to be considered when trying to apply any transfer pricing methods. This section presents an example of a simplified process that could drive decisions on how to apply the policies for intra-group transactions between a principal entity and a routine distribution subsidiary priced using a TNMM. The example is for illustrative purposes only and does not include all of the inputs and outputs that should be considered (*see* Figure 6.4).

Step 1: pricing method to be used

The MNE should evaluate whether, given the current unprecedented economic conditions, the intra-group agreement should still be applied.[47] This decision would need to rely on various elements, including: the content of the agreement (e.g., force majeure clauses), the functional profile of the parties (in particular, *control over risk*, *management of risk,* and *financial capacity to bear risk*), the impact of COVID-19 in terms of possible changes in the functions performed, the economic and financial impact of the pandemic, and the behaviour of independent parties involved in similar uncontrolled transactions. Step 1 of the analysis could result in:

---

44. *Ibid.*, para. 11.
45. *Ibid.*
46. OECD, *OECD Transfer Pricing Guidelines for Multinationals Enterprises and Tax Administrations 2017*, OECD Publishing, Paris, paras 1.129 and 3.65 (2017), and OECD *Guidance on the Transfer Pricing Implications of the COVID-19 Pandemic*, OECD Policy Responses to Coronavirus (COVID-19), OECD Publishing, Paris, paras 38-41 (18 December 2020).
47. *Ibid.*, Chapter II, section 3.

- a decision to deviate from the existing agreement and existing transfer pricing policy (in which case, substantial documentation should be prepared to support this decision, an alternative pricing method should be selected, and analysis under Chapter 9 of the OECD TPG should be performed);
- a decision to apply the existing agreement and policy (in which case, the analysis will move forward to the second step).

Figure 6.4 Decision Tree

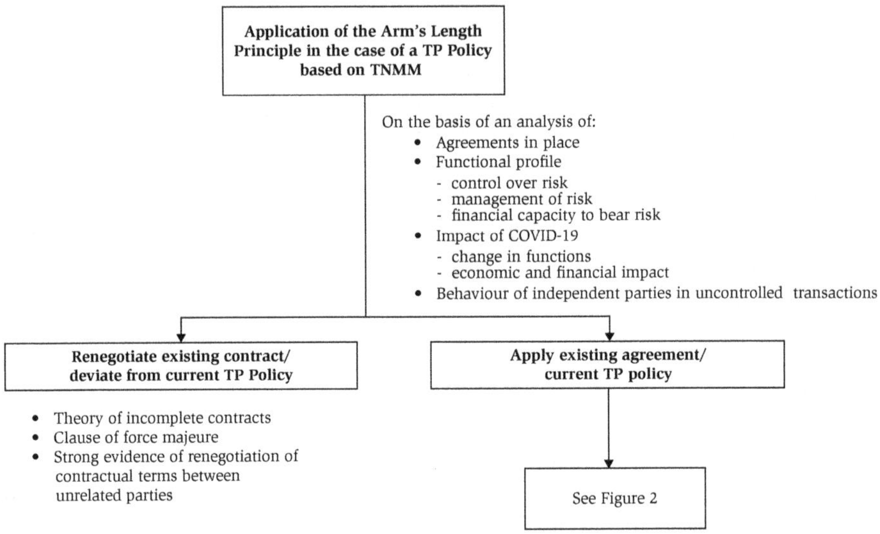

Step 2: Application of the method (*see* Figure 6.5)

Once it is ascertained that it is appropriate to apply the existing TP policy, the MNE needs to decide how the policy should be applied given the unprecedented market conditions. The analysis would rely on the same factual elements indicated in Step 1, i.e., (i) the content of the agreement, (ii) the functional profile of the parties, (iii) the impact of COVID-19 on the transaction (in terms of functions/risks and assets as well as financial results), and (iv) the behaviour of independent parties. Broadly speaking, Step 2 of the analysis could result in:

- a decision to apply the TNMM policy as in previous years (this would be the case, for example, if the transaction has not been impacted by the pandemic);
- a decision to apply the TNMM policy by making adjustments to the financial data of the tested party (i.e., the subsidiary) to exclude (totally or partially) the impact of the pandemic or to dilute it by testing multiple years together (term-test); and
- a decision to apply the TNMM policy by tailoring the selection of comparables to ensure that the comparable data reflect current market conditions.

Figure 6.5 Application of existing agreement / TP policy

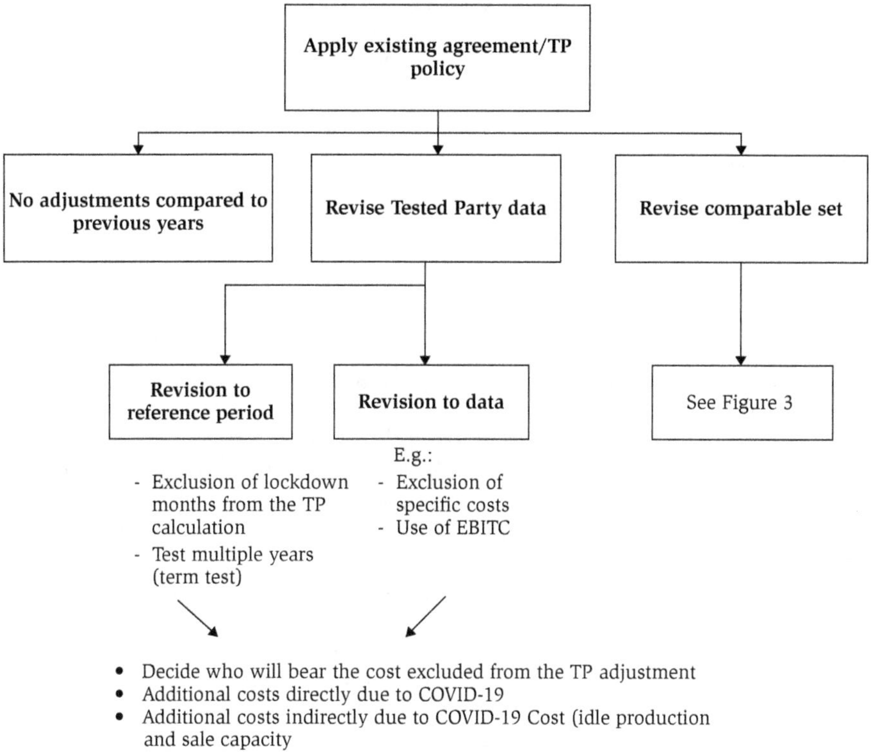

Step 3: Selection and adjustment of comparables

If it emerges in Step 2 of the analysis that, for example, it is appropriate to apply the TNMM as in previous years, but it is necessary to tailor the selection of comparable companies/transactions to better reflect current market conditions, several approaches can be pursued, as summarized in Figure 6.6. These approaches include:

- changing the reference period of the comparables by using, for example, data from the previous economic crisis;[48]
- using 2020 interim data from listed companies; and
- using the most recent data from comparable companies and making comparability adjustments.

48. This approach is not recommended by the OECD, *Guidance on the Transfer Pricing Implications of the COVID-19 Pandemic*, OECD Policy Responses to Coronavirus (COVID-19), OECD Publishing, Paris – *See* para. 25 (18 December 2020).

Figure 6.6 Revision of Comparable Set

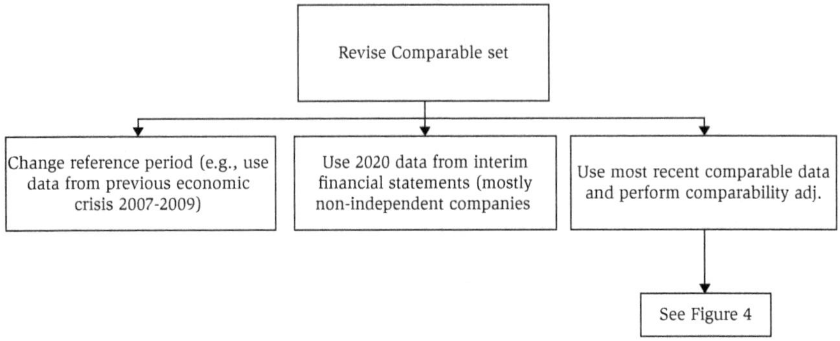

Step 4: comparability adjustments (*see* Figure 6.7)

Several types of comparability adjustments could be considered. Simply identifying the specific part of the profit range that is more comparable to the transaction under analysis would be one possibility. Another would be to perform a statistical/econometrics analysis using data from the previous crisis, current macro-economic or microeconomic data, and data from 2020 interim reports. In most cases, given the current market conditions, loss-making comparables should not be excluded.[49]

Figure 6.7 Application of most recent comparable data

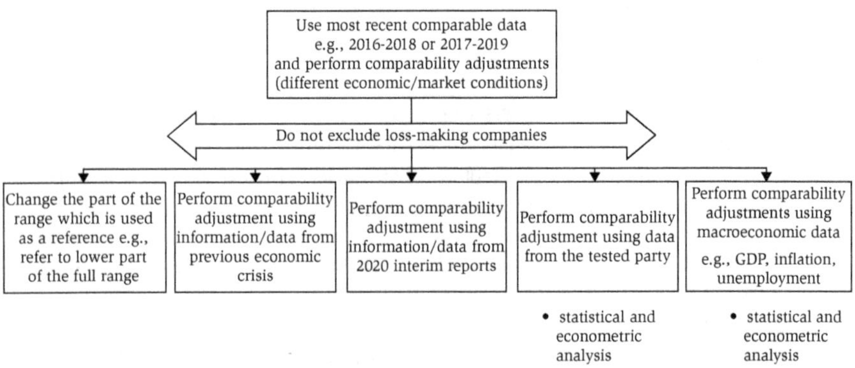

6 COVID-19 AND INTRA-GROUP FINANCIAL TRANSACTIONS

Among the several indirect effects of COVID-19 on the business of MNEs, those experienced by financial treasury operations are particularly notable even though the

49. *Ibid.*

pandemic has not affected the different financial hubs (e.g., in Asia, Europe, North America) at the same time and to the same extent.

In the last few months, intra-group flows of liquidity and transfer pricing policies related to financial transactions have had to be constantly managed and monitored as the environment has been quickly evolving, and the volatility of the financial market has increased. Financial uncertainty at all levels, whether about customers' capacity to spend or government interventions, has had a substantial impact on liquidity flows.

At the outset of the pandemic, the most pressing concern of MNE treasury departments was the increasing risk of liquidity shortages. In certain sectors, sales were frozen at very short notice due to government measures, while expenses could not be reduced at the same pace. Hence, the sharp decrease in revenues was not balanced by a similar trend in costs. MNEs were also concerned about possible delays in payments of outstanding debts and increasing bad debts.

The most common reaction among MNEs was to focus on preserving financial liquidity. In some cases, payment terms were also adjusted/extended in both intercompany transactions and those between unrelated parties. New credit lines were sought to fund short-term needs to meet undeferrable payments. These initial responses were intended to set up a bridge and overcome immediate cash requirements.

Credit lines were obtained either centrally or locally. In both cases, this boosted intercompany financial flows as it was not uncommon to use central credit lines to help subsidiaries and, conversely, to channel locally gathered resources to the holding company or to the central treasuries to meet group-wide obligations. The number of intra-group financial guarantees also increased.

Concerns about outstanding receivables generated new factoring transactions that enabled companies to obtain, in a very short time, additional liquidity from the banking system or from the market. These transactions were frequently handled by central treasuries in order to benefit from economies of scale, thus increasing intra-group financial flows. In the first few months of 2020, the level of uncertainty created significantly volatile interest rates, which, in some cases, indicated anomalous trends. In general, however, the intervention of central banks succeeded in stabilizing financial markets in a relatively short time.

At a time when MNEs were familiarizing themselves with new guidance from the OECD on financial transactions – the *OECD Transfer Pricing Guidance on Financial Transactions* issued in February 2020 (OECD FT Guidance)[50] – the pandemic created additional complexities in the management and pricing of intra-group financial flows.

In terms of transfer pricing analyses, the effect of the pandemic should be evaluated at every stage: from the identification and accurate delineation of a transaction to the selection of the method and how to apply it, i.e., the selection of comparable transactions/prices. The accurate delineation of a transaction and pricing, in particular, should be adapted to the current conditions.[51]

50. OECD, *Transfer Pricing Guidance on Financial Transactions: Inclusive Framework on BEPS Actions 4,8-10*, OECD, Paris (February 2020).
51. OECD, *Guidance on the Transfer Pricing Implications of the COVID-19 Pandemic*, OECD Policy Responses to Coronavirus (COVID-19), OECD Publishing, Paris, para. 10 (18 December 2020).

As for all other transactions, the accurate delineation of a financial transaction is a key step in the transfer pricing analysis. The OECD FT Guidance clearly states that any analysis of the interest rate for an intercompany loan should be preceded by an analysis of the contractual arrangements to ascertain whether the loan should be effectively treated as a loan or should, in part or in total, be delineated as an equity contribution. In doing so, certain elements must be considered. For example, the terms and conditions – for repayment extensions, the renegotiation of interest rates and scheduling of interest payments, or the relative size of debt and equity – must be compared with those applicable on the markets.

During the last few months, as commented in the first section of this chapter, most MNEs have suffered liquidity shortages that have compelled them to change their financing strategies at short notice, at least in the short and medium term. These changes have also impacted intra-group transactions and, in many cases, led to the need to renegotiate their terms and conditions. In parallel, due to liquidity shortages, numerous companies have suffered a rise in debt and a deterioration in their debt-to-equity ratio. These facts will need to be considered when delineating a financial transaction and pricing it, as some MNEs have been heavily affected by non-recurring circumstances. For example, the renegotiation of an intercompany loan due to the unprecedented market circumstances created by the pandemic should not be considered a reason to reclassify the loan as equity but rather as a merely temporary disruption to the company's financial situation.

Similarly, an analysis intended to accurately delineate a cash pooling agreement should consider the unusual 2020 economic conditions. Many companies in the sectors most affected by the pandemic (e.g., fashion retailers, subsidiaries of MNE hotel groups) have turned from being cash generators into being cash absorbers. As a result, the normal functioning of cash pooling in certain industries has been disrupted. Any transfer pricing analysis should consider the peculiarities of the period and should not necessarily re-delineate current transactions on the basis of the unusual circumstances resulting from COVID-19.

Intra-group guarantees are also an area where the pandemic may create challenges in the actual delineation of a transaction. According to the OECD FT Guidance, intercompany financial guarantees must be accurately delineated in order to ascertain whether the overall transaction (guaranteed loan and intercompany guarantee) is correctly delineated or should rather be seen as a capital contribution made by the guarantor to the beneficiary of the guaranteed loan. While this analysis is appropriate in normal economic times, in the current market conditions, it should be evaluated very carefully. Given the economic uncertainty and market volatility, banking institutions may require the issuance of formal parent guarantees also in cases in which they would not normally be requested.

The pricing of intra-group financial transactions requires more caution during economic downturns. On the one hand, interest rates were very volatile at the outset of the pandemic but very low during the year due to interventions by central banks. On the other hand, the probability of companies defaulting has increased significantly because of the recession. Therefore, the selection of comparable market transactions/prices presents several challenges. Further, the use of historical data to benchmark debt-to-equity ratios should be treated with caution due to the unusual market conditions. As stated in the OECD Guidance,[52] historic data may reflect market conditions that are different from those experienced during the pandemic. Therefore, the pricing of financial transactions must take into account the quality of the financial data used in the benchmark, the possible variations in debt capacity, and the probability of companies defaulting.

In conclusion, extreme care must be taken in the accurate delineation of a transaction during an economic downturn as both the tested parties and the market evidence used in the analysis must be contextualized. In 2020, they did not necessarily reflect what would happen in normal circumstances.

7 LONGER-TERM TRANSFER PRICING CONSEQUENCES OF COVID-19

As discussed in section 4 above, many MNEs have centralized structures with organizations based on a principal entity that performs most of the value-adding activities and owns most of the assets as well as on routine or limited-risk entities that carry out manufacturing or commercial activities. They also have long global supply chains with R&D, manufacturing, and commercial activities located in different countries and across different continents.

COVID-19 (together with other macro trends such as increasing tariffs or environmental considerations) has exposed the fragilities of long global supply chains that can be potentially disrupted by events in countries many miles away from the company's customers or headquarters.

In the medium and long term, the pandemic may drive companies to reorganize their operations on a more regional or local basis by onshoring or near-shoring certain activities which, in past decades, were relocated to lower-cost countries. Consequently, some analysts expect a wave of restructuring of global supply chains and a surge of more regional and local structures that are considered to be more resilient and less exposed to events in other geographical areas. Obviously, restructuring and changes in the functional profile would need to be evaluated under Chapter 9 of the OECD Guidelines (the chapter on the transfer pricing aspects of business restructurings).

The impact of the pandemic on globalization and centralization, however, is more complex and multifaceted than it may seem at first sight. At least two other facts need to be considered in evaluating the potential long-term impact of COVID-19 on transfer pricing.

The first fact is that the pandemic has clearly shown how centralized the decision-making process of MNEs really is, with the response to the unusual events of 2020 being, in many instances, driven from headquarters (hence, more centralized than ever). This trend has been facilitated by the digitalization of decision-making, with decisions being made and transmitted very quickly, in real-time, from very far off.

52. *Ibid.*, para. 9.

The second fact is that, while the response to the pandemic has clearly been managed at the headquarters level for many MNEs, what actually constitutes a headquarters has changed. The sudden acceleration of digitalization has resulted in digital and intellectual supply chains becoming longer and more dispersed. People work from different locations, remotely, from home, and from different countries. The increasing centralization of decision-making and flexible working locations not only pose transfer pricing challenges but also have a greater number of tax implications.

To conclude, while MNE operations may become less global and less centralized with a wave of transfer pricing business restructuring, decision-making and control over risk and DEMPE functions may actually go the opposite way and be concentrated increasingly at the headquarters level. At the same time, headquarters may become increasingly difficult to define and attribute to a specific country/tax jurisdiction due to the acceleration of digitalization and flexible working locations.

8 CONCLUSIONS

The current COVID-19 health crisis and the resulting economic slowdown pose many challenges to multinational companies regarding the correct management of intra-group transactions and transfer pricing systems. During recessions, application of the arm's length principle becomes more difficult, especially due to the lack of real-time data from independent comparable companies. As indicated by the OECD, 'it is important not to lose sight of the objective to find a reasonable estimate of an arm's length outcome, which requires an exercise of judgment on the part of taxpayers and tax administrations'.[53]

53. *Ibid.*, para. 5.

CHAPTER 7

Recent Developments on Transfer Pricing and Simplification Measures

Emily Muyaa[*]

[*] The views expressed in this chapter are those of the author.

1 INTRODUCTION

1.1 Initial Thoughts

How much simpler can it be? This is one of the questions that comes to mind whenever this author comes across a discussion on transfer pricing simplification measures. This is a pertinent question given the inherent complexity embedded in the very heart of transfer pricing, i.e., the application of the arm's length principle to related-party transactions. It is undoubtedly remarkable that the arm's length principle has gained much acceptance over the years as a principle applied almost globally, in a uniform manner, and more than most other principles and concepts.[1] The complexity of applying the arm's length principle, exacerbated by the administrative burden resulting from costs and compliance burdens, is part of the reason why simplification measures are worth considering.[2]

Globally, countries are at different levels of development and, most importantly, diverse stages of transfer pricing knowledge and capability. It is crucial to consider ways to apply the arm's length principle and the basic tenets underlying its existence with as minimal inconvenience and/or difficulty as possible. Simplification is necessary in this context. A taxpayer or tax administration in country A should not suffer extra burden in applying an international standard for a transaction involving a taxpayer and administration in country B who do not experience such a burden based on the skill required to apply the standard. How can this be achieved? This is perhaps one of the biggest headaches that tax authorities worldwide have had to deal with over the years. It is a question that continues to generate much debate and interest among all stakeholders. The risk with an improper application of the arm's length principle (be it due to lack of proper legal framework, capability, etc.,) can impact more than one jurisdiction through unrelieved more than single taxation or, at the extreme end of the spectrum, less than single taxation or non-taxation.

1. For example, the concept of the authorized approach to the attribution of profits to permanent establishments has not received as much wide acceptance and/or application, even as a subset to the application of wider transfer pricing rules, and thereby the arm's length principle, to intra-company dealings. For most countries, such non-acceptance is due to the complexity attached to its application but, for other countries, such as those following the UN Model Tax Convention, the concept fails at the foundational base, i.e., the policy reasoning behind it.
2. The OECD recognizes this in its guidance on safe harbours, specifically para. 4.95 of Chapter IV of the OECD Guidelines.

1.2 International Guidance: A Synopsis

In terms of international guidance on transfer pricing simplification measures, the work of the Organisation for Economic Co-operation and Development (OECD) and the United Nations (UN) is notable with current guidance contained in Chapter IV of the OECD Transfer Pricing Guidelines for Multinational Enterprises and Tax Administrations 2017 (OECD Guidelines) and Chapter B.8. of the UN Practical Manual on Transfer Pricing for Developing Countries 2017 (UN Practical Manual).[3] The UN Practical Manual references the OECD in most part but with some additional policy considerations for developing countries.

The work leading up to the current Chapter IV of the OECD Guidelines is important as it gives an overview of the measures implemented by a number of countries. In 2010,[4] the OECD launched a project to improve the administrative aspects of transfer pricing, including a review of techniques that may be implemented by countries to optimize the use of taxpayers' and tax administrations' resources. A survey was conducted as part of this project. The main findings from the survey were released in June 2011 based on the responses provided by thirty-three OECD and non-OECD countries. The OECD subsequently invited more countries to participate in the survey. Consequently, eight countries responded, resulting in a total of forty-one OECD and non-OECD countries providing detailed responses concerning measures currently existing in their domestic law to simplify the application of their transfer pricing rules. The survey focused specifically on simplification measures adopted as part of those countries' transfer pricing regimes. On 6 June 2012, the OECD published the updated survey Multi-Country Analysis of Existing Transfer Pricing Simplification Measures[5] (hereinafter 'OECD Multi-Country Analysis 2012'), which presents the analysis of existing transfer pricing simplification measures as of 1 January 2012. These include not only safe harbours but also measures such as less stringent documentation requirements, alleviated penalties, streamlined procedures, etc.

Some of the key findings as of that date were as follows:

- More than 80% of the respondent countries had transfer pricing simplification measures in place.
- Almost 75% of available simplification measures were in respect of small and medium-sized companies (SMEs), small transactions, and low value-adding intra-group services (LVAS).
- Out of thirty-three respondent countries that have simplification measures, sixteen countries have safe harbours, i.e., simplified transfer pricing method, safe harbour arm's length range/rate, safe harbour interest rate, and

3. The UN Practical Manual also covers safe harbours in Chapters B.1., B.4. in respect of various transactions or frameworks. There is also a discussion of safe harbour rules in the country practices (section D) especially with respect to India and Mexico.
4. OECD – OECD updates the survey 'Multi-Country Analysis of Existing Transfer Pricing Simplification Measures' (7 June 2012), News IBFD.
5. Multi-Country Analysis of Existing Transfer Pricing Simplification Measures – 2012 Update, OECD Committee of Fiscal Affairs, 6 June 2012, available at 50517144.pdf (oecd.org) (accessed 14 January 2021). Hereinafter 'OECD Multi-Country Analysis 2012'.

exemption from transfer pricing rules/adjustment. Of those sixteen countries, ten have simplified transfer pricing methods, safe harbour arm's length range/rate, and safe harbour interest rates.

The OECD Guidelines were subsequently updated in 2013 to reflect discussions and comments received as part of the above project. The guidance covers the basic tenets of safe harbour regimes, including the advantages and disadvantages. An important piece of additional guidance is the Annex to Chapter IV that provides a sample memorandum of understanding for competent authorities to establish bilateral safe harbours.[6]

Countries have continued to revise or introduce simplification measures aimed at making compliance with transfer pricing regulations less costly and burdensome for all stakeholders. This is a welcome move. However, as with other unilateral measures, it is important to bear in mind the impact that such measures might have including, but not limited to, double taxation or non-taxation, tax competition, etc.

Generally, the design of safe harbour rules varies from country to country and may include provisions whereby, if a taxpayer's reported profits are within a certain range or percentage or certain amount, the taxpayer is not required to follow a complex and burdensome rule such as applying the transfer price methodologies.[7]

Safe harbours may typically target types of transactions (small transactions) or, more generally, taxpayers (e.g., SMEs). The thresholds for determining what transaction or taxpayer falls within the definition is a matter of domestic law. The UN notes that safe harbours 'may only be used by taxpayers at their option'. This statement supports the position of rebuttable safe harbours.

One of the benefits of well-designed safe harbour regimes is that they do away with the need to undertake a complex transfer pricing analysis for otherwise simple transactions, especially in situations where there is a lack of uncontrolled comparables data needed to undertake a proper analysis. This is because, at the point of designing the safe harbour, it is assumed that the tax administration would have made reference to comparables data that is not likely available in the public domain[8] that would not normally be applicable (or even acceptable) during a normal transfer pricing analysis (outside a safe harbour context) as the comparables data would qualify as 'secret', i.e., not necessarily available to the taxpayer(s). However, a well-designed safe harbour

6. However, the memorandum covers types of services that are not commonly addressed by safe harbours such as low-risk distributors, contract manufacturers, and contract research and development. *See further* C. Silberztein, OECD: Transfer Pricing Safe Harbours, 20 Intl. Transfer Pricing J. 2 (2013), Journal Articles & Papers IBFD, section 4.2.
7. Paragraph B.1.7.6. of the United Nations Practical Manual on Transfer Pricing (2017) available at https://www.un.org/esa/ffd/wp-content/uploads/2017/04/Manual-TP-2017.pdf (accessed 11 January 2021).
8. *See* https://www.oecd.org/ctp/transfer-pricing/oecd-and-brazil-federal-revenue-authority-invite-taxpayer-input-on-transfer-pricing-issues-relating-to-the-design-of-safe-harbour-provisions-and-other-comparability-considerations.htm#:~:text=30%2F07%2F2020%20%E2%80%93%20As,well%20as%20other%20simplification%20measures (accessed 8 January 2021). The OECD /RFB Safe Harbours Survey Document is downloadable as a Word document in that link. *See* specifically para. 17.

regime would have allowed for the impacted taxpayers to give input into the tax administration's process and thereby accept the outcome.

The UN Practical Manual cautions as follows:[9]

> There are some risks to safe harbours, such as arbitrariness in setting parameters and range; equity and uniformity issues; incompatibility with the arm's length principle; opportunities for tax planning and tax evasion and potential risk of double taxation. In any case ... introducing a safe harbour rule should involve analysis of whether, in a broad sense, the administrative and simplification benefits of a safe harbour outweigh the potential costs of applying something other than the arm's length principle.

Some of the avenues to mitigate or even eliminate some of the often-mentioned drawbacks of safe harbours include the use of bilateral or multilateral safe harbours (thereby avoiding unilateral measures that might not be acceptable to the other tax administration); restricting the scope of safe harbours to only relatively low risk and straightforward transactions (this avenue has presently been explored quite remarkably by most countries. However, there is a call for more boldness in adopting safe harbour rules, including for somewhat complex transactions) and preserving the arm's length principle by allowing multinational enterprises (MNEs) to apply a traditional transfer pricing analysis as an alternative to a safe harbour if it is more appropriate (this can be achieved by designing safe harbours to allow taxpayers to opt in or out but with properly designed criteria in order to avoid unwanted outcomes and/or having rebuttable safe harbours).[10]

1.3 Recent Developments: A Quick Note

1.3.1 Brazil

The Brazilian transfer pricing regime is characterized by an approach based on fixed margins derived from industry practices. For example, under the system, different rules apply to export and import transactions. Although the rules are inspired by the traditional transfer pricing methods (under the OECD Guidelines/UN Practical Manual), the Brazilian methods adopt predetermined fixed margins under its equivalents of the resale and cost-plus methods that are encompassed within the OECD/UN guidance for such transactions.[11]

9. Paragraph B.1.7.6. of the United Nations Practical Manual on Transfer Pricing (2017) available at https://www.un.org/esa/ffd/wp-content/uploads/2017/04/Manual-TP-2017.pdf (accessed 11 January 2021).
10. J. Walls, A Closer Look, Transfer Pricing Safe Harbors: The New Arm's Length Standard?, 24 Global Tax Weekly, 7 (April 2013), cited in R.S. Critchley, Dispute Prevention Avenues for Permanent Establishments, 24 Intl. Transfer Pricing J. 4 (2017), Journal Articles & Papers IBFD, section 3.1.1.
11. L.E. Schoueri and R.A. (Jr.) Galendi, Challenges to Brazilian Transfer Pricing Rules upon Accession to the OECD, 26 Intl. Transfer Pricing J. 6 (2019), Journal Articles & Papers IBFD, pp. 434 & 435. The authors explain that the methods concerning the import of goods, services, or rights are: the comparable independent price method (PIC); the resale price less profit method (PRL); the production cost-plus profit method (CPL); and the quotation price on imports method

In the 2019 Joint Statement[12] issued by the OECD and the *Receita Federal do Brasil* (RFB), a number of benefits and shortcomings of the predetermined margins approach are set out. Some of the benefits are the fact that the approach is predictable and provides certainty to taxpayers. One of the mentioned disadvantages of the approach is that it can result in double taxation, and the implied predictability and certainty only applies in a domestic (not cross-border) situation.[13]

A report by the OECD and RFB,[14] setting out the outcomes of the work to assess the similarities and differences between the Brazilian and OECD transfer pricing frameworks, notes as follows with respect to Brazil's transfer pricing regime with specific reference to simplification: 'At least three aspects of the Brazilian transfer pricing system simplify compliance and administration – fixed margins, freedom of selection of the method, and safe harbour regimes – but raise concerns because they fail to achieve the dual objective of transfer pricing rules.'

The OECD/RFB Joint Statement sets out a succinct analysis of the Brazilian regime with respect to simplification measures, including the benefits and shortcomings. That analysis is not repeated here.[15] The joint statement cautions that the safe harbours currently in place may provide unintended tax benefits by deactivating the existing transfer pricing rules.[16] Some of the difficulties encountered in applying the arm's length principle can be addressed through carefully designed and regularly reviewed safe harbour rules.[17]

The OECD/RFB Joint Statement,[18] while identifying the strengths and weaknesses of the features of the Brazilian transfer pricing regime, sets out two options for Brazil to converge with the OECD standard while enhancing the positive attributes of its existing transfer pricing framework. Both options contemplate full adherence to the arm's length principle that is at the core of the OECD standard while seeking to preserve

(PCI). In the case of exports, the applicable methods are the export sales price method (PVEx); the resale price method (RPM), the purchase or production cost-plus tax and profit method (CAP); and the quotation price on exports method (PECEX).

12. Joint Statement on the OECD-BRAZIL Transfer Pricing Project issued on 11 July 2019 available at http://www.oecd.org/tax/transfer-pricing/joint-statement-oecd-brazil-transfer-pricing-project-july-2019.pdf (accessed 5 January 2021) – hereinafter 'OECD/RFB Joint Statement'. *See also* OECD/Receita Federal do Brasil (2019), Transfer Pricing in Brazil: Towards Convergence with the OECD Standard, OECD, Paris, www.oecd.org/tax/transfer-pricing/transfer-pricing-in-brazil-towards-convergence-with-the-oecd-standard.htm, at para. 224.
13. OECD/RFB Joint Statement, *supra* n. 12, at p. 4.
14. Transfer Pricing in Brazil: Towards Convergence with the OECD Standard – Highlights (at p. 8) available at https://www.oecd.org/tax/transfer-pricing/transfer-pricing-in-brazil-towards-convergence-with-oecd-standard-brochure.pdf (accessed 4 January 2021).
15. Transfer Pricing in Brazil: Towards Convergence with the OECD Standard – Highlights, *supra* n. 14. *See* especially pp. 8 & 9 for a discussion of the existing rules.
16. Transfer Pricing in Brazil: Towards Convergence with the OECD Standard – Highlights, *supra* n. 14, at p. 14.
17. Transfer Pricing in Brazil: Towards Convergence with the OECD Standard – Highlights, *supra* n. 14, at p. 17.
18. OECD/RFB Joint Statement, *supra* n. 12.

simplicity and certainty. Accordingly, the work on safe harbours will give consideration to incorporating targeted, carefully designed safe harbours in appropriate circumstances.[19]

In 2020, the OECD Secretariat[20] and RFB launched a survey to seek public input to inform the work related to the development of safe harbours as well as other simplification measures and mechanisms that can contribute to enhanced tax certainty. This survey was released as part of the wider project being undertaken as a precursor to Brazil's accession to the OECD.

The survey puts forth a total of seventeen questions[21] for which comments will be taken into account when pursuing the work on safe harbours for Brazil. The key considerations of the questions include the following: an interrogation regarding the relevance of designing the safe harbours; input on the commonalities of the respondent's transactions with other taxpayers in a bid to ensure that the designed rules cover large numbers of transactions/taxpayers; the appropriate transfer pricing method for each of the specific cases mentioned by the respondent; an economic analysis of the specific cases presented; the step of the transfer pricing analysis that a safe harbour would be able to provide relief in terms of compliance efforts; specific cases for which lack of comparables data is foreseen; any challenges to the application of comparability adjustments to foreign comparables in instances involving lack of local comparables; whether there is a need for sector-specific advance pricing agreements (APAs); whether there is a need for other simplification measures to enhance tax certainty and, if so, what measures.

It is mentioned that comments received from stakeholders will be treated confidentially, and only 'aggregated comments' of the responses will be made available to the public. At the time of writing this chapter, the official aggregated comments in response to the survey questions had not yet been published.

This chapter[22] discusses various measures already in existence, more like a pre-emption of what might be the outcome of the survey questions that were raised. With the main objective of the joint project being to align Brazil's transfer pricing regime with the OECD standards, it is logical to assume that the measures that are eventually set out for Brazil will be close to, if not aligned with, those already in existence in most (OECD member) countries. This is further supported by the response of a number of countries to the OECD Multi-Country Analysis 2012, viz. none of the countries from the sample were aware of any cases of double taxation occasioned by the application of their unilateral measures.

However, as the world works towards achieving unification in taxation principles (especially in the context of taxation of the digital economy), additional questions arise, such as if and the extent to which Brazil's regime will be adjusted with safe harbours that are outside those currently being tackled in the international arena

19. OECD/RFB Safe Harbours Survey Document, *supra* n. 8, at para. 1.
20. *Supra* n. 8.
21. OECD/RFB Safe Harbours Survey Document, *supra* n. 8, at pp. 7-9.
22. This chapter does not presume to be exhaustive on the work on simplification measures but provides some ideas that guide the reader on the kind of measures in place in a number of countries.

and/or how any proposed safe harbours will interact with other rules being discussed globally. It is important to ensure that any regime proposed for Brazil is looked at in the context of the work currently ongoing in the international tax arena as this would not only save resources for Brazil (having to consider the measures together in one instance) but also gives comfort and certainty to the taxpayers who will be impacted by Brazil's domestic regime and its interaction with the global regime.

1.3.2 Other Recent Developments

A short synopsis is included regarding the simplification measures proposed in the ongoing discussions under the Inclusive Framework, specifically regarding Amount B under Pillar One. For a more detailed discussion on the work regarding tax challenges of the digitalization of the economy, *see* Chapter 5 of this book.

One of the most notable recent developments in the area of simplification measures that has also received wide acceptance is with regard to the LVAS that was introduced as a result of the outcome of the OECD/G20 BEPS Project. Although most countries already provided one form or another of simplification for the type of services tackled as part of the OECD BEPS Report on Action 10, more pronounced acceptance was achieved in the context of the BEPS Project.[23]

The COVID-19 pandemic has impacted global economies. As countries look to recover from the impact of the pandemic, the question that arises is: what can be done in a transfer pricing context in order to ease the burden for taxpayers and tax authorities. For the former, it is important to continue to comply with the set rules. For the latter, it is still an objective to collect much-needed revenue to supplement depleted economic resources. What role can simplification measures play in this regard? A more detailed discussion on transfer pricing and COVID-19 is provided in Chapter 6 of this book. *See also* section 6.

1.4 Cursory Definition of Terminologies

Simplification measures go beyond just safe harbours and encompass other measures designed to aid taxpayers in complying with transfer pricing obligations as well as ensuring certainty and predictability of the tax system. If properly designed, these measures are also beneficial to tax administrations, at the very least, to the extent that they free up the resources of the tax administrations from small transactions and/or taxpayers and allow for focus to be placed on complex transactions. This has the spillover effect of ensuring proper skill is developed to examine these cases with the expected outcome of protection of the tax bases of the countries involved.

As noted by the OECD, the main objective of a safe harbour regime is to provide for a standardized approach to determine or approximate the arm's length outcome for

23. Paragraph 13 of the OECD Multi-Country Analysis 2012 (*supra* n. 5) notes that sixteen of the surveyed countries have a total of twenty-three safe harbours with 30% of the safe harbours directed at the LVAS. In the EU, for example, the Joint Transfer Pricing Forum in the area had already provided guidance in the area of the LVAS even before the BEPS Project.

groups of taxpayers or to provide simplified guidance on compliance with otherwise complex and burdensome processes when it is reasonable to standardize these outcomes.[24]

Safe harbours do not work in all situations. For more complex and higher risk transfer pricing matters, a more targeted application of the arm's length principle through a complete transfer pricing analysis is still necessary. This is mainly due to the fact that the unique and complex features of the transactions, as well as important differences between such complex transactions, do not make it possible to develop a reliable and standardized approach (which is the intended purpose through a safe harbour) that could be equally relevant and applicable to other taxpayers.[25]

For purposes of this chapter and for ease of discussion, 'substantive simplification measures' mean regimes/measures that go to the very heart of a transfer pricing analysis, e.g., determining who is subject to transfer pricing rules, determining what transactions are covered, the applicable transfer pricing method, its mode of application including the profit level indicator, the margins, etc.

Some measures are intended to aid the taxpayer in complying with transfer pricing obligations. Some countries offer simplification in the form of compliance with procedures, alleviated penalties, mode of dispute resolution, etc. These measures will be referred to as 'procedural simplification measures'.

All in all, transfer pricing simplification measures should satisfy certain purposes, i.e., be beneficial, for them to be fully appreciated. From a taxpayer's perspective, such simplification measures should facilitate transfer pricing compliance, reduce related costs and transfer pricing litigation, as well as guarantee certainty with regard to tax positions. Conversely, from a tax administration perspective, such measures eliminate the risk of tax base erosion and create the opportunity to focus their limited resources on higher risk transfer pricing cases.[26]

Speaking on a more general note, simplification measures (or safe harbours, as the case might be) apply to related-party cross-border situations. This might raise some questions depending on the domestic or treaty law of a country, e.g., whether the tax system is discriminatory by promoting inequality between domestic and foreign investors.[27] That discussion is beyond the scope of this chapter. Mention of the scope of application is made in this instance only to distinguish the practice in some countries that apply such measures to domestic related parties. In some instances, these parties enjoy some additional simplification measures. Examples of countries that extend the application of these measures to domestic related-party situations include Israel, Poland, and Turkey.[28]

24. OECD/RFB Safe Harbours Survey Document, *supra* n. 8, at para. 14.
25. OECD/RFB Safe Harbours Survey Document, *supra* n. 8, at para. 14.
26. P. Valente, Transfer Pricing: Valuation of Intangibles and Simplification – A Summary of Key Issues at the International Level, 52 Eur. Taxn. 12 (2012), Journal Articles & Papers IBFD.
27. *See* UN Practical Manual caution in (para. B.1.7.6. of the United Nations Practical Manual on Transfer Pricing (2017) available at https://www.un.org/esa/ffd/wp-content/uploads/2017/04/Manual-TP-2017.pdf (accessed 11 January 2021).
28. OECD Multi-Country Analysis 2012, *supra* n. 5, at p. 30.

2 SUBSTANTIVE SIMPLIFICATION MEASURES

2.1 Overview

Some of the related-party transactions for which there has been wide simplification either in terms of the applicable methodology (or indices), arm's length ranges and rates, etc., include those in respect of commodity pricing, services, debt transactions, etc. In most cases, the transactions covered by simplified methodology are simple transactions for which simplification is justified to the extent that the compliance burden is lifted for both taxpayers and tax administrations. General observations in terms of methodology are that the cost-plus method is applied mostly for the LVAS and exceptionally for small transactions; the comparable uncontrolled price method mostly for interest rates on loans; and the transactional net margin method and the transactional profit split methods applied in certain cases for loans and other transactions. Examples of countries that apply a simplified transfer pricing methodology for prescribed transactions include Australia, Austria, Japan, Mexico, the Netherlands, New Zealand, Slovenia, and the United States.[29]

In some cases, the application of a prescribed transfer pricing methodology is coupled with a prescription on the acceptable arm's length rate/range, industry averages, and other prescribed indicators, e.g., for commodities. The prescriptions themselves also serve as a form of simplified application for transfer pricing purposes as they provide guidance to the taxpayer on what the tax administration will likely accept for certain (groups of) transactions. However, prescription comes with the risk that the outcome might not always be at arm's length hence the need to check the set prescriptions from time to time to ensure they are still sound and reflect the market conditions.

The use of fixed returns, such as those adopted in the context of the LVAS, seems widely acceptable to many tax administrations.[30] Some authors[31] observe that fixed returns could work well in developing countries, with proper adjustments made to reflect the heightened risks of operating in those countries. Perhaps this would aid in gathering acceptance of the measure more widely across countries where the measure has yet to be implemented.

Some aspects warrant discussion in the context of recent developments with regard to substantive simplification measures, namely: commodities pricing; intra-group services, specifically, the LVAS and interest rates.

29. OECD Multi-Country Analysis 2012, *supra* n. 5.
30. Based on a regional outlook, the measure on the LVAS was least adopted in Africa, with only one country (Zambia) having legislated such a measure. However, this measure has yet to be implemented in practice, and it is not yet possible for the author to gauge the effectiveness and/or possible lessons learned, and therefore accepted, by other tax administrations in Africa.
31. *See*, for example, S. Gonnet et al., *Proposed Framework for Foreign Comparables Selection and Adjustment* (pp. 4 & 11) available at https://tped.eu/wp-content/uploads/2019/12/TPED-FINAL-PAPER-1.pdf (accessed 9 January 2021).

2.2 Commodities Pricing

A number of countries, notably Latin American countries, apply the so-called sixth method or commodity rule, although the name of the rule or the method applied may differ from country to country. Historically, this approach has been used for commodities by several countries. The common feature of these rules is that they rely on the quoted prices of the commodities market to price commodity transactions between associated enterprises. The workings of the sixth method may resemble the comparable uncontrolled price method and, despite its more general title, considering its operation, the sixth method (depending on how it is applied) could be considered as an anti-abuse rule, an abuse-deeming rule, or even presumed a form of safe harbour.[32]

In the author's view, the sixth method is simplified in its application to the extent that it gives an indication of where information to a price commodity transaction is to be obtained, thereby giving some level of certainty for the taxpayer in the form of knowing that, for that particular kind of transaction, the tax administration will take a defined approach. This is especially due to the fact that, in practice, it is not always the case that what the taxpayer considers as the most appropriate method for a particular transaction will be the same as the one that the tax administration determines.

The pricing of commodities was considered during the BEPS Project (Action 10) and the guidance (both OECD and UN) updated in that regard. Although, as mentioned earlier, the sixth method was already being applied by a number of Latin American countries, some developments have occurred in this regard between 2017 and now. Examples of developments for some countries are highlighted below.

Zambia extended the application of 'reference price' as defined to cover also the purchase price, effective 1 January 2020. Previously, reference price covered only the sale price. The reference price is used as the arm's length price in any transaction involving the sale or purchase of minerals (minerals, in this case, are restricted to base metals or any substance containing base metals or precious metals) by a company carrying out mining operations, directly or indirectly, to related or associated entities. Additionally, effective 1 January 2020, the law allows premiums to be taken into account as one of the adjustments that may be made to the reference price on account of quality or grade of the metal in order to reflect what would have happened at arm's length. Previously, only discounts were allowed as adjustments.[33]

32. UN Practical Manual (2017) paras B.3.4.1.3. & B.3.4.1.4.
33. I. Kawaza Mvula, Zambia: Corporate Taxation Section 7, Country Tax Guides IBFD. An additional change made to reference pricing (although this is more of an anti-abuse provision) is that it now also applies when a sale of a mineral is made to a third party (unrelated person) by a resident or non-resident company and the following conditions apply: (1) the sale to the third party is at a higher selling price than the reference price in the month that the mineral was sold by the resident or non-resident person to a related or associated person and (2) the sale of the mineral to the third party did not involve any further processing or transformation. If both conditions are met, the higher agreed selling price with the third party becomes the reference price in the transaction between the related or associated persons (effective 1 January 2020).

Ecuador modified its transfer pricing regulations in order to prescribe the pricing of exports of bananas, among other changes, vide Resolution No. NACDGERCGC20-00000046,[34] effective 1 July 2020. The new resolution establishes procedures for calculating the monthly comparable price for defined types of bananas (box type 22XU) according to defined parameters which depends on the country of destination and the calendar month.

Malawi implemented provisions regarding the pricing of commodities in 2017 to reflect some of the (alternative) recommendations pursuant to the BEPS Project, i.e., a deeming price. Accordingly, the arm's length price for specified commodities is determined on the basis of publicly quoted prices as defined on the date of shipment regardless of the price agreed upon between the parties unless the taxpayer provides the necessary evidence to show that adjustments are appropriate to the quoted price to arrive at the arm's length price. In the case of exports from Malawi, however, where the price agreed upon between the related parties is higher than the publicly quoted price on the date of shipment, the agreed-upon price shall be considered for purposes of computing the taxable income.[35] The provision operates as a rebuttable anti-abuse rule and is considered here mainly due to the fact that the prescription of what is expected gives the taxpayers certainty about how the tax administration will approach the covered transactions.

2.3 Intra-group Services (LVAS)

The transfer pricing of intra-group services is an area of concern for most countries, with enormous obligations placed on the taxpayer with regard to proving the benefit obtained by the service recipient and the breadth of documentation required to support intra-group service transactions. As a result, and in order to ease the administrative burden for taxpayers and tax administrations, the LVAS has been a good candidate for simplification, as seen in a number of countries such as Australia, Austria, Hungary, Japan, the Netherlands, New Zealand, Singapore, and the United States.[36] Latvia[37] implemented the guidance on the LVAS in its domestic law in July 2019. According to the guidance, if the criteria for categorization as the LVAS are met, a markup of 5% on costs apply, and a simplified transfer pricing documentation (without separate benchmarking analysis) instead of a local file may be prepared by the taxpayer.

The LVAS was considered under the BEPS Project (Action 10) with a recommendation for simplification in terms of the selection and application of the transfer pricing

34. For a detailed discussion of this measure, *see* https://www.ey.com/en_gl/tax-alerts/ecuador-modifies-transfer-pricing-rules (accessed 10 January 2021). This resolution modifies Resolution No. NAC-DGERCGC16-00000531 which establishes the procedures for calculating comparable prices for transactions involving exports of bananas and other musaceae to related parties.
35. V. Moyo, Malawi: Corporate Taxation Section 7.2, Country Tax Guides IBFD. The provision is contained in section 127A(7) of the Taxation Act 2006, as amended, and in the Transfer Pricing Regulations 2017.
36. OECD Multi-Country Analysis 2012, *supra* n. 5.
37. Through Government Regulation 677 of 18 July 2019. *See* T. Koncevaja, Latvia: Transfer Pricing, Country Tax Guides IBFD, section 12.

method. The recommendation for the LVAS is that a prescribed cost plus markup will apply based on defined parameters and requirements. Examples of countries that recently implemented a rule on the LVAS in one form or another include Israel and Zambia.[38] A number of European Union (EU) countries[39] already applied a rule on it with a cost-plus markup, but instead using a range of markups (as opposed to a single markup as advocated in the BEPS Project). This is in line with the report of the EU Joint Transfer Pricing Forum, which sets a range of markups (i.e., between 3% and 10%, normally 5%, but a different markup might be determined based on the specific facts and circumstances).[40]

Additionally, when the simplified approach for the LVAS is applied, the determination of the benefit test is simplified to the extent that tax administrations are encouraged to generally refrain from reviewing or challenging the benefit test when the simplified approach has been applied under the conditions and circumstances governing the approach and, in particular, in conformity with the documentation and reporting requirements for that approach. Furthermore, the Actions 8-10 Final Report notes that, while the LVAS may provide benefits to all recipients of those services, questions may arise about the extent of the benefits and whether independent parties would have been willing to pay for the service or perform it themselves. When the MNE group has followed the guidance of the simplified approach, including the documentation and reporting requirements thereunder, that should provide sufficient evidence that the benefit test is met given the nature of the LVAS. In evaluating the benefit test, tax administrations should consider benefits only by categories of services and not on a specific charge basis.[41]

As mentioned earlier, based on a regional outlook, the recommendation on the LVAS has not yet been accepted by most countries in Africa. One of the often-mentioned reasons for this is that the determination of the fixed markup does not take into account the unique situation of operating an entity in Africa, e.g., given the risks associated with the region, theoretically, it is expected that the return of the entity in the risky region would be higher. Although no concrete evidence has been given to prove this position or whether indeed applying the full transfer pricing analysis would give a

38. M. Lang and R. Petruzzi, Transfer Pricing Developments Around the World 2020, Wolters Kluwer, at p. 98.
39. These include Belgium (based more on the EU Joint Transfer Pricing Forum (JTPF) Report), Czech Republic and Hungary. *See further infra* n. 40.
40. EU JTPF Report: Guidelines on Low Value Adding Intra-Group Services, available at https://ec.europa.eu/taxation_customs/sites/taxation/files/docs/body/jtpf_020_rev3_2009.pdf (accessed 8 March 2021). *See* specifically, para. 63.
41. OECD (2015), *Aligning Transfer Pricing Outcomes with Value Creation, Actions 8-10 – 2015 Final Reports*, OECD/G20 Base Erosion and Profit Shifting Project, OECD Publishing, Paris, at pp. 156-157. *See also* S. Biswas, Intra-group Services: Issues, Solutions and Issues in Solutions, 23 Intl. Transfer Pricing J. 5 (2016), Journal Articles & Papers IBFD, section 5.2., where a succinct analysis and comparison of the 'safe harbour' rules for the LVAS under various international organizations' guidance and country perspectives are given.

higher markup or range of markups, the author believes that the position might have been different if the discussion of the Actions 8-10 (and thereby the LVAS) had taken place in an inclusive manner. At that point, (non-OECD) countries would have had the opportunity to contribute to the design of the simplification measure.

Services (the LVAS and core services) are an area of great focus for most developing countries. With often little or no information available to undertake a comparability analysis, it gets trickier when an outcome is proposed without much insight into how the figure (of 5%) was arrived at for the definition/categorization of services such as the LVAS, etc. However, some commentators are of the view that, if countries globally were to adopt a safe harbour rule based on each country's economic situation or circumstances, it would be more detrimental for MNEs than helpful as there would be instances of double taxation, and MNEs may be disallowed expense deductions despite valid commercial reasons for incurring such expenses.[42] In the author's view, some comfort could be achieved for all stakeholders by reopening the main issues regarding simplification measures (being also one of the BEPS outcomes with the list uptake by some regions) and allowing discussions with other countries. In the meantime, a range of markups[43] might help.

Although simplification was achieved through the defined cost-plus markup for the LVAS, there are still some aspects on the transfer pricing of other intra-group services that are generally ripe for some simplification, for example, regarding the operation of the benefit test,[44] especially as the current requirement for accurately delineating the transaction and recognition of the delineated transaction is thought to take care of the intended outcome with the benefit test. Alternatively, a threshold could be introduced as a safe harbour under which the taxpayer would not be required to produce specific documentation in order to pass the benefit test.[45] Another aspect of intra-group services is proving that a service was not duplicated and that a benefit with respect thereto was accorded to the recipient of the service. In practice, a huge compliance burden is placed on taxpayers, especially in instances involving shared service centres where the taxpayer also provides the service for itself at the local country level.[46]

42. OECD, Comments Received on Public Discussion Draft – BEPS Action 10: Proposed Modifications to Chapter VII of the Transfer Pricing Guidelines relating to Low Value-Adding Intra-Group Services (OECD 2015), Comments by EBIT, at 145; cited in S. Biswas, Intra-group Services: Issues, Solutions and Issues in Solutions, 23 Intl. Transfer Pricing J. 5 (2016), Journal Articles & Papers IBFD, section 5.4.2.
43. Such as those recommended by the EU JTPF guidance on LVAS (*supra* n. 40).
44. G. Capristano Cardoso and R. Petruzzi, Simplifying the Transfer Pricing Analysis: An Illusory Chimaera or a Realistic Ambition?, 11 World Tax J. (2019), Journal Articles & Papers IBFD, section 2.2.
45. The OECD Guidelines recommend the implementation of a threshold for the LVAS (para. 7.63). Similar guidance would help with respect to core services.
46. *See* G. Capristano Cardoso, Global Transfer Pricing Conference 2019: Transfer Pricing Developments Around the World, 26 Intl. Transfer Pricing J. 5 (2019), Journal Articles & Papers IBFD, section 4.1.

2.4 Interest Rates[47]

The use of a safe harbour in respect of interest rates for debt transactions between related parties is an area that has continued to gain momentum in recent times. In some cases, the tax administration applies the interest rate under the safe harbour in the form of a rebuttable presumption, i.e., that the taxpayer can show that a different rate applies at arm's length, and some tax administrations apply the interest rate as a definitive threshold. Although the latter instance can result in taxation that is not in accordance with the arm's length principle, it does provide some level of certainty for taxpayers. It can also have the negative effects of double taxation (especially if the other tax administration does not accept the figure as determined), unwarranted tax planning opportunities, etc. That notwithstanding, the simplicity and predictability provided by such a measure are undeniable.

In 2017, Korea[48] introduced a safe harbour rule for interest rates applicable to cross-border intercompany borrowing and lending transactions. If a taxpayer applies an interest rate under the safe harbour rule, it will be respected at arm's length as it is. When a Korean resident lends funds to a foreign-related party, the applicable interest rate is the bank overdraft rate as prescribed periodically, currently 4.6%. When a resident borrows funds from a foreign-related party, the applicable rate is the twelve-month London Inter-bank Offered Rate (LIBOR) of the currency of the loan at issue as of the last day of the preceding fiscal year plus 1.5% – if the LIBOR is not available for the currency of the loan at issue, the USD-based LIBOR shall apply.

Switzerland applies safe harbour interest rates that are distinguished depending on various factors, such as the denomination of the loan (i.e., local versus foreign currency); the type of loan, e.g., real estate, operational production company; who grants or is granted the loan, i.e., related party to shareholder and vice versa, etc. The rates are published periodically. In certain situations, different interest rates based on the arm's length principle can be paid if they are justified by a business purpose.[49]

India[50] also applies safe harbour interest rates to intra-group loans, distinguishing them based on the currency in which the loan is denominated. A 'threshold' in this instance is the CRISIL[51] rating of the associated enterprise. A range of 'rates' applies as determined. For the financial year 2019-2020, the safe harbour rates are as follows (depending on CRISIL rating):

47. This part does not consider developments regarding rules limiting deductibility of interest based on considering, e.g., the gearing of an enterprise (like thin capitalization rules) or provisions akin to earning stripping rules such as the rule developed pursuant to the BEPS Project (Action 4).
48. S.L. Moller et al., Korea (Rep.): Transfer Pricing, Country Tax Guides IBFD, section 12.
49. For the 2020 rates, *see* Switzerland – Safe haven interest rates for 2020 – announced, News IBFD.
50. Deloitte Tax Alert, India Issued Safe Harbour Rates for FY 2019-20 for Determining Arm's Length Price for certain Specified Transactions available at https://www2.deloitte.com/content/dam/Deloitte/in/Documents/tax/Transfer%20Pricing/in-tax-tp-alert-india-issued-safe-harbour-rates-for-fy-2019-20-for-determining-arms-length-price-for-certain-specified-transactions-noexp.pdf (accessed 15 January 2021).
51. CRISIL is an Indian analytical company providing ratings, research, and risk and policy advisory services and is a subsidiary of American company S&P Global (*see* https://en.wikipedia.org/wiki/CRISIL (accessed 17 January 2021)).

- Intra-group loan denominated in local currency: the one-year marginal cost of funds lending rate of the State Bank of India as of 1 April 2019 plus 175-425 bps depending on the CRISIL rating.
- Intra-group loan denominated in foreign currency: six months' LIBOR of the relevant currency as of 30 September 2019 plus 150-600 bps depending on the CRISIL rating.

Other countries with safe harbour interest rates include Slovenia.[52] The rates are published by the tax administration on a monthly basis. If the interest rate charged in the related-party transaction is lower than the rate determined by the tax administration, the income is correspondingly increased for tax purposes. If the interest rate charged is higher than the rate so determined, the excess interest expense is not recognized for tax purposes. However, the taxpayer may use an interest rate different from the rate officially determined if he proves that that other rate is at arm's length.

2.5 Other Notable Measures

India[53] prescribes a number of 'safe harbour rates' for various international transactions undertaken with associated enterprises. The rates vary depending on the type of transaction and the monetary threshold involved. For the financial year 2019-2020, a number of safe harbour rates apply for various international transactions, including the following (based on various measures and thresholds):

- software development services and information technology-enabled services - 17% or 18%;
- knowledge process outsourcing services - 18%, 21%, or 24%;
- contract research and development services relating to software development - 24%;
- contract research and development services relating to generic pharmaceutical drugs - 24%;
- corporate guarantee - 1% of the guaranteed amount;
- manufacture and export of core auto components - 12%;
- manufacture and export of non-core auto components - 8.5%;
- receipt of the LVAS;[54] the value of transactions cannot include a margin of more than 5%.

Unlike previous years, the safe harbour notification issued by the Central Board of Direct Taxes is only for one financial year, i.e., 2019-2020.[55]

52. B. Pate, Slovenia: Transfer Pricing, Country Tax Guides IBFD, sections 8.1.2.1. and 12.
53. Deloitte Tax Alert, India, *supra* n. 50.
54. It is important to note that India, unlike many other countries, sets a threshold for the LVAS to which the safe harbour rate applies, i.e., total value of the LVAS does not exceed INR 10 crores.
55. Furthermore, Finance Act 2020 amended safe harbour provisions in the Income Tax Act, 1961, to cover profit attribution for permanent establishment. However, the CBDT's notification did not specify profit attribution for permanent establishments.

Generally speaking, India's safe harbours are governed by detailed legal provisions including with respect to the mode of compliance. An anti-abuse rule operates to the effect that the safe harbour shall not apply in respect of eligible international transactions entered into with an associated enterprise located in any country or territory notified under section 94A[56] or in a no-tax or low-tax country or territory (i.e., a maximum rate of income tax is less than 15%). Additionally, taxpayers who invoke the safe harbour cannot opt for a mutual agreement procedure (MAP). The rules incorporate a time limit up to which the tax authorities can challenge the validity of the safe harbour option exercised by taxpayers in order to provide certainty for them.[57]

New Zealand[58] provides various administrative simplification measures, including with respect to small wholesale distributors as defined for which benchmarking may not be necessary. The tax administration considers weighted average earnings before interest, tax, and exceptional items ratio of 3% or greater to be broadly indicative of an arm's length result for foreign-owned wholesale distributors with an annual turnover not exceeding NZD 30 million. This safe harbour may be applied in the absence of readily available transactional data for that distributor's transfer pricing transactions or other comparable market data for distributors operating with similar risk characteristics. The measure is reviewed periodically.[59]

When deliberating substantive simplification measures, an important consideration might be how the process of accurately delineating the transaction can be made a little easier for stakeholders to understand and apply. In this regard, some authors[60] have suggested that perhaps the process could be 'simplified' by providing a more step-by-step guidance (such as the six-step risk analysis process contained in the OECD Guidelines and UN Practical Manual). The author agrees with this observation but cautions that, although this might be useful especially in situations where the capability to tackle transfer pricing matters is limited, in theory, this approach can be quite prescriptive and might therefore not allow for a more informed analysis of the transaction(s) at hand. As such, if this suggestion was to be included in the respective guidance on transfer pricing, maybe it would be better to regard it as a 'possible' way to consider the transaction at hand and not the only way.

Measures such as those that limit the deductibility of various expenses (such as interest, management fees, etc.) can also arguably be viewed as a simplification to the process requiring accurate delineation of the transaction, at least to the extent that they do not necessarily require such an exercise. These measures are viewed more as a way

56. Section 94A deals with certain jurisdictions with which India has no exchange of information arrangements in place and when no tax information exchange mechanisms exist.
57. V. Chhabra et al., India: Transfer Pricing, Country Tax Guides IBFD, section 12.
58. L. Prescott-Haar and S. (Sophie) Day, New Zealand: Transfer Pricing, Country Tax Guides IBFD, section 12. The other transactions for which administrative simplification is provided include the LVAS and small value loans.
59. *See also*, Simplification measures for transfer pricing available at https://www.ird.govt.nz/international-tax/business/transfer-pricing/simplification-measures (accessed 12 January 2021).
60. *See* Cardoso, *supra* n. 46, section 2.1.

for countries to protect their tax bases and less as propagating (a strict) application of the arm's length principle.[61]

3 PROCEDURAL SIMPLIFICATION MEASURES

3.1 Overview

In the context of this chapter, procedural simplification measures are understood to mean measures that apply as part of the administrative processes/practices required in transfer pricing compliance. Accordingly, these measures are distinguishable from substantive simplification measures (*see* section 2) to the extent that they speak more to procedural issues as opposed, e.g., to the more complex determination of the appropriate application of the arm's length principle in the context of a simplification regime. However, it is important to note that administrative measures exist to aid the application of substantive measures, and, therefore, the measures discussed in this part must be viewed as supporting those discussed in section 2.

3.2 Less Stringent Documentation Requirements

Documenting transactions between related parties for transfer pricing purposes can be quite a costly and burdensome exercise, especially if the requirements for documentation are not distinguished, e.g., on the basis of the size of the taxpayer or, more specifically, the size of the transaction. A simplification measure in this regard could involve the exemption of SMEs from the requirement to file transfer pricing documentation or limiting the information required to be provided by such enterprises. This notwithstanding, such enterprises should be obligated to provide information and documents about their material cross-border transactions upon a specific request of the tax administration in the course of a tax examination or for transfer pricing risk assessment purposes.[62]

Examples of countries that reported less stringent documentation requirements in their domestic legislation in the OECD Multi-Country Analysis 2012 include Australia, Belgium, Denmark, Estonia, Finland, France, Germany, Hungary, India, Israel, Italy, Mexico, Norway, Poland, Spain, Sweden, and Turkey.[63]

Belgium,[64] for example, avoids excessive requests for documentation, stating that the appropriateness of asking for certain information has to be assessed in light of the factual circumstances of each case. Furthermore, when information is required from the taxpayer, e.g., through questionnaires, the list of questions has to be adjusted to each case and sending out general questionnaires has to be avoided. All in all, the requested information must consequently be limited to that which is relevant on the basis of the specific characteristics of the enterprise and of the group to which the

61. Lang and Petruzzi, *supra* n. 38, at pp. 99-100.
62. OECD Guidelines para. 5.33.
63. OECD Multi-Country Analysis 2012, *supra* n. 5, at p. 13.
64. OECD Multi-Country Analysis 2012, *supra* n. 5.

enterprise belongs. All this is done on a case-by-case approach with a lighter touch for SMEs and simple transactions.

Australia[65] provides at least eight simplified transfer pricing record-keeping options: small taxpayers; distributors; intra-group services; low-level inbound loans; low-level outbound loans; materiality; management and administration services; and technical services. Specified rules apply to each category based on various parameters that vary from one category to the other, e.g., turnover, if the enterprise has undergone a restructure during the year under consideration, etc.

Some countries do not require taxpayers to maintain contemporaneous transfer pricing documentation if certain criteria are not met. For example, Portugal[66] does not require companies for which turnover in a given financial year does not exceed EUR 3 million to retain contemporaneous transfer pricing documentation as part of the general self-assessment system.

Singapore[67] exempts taxpayers from the requirement to maintain contemporaneous transfer pricing documentation, effective from the year of assessment 2019, if two cumulative conditions are met: (1) the entity has an annual gross revenue from its trade or business for the basis period concerned that does not exceed SGD 10 million; and (2) the entity was not required to prepare transfer pricing documentation for the immediately preceding year (year of assessment 2020 would be the first year for which this test will be applicable). However, if the entity does not meet this condition (i.e., it was required to prepare transfer pricing document for the immediately preceding year), but its annual gross revenue does not exceed SGD 10 million for the two years immediately preceding, the entity is considered to have met the condition. Furthermore, if the taxpayer does not meet the conditions for this general exemption, it may still avail itself of the transaction-based exemptions set out in the Income Tax (Transfer Pricing Documentation) Rules 2018.

In 2019, Argentina[68] revised its transfer pricing regulations in order to provide *de minimis* thresholds for filing certain transfer pricing forms.

In 2020, Rwanda gazetted its new transfer pricing rules (which replaced the 2007 rules). Among the changes introduced by the rules are the requirements for documentation, including for country-by-country reporting, in prescribed situations. Taxpayers with an annual turnover below RWF 600 million and whose controlled transactions have the value below RWF 10 million individually, or the aggregate value below RWF 100 million, are not required to prepare transfer pricing documentation.[69]

65. M.St.J.R. Butler, C. Vu and L. Wang, Australia: Transfer Pricing, Country Tax Guides IBFD, section 12.1.
66. G. Teixeira and R. Tavares de Pina, Portugal: Transfer Pricing, Country Tax Guides IBFD.
67. J.C. See and S.Y. Lee, Singapore: Transfer Pricing, Country Tax Guides IBFD, section 12. The conditions are prescribed pursuant to section 34F of the Income Tax Act.
68. *See* EY Tax Alert, Argentina amends transfer pricing compliance obligations https://www.ey.com/en_gl/tax-alerts/argentina-amends-transfer-pricing-compliance-obligations (accessed 14 January 2021).
69. Rwanda – Rwanda Introduces New Transfer Pricing Rules, News IBFD. The new TP rules, as outlined in Ministerial Order No. 003/20/10/TC of 11/12/2020, were gazetted vide Official Gazette No. 40 of 14/12/2020.

Ultimately, the question of how to adopt simplified documentation requirements is, like all other issues discussed in this chapter, one for a particular country to consider based on its tax policy. However, it is recommended to look for ways to minimize the costs and burden for taxpayers in the nature and breadth of information or documentation required, especially in order to assess the arm's length position of simple transactions. Conversely, tax administrations' efforts could be focused on larger, more complex transactions and, as in the Belgium example above, call for information only if it is useful for either risk assessing the taxpayer or undertaking an audit.

3.3 Alleviated Penalties

The general trend across most countries has been the increase of administrative penalties, be it in the context of non-compliance with transfer pricing documentation requirements, failing to submit relevant data to the tax authorities, a transfer pricing adjustment, etc.

The OECD,[70] while discussing penalties in the context of (non)compliance with documentation requirements and/or provision of relevant information, advises that care should be taken in designing penalties in order to avoid those that will have the result of placing a burden on the taxpayer that would be impossible to fulfil, e.g., requiring submission of information that would be impossible for the taxpayer to access in the first place. Alleviated penalties help to ease the monetary burden for taxpayers but may result in unwarranted effects such as promoting a cherry-picking of jurisdictions among taxpayers or good corporate citizenship in countries that levy heavy penalties.

Some countries, e.g., Canada,[71] alleviate penalties in certain defined instances when a transfer pricing adjustment is made if the taxpayer demonstrates that he took all reasonable efforts to determine the arm's length price.

3.4 Streamlined Procedures

Transfer pricing audits are an area in which most taxpayers' and tax administrations' resources are channelled, especially in developing countries where the numbers of transfer pricing cases going to audit are still high. Undoubtedly, this is an area that would benefit a lot from simplification, even if just in the form of more tax certainty being provided.[72] One of the preliminary steps towards an audit that could be simplified is by having guidance on how risk assessment for case selection is carried out. Some countries do not provide such information publicly. As a result, resources on

70. OECD Guidelines (2017), paras 5.40 & 5.42.
71. OECD Multi-Country Analysis Report, *supra* n. 5, at p. 45. In Canada, a transfer pricing penalty provision applies subject to a threshold. Accordingly, the penalty does not apply when; (i) the transfer pricing adjustments do not exceed the lesser of: – 10% of the taxpayer's gross revenue for the year, and CAD 5 million, or (ii) the taxpayer has made reasonable efforts to determine and use arm's length transfer prices.
72. Relevant work in this area includes, e.g., that of the OECD FTA.

both ends are utilized almost in the same proportion for all transactions, including those for which the tax authority might not even deem 'risky'. If the case selection criteria are not understood by the taxpayer, there is a chance that there will be controversy at the audit stage as the outlook of the taxpayer and tax administration is evidently at variance. Extending a number of transaction-based thresholds already in existence under various other measures could serve as a starting point, e.g., for exempting certain transactions or taxpayers from the audit.

As an example, although, in principle, Belgium[73] does not have criteria or thresholds below which it would not audit or adjust a controlled transaction for transfer pricing purposes; generally, SMEs (or small groups) do not undergo an in-depth transfer pricing audit. In any event, it is stated that most of the SMEs are not active internationally or have only limited international activities.

Additionally, although the United Kingdom (UK) does not have safe harbour arrangements, in practice, the Her Majesty's Revenue & Customs is likely to consider as 'low risk' certain transfer pricing policies in the process of applying a risk assessment process before commencing a detailed transfer pricing enquiry. In particular, a UK provider charging for low-value services (such as accounting or payroll administration) with a markup of 5%-10% is likely to be regarded as low risk; and simple UK distribution functions for overseas manufacturers that reward the UK operation with a return on sales of, say, 3%-5% supported by reasonable comparable data are also likely to be regarded as low risk.[74]

Other examples of streamlined procedures include those regarding dispute prevention and resolution. Some countries have streamlined their procedures with respect to APAs. For example, Canada has separate rules governing APAs for small businesses, and Norway does not charge fees for the application for an APA.

4 SIMPLIFICATION IN THE CONTEXT OF DIGITALIZATION: AMOUNT B

4.1 Overview

Following the ongoing discussions around the tax challenges of the digitalization of the economy, in October 2020, the OECD released a report on the current status of the work undertaken with respect to Pillar One (hereinafter the Pillar One Blueprint).[75] Of importance to the discussion in this chapter is the text on Amount B.

The Pillar One Blueprint discusses the use of fixed returns specifically with reference to certain baseline marketing and distribution activities taking place physically in a

73. OECD Multi-Country Analysis 2012, *supra* n. 5.
74. A.J. Casley, United Kingdom: Transfer Pricing, Country Tax Guides IBFD, section 12.
75. OECD (2020), *Tax Challenges Arising from Digitalisation – Report on Pillar One Blueprint: Inclusive Framework on BEPS*, OECD/G20 Base Erosion and Profit Shifting Project, OECD Publishing, Paris https://doi.org/10.1787/beba0634-en, hereinafter, 'Pillar One Blueprint'.

market jurisdiction.[76] The Pillar One Blueprint identifies the intended purpose of Amount B as two-fold, viz.: (i) simplification of the administration of transfer pricing rules for tax administrations and lower compliance costs for taxpayers; and (ii) to enhance tax certainty and reduce controversy between tax administrations and taxpayers.[77]

The key aim of safe harbours (and, more widely, simplification measures) is to provide a standardized approach to the determination of the arm's length nature of related-party transactions that are viewed to be 'simple' by virtue of the functions performed, assets used, and risks assumed in the course of performance of such transactions. Accordingly, Amount B is intended to provide a standardized approach to the remuneration of related-party distributors that perform 'baseline marketing and distribution activities' in the market jurisdiction.[78]

Amount B undoubtedly considers a key area of transfer pricing controversy, namely, distribution arrangements in a related-party context. In situations where there are bilateral tax treaties in place, any disputes arising as a result of an adjustment by one tax administration can normally be dealt with under a MAP. The problem worsens in cases when there are no bilateral tax treaties or other legal frameworks allowing for the use of a MAP. Amount B will deal with complications presented by the latter situation.[79]

The Pillar One Blueprint emphasizes the importance of accurately delineating the controlled transaction in order to determine if the activities of a given entity fall within the in-scope activities. Accordingly, no assumptions are to be made regarding the functional profile of an entity based on the labelling or characterization accorded to such an entity by the MNE group of which it is a member.[80] This emphasis serves to draw the attention of stakeholders to the fact that safe harbours and/or simplification measures are not intended to do away with the crucial steps of a transfer pricing analysis, viz. identifying the transaction, determining the financial and commercial

76. Fixed returns for the said activities are discussed in the context of Amount B under Pillar One. Amount B is one of three components of Pillar One with the other two components being: (1) a new taxing right for market jurisdictions over a share of residual profit calculated at the multinational enterprise group (or segment) level (Amount A); and (2) processes to improve tax certainty through effective dispute prevention and resolution mechanisms. The most recent output of the OECD/Inclusive Framework work on the subject is contained in the blueprint issued in October 2020. *See* Pillar One Blueprint, para. 7.

77. Pillar One Blueprint, paras 11-15. It is noted that, due to the identified intended purposes of Amount B, '*it has been acknowledged by a number of Inclusive Framework members and MNEs as a key deliverable of Pillar One on the presumption that the intended benefits may be achieved*'.

78. According to the Pillar One Blueprint, the definition of baseline marketing and distribution activities covers distributors that (i) buy from related parties and resell to unrelated parties; and (ii) have a routine distributor functionality profile. Furthermore, the definition is further determined by reference to a 'positive list' of the functions, assets, and risks that would typically be expected at arm's length among routine distributors (based on a narrow scope akin to limited risk distributors) complemented by a 'negative list' of functions, assets, and risks that are not seen among such a class of distributors and the application of qualitative measures and quantitative indicators, as described, in order to determine in-scope activities. *See* Pillar One Blueprint, paras 11-13, 663 & 664.

79. *See also* Pillar One Blueprint, para. 650.

80. Pillar One Blueprint para. 161.

relations/conditions of the transaction and, more importantly, accurately delineating the transaction. What safe harbours do is offer an easier way to deal with the subsequent steps of a transfer pricing analysis. It would be impossible to apply even the best designed safe harbour regime if the crucial steps were not followed. It is important to note that following those steps helps in determining whether the subject transaction or taxpayer is eligible for the measure under consideration.

As the Amount B fixed return will be determined through a benchmarking analysis based on third party comparables, it is intended to approximate results determined under the arm's length principle and hence existing domestic and treaty law.[81] In the author's view, this goes a long way in preventing disputes and also ensuring that, if any disputes arise, the usual remedies under domestic and treaty law will be available. As a result, Amount B will, once the technical work pending on various issues is finalized, provide an avenue that has not been achieved by any 'safe harbour' so far on a global scale, i.e., achieve the objective of avoiding double or non-taxation and preventing disputes (or allowing quick resolution thereof) as well as providing certainty for taxpayers and tax administrations alike. As a result, tax administrations, especially in developing countries, will have some comfort in taking on this measure and thereby freeing their valuable resources to focus on complex transactions, which undoubtedly require much effort and focus in order to ensure that their tax bases are protected.

It is expected that any activities that do not fall within the defined in-scope activities will be considered outside the scope of Amount B and continue to be remunerated through application of the arm's length principle as it is currently being used. This would be the case, for example, if the in-market enterprise is found to either be performing fewer functions and assuming less risk than what is defined under the baseline marketing and distribution activities or if the in-market enterprise is performing more than routine functions and assuming more than routine risks than are defined under the baseline marketing and distribution activities.[82]

In the author's view, the relative simplicity obtained through the application of Amount B is reduced in the case of multifunctional entities,[83] i.e., an entity performing in-scope activities and other additional activities that are out-of-scope. The Pillar One Blueprint notes that the application of Amount B should still be possible based on the foundational principle of a transfer pricing analysis, i.e., on a transaction by transaction basis, and when it can be shown, e.g., that the additional activities do not relate to the product being distributed. In such a case, Amount B applies to the in-scope

81. Pillar One Blueprint para. 687.
82. Pillar One Blueprint para. 665.
83. This is because great skill is required to be able to 'segregate' transactions undertaken by a single taxpayer into clusters of what falls within the safe harbour and what does not, especially for 'similar' transactions. Although most countries' tax administrations and taxpayers are now able to undertake a normal transfer pricing analysis and therefore able to analyse a case on a transaction by transaction basis, tax administrations and taxpayers in some mid-level and least developed countries would find this a daunting task. However, it is possible to cure this void by consistent, targeted capacity development especially in countries where transfer pricing expertise is needed most.

activities, with a full transfer pricing analysis being undertaken with respect to the additional activities.[84]

The Pillar One Blueprint notes as follows:[85]

> While this Blueprint contains an outline of a solution that assumes that in-scope distributors are to be identified based on a narrow scope of baseline activities, there is interest by some members to explore the feasibility of broadening the scope of Amount B. Some Inclusive Framework members have expressed the need to further refine the design of Amount B such that the intended simplification benefits are achieved, and further consider that implementation through a pilot programme at first may allow for some evaluation of the benefits in practice. The Inclusive Framework will therefore need to decide how to proceed.

For a more detailed discussion on the work regarding tax challenges of the digitalization of the economy, *see* Chapter 5 of this book.

4.2 Selected Transfer Pricing Method

Amount B is intended to approximate results determined according to the arm's length principle and would therefore be based on comparable company benchmarking analyses undertaken using the transactional net margin method with the quantum potentially varying by industry and region[86] provided any such variation is supported by the relevant benchmarking analysis. It is noted that this might result in a range of fixed returns depending on, *inter alia*, the region of the tested party. This is a welcome development in the proposal for fixed returns as it might take into account the unique positions of countries and could have the positive effect of wide acceptance among developing countries. This is seen when the Pillar One Blueprint continues to state that there has been a call by a number of Inclusive Framework members, especially developing countries, to explore the possibility of widening the scope of Amount B. The view expressed by some Inclusive Framework members to explore the implementation of Amount B initially through a pilot programme in order to measure how simplification measures may be achieved is a welcome move and will hopefully provide better insights into its effectiveness in achieving the intended policy objectives.[87]

It is not unusual to see the transactional net margin method used in a normal transfer pricing analysis for the kind of activities that will fall under Amount B. This is based on the advantage of the method (compared with the resale price method, which could be ideal in some cases) that net profit indicators are less affected by transactional differences and more tolerant to some functional differences between the transactions being compared. While noting that further work is still needed to define some aspects

84. Pillar One Blueprint para. 680.
85. Pillar One Blueprint, p. 12. *See* subheading, 'Scope and application of Amount B'.
86. *See* further, Pillar One Blueprint paras 688-691. Notably, the Pillar One Blueprint indicates that further technical work is required on various aspects as set out in para. 689.
87. Pillar One Blueprint para. 15.

of the determination, the Pillar One Blueprint notes that a return on sales could be used as the appropriate profit level indicator.[88]

The Pillar One Blueprint discusses certain aspects regarding the possibility of using standardized benchmarking references with respect to Amount B. This is discussed briefly in section 5.

4.3 Operation of Amount B

Some of the proposals put forward for the application of Amount B is that it would operate on the basis of a rebuttable presumption.[89] This would operate to the effect that an entity that is found to perform the baseline activities within the scope of an Amount B fixed return can rebut its application by providing evidence that another transfer pricing method would be the most appropriate to use under the arm's length principle, i.e., based on the specific facts and circumstances. However, the question on the operation of Amount B as a rebuttable presumption is still open for discussion under the Inclusive Framework.[90]

5 STANDARDIZED BENCHMARKS AS SIMPLIFICATION MEASURES

5.1 Overview

Application of the arm's length standard calls for a critical examination of the transactions between related parties in order to establish if the price is what could have been agreed by unrelated parties in similar circumstances. In order to do so, the OECD and UN[91] set out the critical steps to undertaking a proper analysis. In this particular instance, a comparability analysis is a critical consideration to the extent that it sets the tone and determines if the other steps of a transfer pricing analysis will be applied appropriately.

The performance of a broad functional analysis that allows a taxpayer to demonstrate that the value creation has been properly allocated between the parties to the transaction is necessarily the first step to a comparability analysis. This analysis cannot be properly undertaken if only based on standardized commercial database searches. As such, the search should be complemented by a critical analysis of other publicly

88. Pillar One Blueprint paras 685 & 686.
89. Pillar One Blueprint para. 687.
90. *See supra* n. 4 to para. 653 of the Pillar One Blueprint. Some commentators have expressed the opinion that the safe harbour rule for Amount B should not have an arm's length 'let-out', which is read to mean an option for taxpayers to opt for the 'arm's length position' to apply instead, due to concerns that this might be burdensome for tax administrations that do not have adequate capacity (*see*, for example, comments by the African Tax Administration Forum Technical Note, para. 3.6. available at https://events.ataftax.org/includes/preview.php?file_id=40&language=en_US (accessed 18 January 2021).
91. OECD Guidelines (section D. and Chapter III), UN Practical Manual (section B.2.2.).

available information (e.g., on websites, financial statements, etc.) in order to properly interrogate the data obtained in the databases.[92]

In practice, however, the process is complex and presents some challenges, as discussed below.

5.2 The Dilemma

Lack of comparables data in transfer pricing in order to undertake a sound benchmarking analysis of related-party transactions against uncontrolled transactions is one of the biggest difficulties encountered by tax administrations and taxpayers, especially those in developing countries and notably in Africa.

Some of the difficulties in accessing comparables data for benchmarking, especially for developing countries, include the following:

- financial constraints, i.e., the tax administrations do not have the necessary financial resources to access commercial databases;
- lack of publicly available information on local companies either because there is no obligation for that information to be provided publicly, or there is lack of compliance on the part of the persons required to file such information;
- lack of comparables data either because domestic companies do not perform the kind of transactions carried on by the related-party company.

The issue gained more light post-BEPS when, after the substantive discussions on the BEPS Action Points, developing countries called for certain issues to be tackled that are more specific to operating in those regions. From the perspective of those developing countries, the issues had not been or not sufficiently tackled during the BEPS Project. One of those issues was regarding the lack of comparables. A toolkit was eventually developed by the Platform for Collaboration on Tax to provide some recommendations and insights to be taken into account when dealing with situations when there are no comparables.[93]

The toolkit explores various options that may be adopted by developing countries in instances when there are no local comparables, such as allowing the use of foreign comparables.[94] However, preference is given to the use of domestic comparables when

92. Paragraph 3.33 of the OECD Guidelines notes that such a refinement of the database search with other sources of information is meant to promote quality over standardized approaches and is valid for both database searches made by taxpayers/practitioners and for those made by tax administrations. The OECD cautions that the compliance burden for taxpayers should be taken into account.
93. A Toolkit for Addressing Difficulties in Accessing Comparable Data for Transfer Pricing Analyses, in https://www.oecd.org/tax/toolkit-on-comparability-and-mineral-pricing.pdf (accessed 17 January 2021).
94. Some recent notable literature in this regard includes the practical testing of the viability of foreign comparables in situation where there are no local comparables. *See*, for example, Gonnet et al., *supra* n. 31, where the authors explore the use of foreign comparables on a tested party in Ghana.

those are available, as that disburses the need to undertake often complex comparability adjustments, in this instance, geographic market differences.[95] However, when local comparables are not available, it is not always clear, unless specifically indicated in domestic legislation or administrative guidance,[96] that the tax administration will accept the use of foreign comparables and, if such comparables are acceptable, the preferred region from which such comparables should be drawn. This exacerbates the complexity of applying the arm's length principle for developing countries.

The dilemma that most tax administrations face in such situations is determining the veracity of comparables data that is used, especially if such data is not immediately available or verifiable by the tax administration. This is especially the case as some tax administrations do not have access to the commercial databases used by taxpayers to support their transfer pricing benchmarking analysis. This notwithstanding, the use of foreign comparables (even if only from the same region as the subject country) is not as straightforward for some developing countries as it is, e.g., for most of their developed country counterparts. Taxpayers face the uncertainty of not knowing if their set of comparables will be accepted and/or if any adjustments will be made by the tax administration or what the general outcome of the transfer pricing analysis will be.[97]

The above constraints to accessing comparables can be mitigated by, *inter alia*: financing developing countries in order to be able to obtain access to commercial databases; targeting capacity building efforts towards enhancing tax administrations' capability to be able to use and interrogate foreign comparables data, including with respect to any required comparability adjustments; requiring and encouraging local companies to file financial statements publicly.[98]

Against this backdrop, maybe there is a place for standardized benchmarks with a view to simplification, particularly guidance on the practical considerations of the use of foreign comparables is welcome, e.g., regarding the selection of foreign comparables and their adjustment to reflect the economic circumstances of the domestic market of the tested party.[99]

5.3 The Proposal

There has been some discussion on the possible use of (and the provision of guidance regarding) standardized benchmarks, but not much concrete work has been done in that area.

In 2019, the OECD Forum on Tax Administration (FTA) indicated that it will continue its work regarding the tax certainty agenda and will expand it to include the

95. Comparability Toolkit, *supra* n. 92, at p. 41.
96. In terms of prescribing/allowing the use of foreign comparables according to administrative guidance, South Africa allows the use of comparables from certain countries (e.g., UK, Australia), in situations where it is not possible to get local comparables. *See* Practice Note 7, para. 11.2.1.
97. *See further*, Gonnet et al., *supra* n. 31, at p. 8.
98. *See also* Comparability Toolkit, *supra* n. 92, at pp. 37-38.
99. *See also* Gonnet et al., *supra* n. 31, at p. 8.

exploration of the potential use and sharing of benchmarks for standard situations in the area of transfer pricing.[100]

The Pillar One Blueprint states that, with respect to establishing the quantum for the fixed return under Amount B,[101] establishing the specific fixed return for the baseline marketing and distribution activities will require the preparation of reference benchmarking sets for each of the regions to which differentiated returns should apply. It then goes on to set out some of the important considerations in this regard, including the following:[102]

- development of a consistent definition of the industries for which a reference benchmarking set will be developed;
- searching for comparables geared towards independent parties within the industry and region for which a benchmarked return on sales will be calculated;
- development of a specific strategy in that regard, including a fixed definition of independence, the specific use of industry classification codes, and other qualitative and quantitative criteria by which potentially comparable companies may be reviewed to ascertain whether or not they should be included in the reference set;
- calculation of the profit level indicator (with the potential to make certain comparability adjustments that are to be defined) to establish the range of potentially appropriate fixed returns.

In order to promote consistency with the arm's length principle, the determination of the quantum of fixed returns for Amount B should be informed by benchmarking studies based on publicly available information. The Pillar One Blueprint sets out some further considerations to this end:[103]

- the choice of the time period of the data to be used, i.e., single year or a weighted average of multiple years;
- the selection of the database(s) to be used for the benchmarking exercise;
- the selection of the search strategy, which includes the search parameters and screening criteria, for instance, identification of the relevant industry classification codes to capture the scope of Amount B and the identification of the filters to be applied in the screening procedure (number of years of available financial data, independency criteria, consolidation, etc.); and
- the evaluation of necessary adjustments to enhance comparability.

100. *See* https://www.oecd.org/tax/forum-on-tax-administration/events/forum-on-tax-administration-communique-2019.pdf at p. 2 (accessed 14 January 2021). Other items on the FTA's tax certainty agenda include bilateral and multilateral mutual agreement procedures, the International Compliance Assurance Program, and advance pricing arrangements.
101. For more details regarding Amount B, *see* section 4 of this chapter.
102. Pillar One Blueprint para. 693.
103. Pillar One Blueprint para. 694.

Regarding the issue of industry codes, some authors see this as a difficulty when trying to arrive at a reliable set of comparables. Industry codes are, to a great extent, not identical across all countries or regions, and a company can be presented with different codes across various countries/regions.[104] Even with a normal benchmarking analysis, the fact that different regions use different codes for various industries/activities means that a reliable set of comparables cannot be arrived at by just using industry codes. In such cases, the search should be supplemented by the use of other 'tools', e.g., keyword searches. However, if standardized benchmarks are to be developed more widely on a global scale, it would serve as a good starting point to check that the industry codes to be adopted for the particular taxpayers to be brought within the simplification measure net are largely uniform across all regions. This will give some comfort, especially for countries that already experience difficulties in searching for comparables for 'normal' transactions. To begin with, however, it might help if uniform coding is adopted by commercial databases.

Additionally, the Pillar One Blueprint notes the following:

> Further work will also need to be undertaken regarding analysing how often the benchmarking will need to be updated and how often the underlying search process to develop the reference sets will need to be reviewed. The specific benchmarking with regional and industry variation will be developed alongside the current FTA MAP forum benchmarking exercise.[105]

A development such as this calls for careful consideration and transparency. It is an added advantage that the discussion is happening in the context of the Inclusive Framework, and it can be assumed that participants had or will have the opportunity to look at the proposal in their own country's context. Of great importance is that the process of determining such standardized reference benchmarks is made transparent; clearly documented (setting out all the assumptions made, e.g., the selection of the comparables, the set perimeters, the expected review period in the event of 'extraneous circumstances' occurring that were not foreseen when designing the indicator). On a more general note (not necessarily in the context of Amount B), it would appear that the process of setting standardized benchmarks is already one that is familiar in the context of the sector-specific APA programmes. Countries within the same region that have such mechanisms could use the guidance there to inform the design of the process to be followed when designing the steps for the standardized benchmarks for other transactions outside the scope of Amount B.

104. European Commission, Study on Comparable Data used for Transfer Pricing in the EU, December 2016, at pp. 20, 26, 30 & 31 available at https://www.deloitte-tax-news.de/transfer-pricing/files/study-on-comparable-data-used-for-transfer-pricing-in-the-eu.pdf (accessed 14 January 2021).

105. Pillar One Blueprint para. 695. The OECD FTA continues its work in the area of tax certainty. In 2019, it indicated that it will continue its work including the exploration of the potential use and sharing of benchmarks for standard situations in the area of transfer pricing.

Some of the benefits that could be obtained by using standardized benchmarks and/or developing guidance thereon include the following:[106]

- reducing the burden on both taxpayers and tax administrations with respect to the type of comparables that would fit within the prescribed 'safe harbour' rule;
- reducing the uncertainty in terms of the selection of the comparables;
- improving the reliability of the analyses. In the context of simplification measures, this would give comfort to tax administrations and taxpayers that the result obtained is acceptable by both parties.

As one commentator put it, perhaps the clearest case for standardized benchmarks is the fact that tax authorities come across the same cases over the course of transfer pricing practice that would justify advocating for or at least giving a chance to such measures.[107] However, one of the questions that should be answered here is: how transparent is the information if other taxpayers do not have access to it? If the measure succeeds in the context of Amount B, then it will be a good candidate for wider consideration, especially with respect to other 'simple' transactions.

The author supports other authors[108] calling for careful consideration of the inherent risk in operating in some countries (especially developing countries) and giving a determination of how such risk can be accounted for, i.e., a standard fixed return at the international level might not properly take into consideration the unique risk situation of some countries. The specific risks referred to in this context are those that cannot sufficiently be compensated in the MNE group transfer pricing policy. Alternatively, guidance should be provided for reference by tax administrations in developing countries in establishing whether and to what extent such risks have been compensated in the pricing policy. This latter point also calls for targeted capacity enhancement and/or development post the digitalization debate.

6 CONCLUSIONS AND RECOMMENDATIONS

In the OECD Multi-Country Analysis 2012, there was a unanimous response by the surveyed countries that they were not aware of any cases of double taxation occasioned by the application of their unilateral simplification measures. However, it must be borne in mind that, for most of the countries that participated in the survey, especially the EU countries, there might be other administrative measures in place in a common market perspective to ensure somewhat uniform rules. For example, pursuant to

106. EU JTPF Report, *supra* n. 40, p. 18. Although the benefits are mentioned in the general context of developing guidance on searching for comparables widely, i.e., not in the context of standardized benchmarks, the remarks are applicable also in the context of standardized benchmarks.
107. *See*, for example, a report by EY on the OECD virtual webinar on tax certainty available here https://www.ey.com/en_gl/tax-alerts/oecd-holds-second-tax-certainty-day (accessed 13 January 2021).
108. The proposals for country risk adjustment by Gonnet et al. are informative in this regard (*supra* n. 31, at pp. 19-22).

Directive 2018/822 of 25 May 2018 (DAC6), cross-border arrangements within the EU and between the Member States and third countries (as of 1 July 2020) involving the use of unilateral safe harbour rules will be reportable and subject to automatic exchange of information. As such, it is important for MNEs to keep up to date with the developments in various countries so as to ensure effective and efficient compliance.

It is important for countries to carefully assess their particular situation in order to determine the effect of their simplification measures or the spillover effect that these measures in neighbouring countries might have on their own economic situation.

For developing countries that still encounter great difficulty in terms of capability to undertake transfer pricing analysis/audits, it might be worth considering creating safe harbour rules for simple transactions in order to allow tax administrations to focus and develop their expertise to audit complex cases. In the beginning, however, it could be worth considering extending the scope of any safe harbours beyond the 'normal' transactions with clearly designed rules about when the rules will cease to apply in order to ensure that some revenue is collected.[109] However, care should be taken so that unwanted effects, e.g., artificial tax arrangements, are avoided.

Capacity development remains a key agenda item for ensuring that international principles are understood and applied by tax administrations (and taxpayers). As the world moves towards achieving unification in taxation rules, e.g., in the ongoing discussions on digitalization of the economy, it is crucial to ensure that no country is dropped along the way. As such, clear capacity development strategies need to be created by countries in need of capacity development as well as by international organizations that wish to support such countries. There is no one-size-fits-all in this regard as developing countries, even within one particular region, are at different stages of expertise. It is important that the strategy appreciates the level and the nature of assistance needed by particular countries, e.g., some countries might need training for tax administration personnel while others need access to commercial databases. Other countries might need capability with regard to dispute (prevention and) resolution. Other ways through which developing countries can continue to provide certainty and predictability for taxpayers while protecting the countries' databases include anti-avoidance rules limiting the deductibility of certain expenses. This is mainly with respect to transactions that a country determines that they are not able to verify easily or the effort is not commensurate with the income obtained. Most such rules limit the deductibility of expenses such as interest, technical services, royalties, etc. Examples of countries that implemented measures in this regard between 2018 and now include Algeria, Benin, Ivory Coast, Malaysia, Peru, Senegal, Uganda, etc.[110]

Knowledge sharing, e.g., through exchange programmes by tax administrations, is encouraged. In the context of simplification measures, countries would benefit from an

---

109. *See also* A. Ezenagu, Safe Harbour Regimes in Transfer Pricing: An African Perspective Other Authors, ICTD Working Paper 100, August 2019, at p. 26 available at https://opendocs.ids.ac.uk/opendocs/bitstream/handle/20.500.12413/14620/ICTD_WP100.pdf?sequence=1&isAllowed=y (accessed 16 January 2021); the author calls for a bolder move by African countries in developing safe harbour regimes.

110. For more details, *see* Lang and Petruzzi, *supra* n. 38, at pp. 99-100. Peru's provisions took effect in January 2021.

evaluation of the effectiveness of the safe harbour/simplification measure in other jurisdictions. This could be useful as then countries that have been routinely opposed to such measures can gauge the effectiveness in other jurisdictions in a bid to extrapolate the results into their own domestic situation.

Although APAs are not safe harbours, their application to transfer pricing is important. This is especially in the case of more complex transactions that cannot be covered in the context of a safe harbour regime and require a rigorous transfer pricing analysis on a case-by-case basis.[111] Simplified application of the arm's length principle to such transactions can be achieved by designing an APA regime about which taxpayers can obtain certainty, among other things, the expected transfer pricing method, margins, etc. APAs operate to ease transfer pricing practice, and more efforts in this regard will help in dispute prevention and resolution.

With regard to the ongoing project regarding Brazil's transfer pricing system, some authors[112] have expressed the view that some of the foreseen challenges with the current project include the development and implementation of safe harbour regimes that streamline and provide assertiveness to the taxpayer since transactions covered by such mechanisms would require a much lower level of documentation than what is required in a conventional analysis. In any case, it is important for MNEs to prepare for the overhaul of the transfer pricing regime as Brazil moves towards alignment with the OECD standard.

Without pre-empting the outcome of the ongoing comments process, the author supports the view espoused by some authors[113] that there could be some element of a 'hybrid' system, i.e., retaining some of the features of the Brazilian safe harbour regime that have been proven successful, albeit in a domestic perspective, and complemented by new rules that align with the arm's length principle. Authors supporting this perspective advocate for the continued use of optional safe harbours that are compatible with the arm's length principle but extending the scope to cover not only the LVAS (or low risk) functional profiles but also other types of transactions. This 'bold' approach to safe harbours could make Brazil's regime unique and, if it proves successful, can then serve as an example/sample of a safe harbour regime for other jurisdictions.

Global economies have undergone a massive shock since the COVID-19 pandemic hit the world. The uncertain economic times have caused the depletion of economic (and social) resources. As countries look towards economic recovery in what will undoubtedly be one of the harshest economic crises ever, it is important to think forward on the role that simplification measures can play.

111. *See also* paras 15 and 16 of OECD/RFB Safe Harbours Survey Document, *supra* n. 8.
112. *See*, for example, C. Ayub, *Brazil: Advancing Towards Global Transfer Pricing Convergence*, ITR available at https://www.internationaltaxreview.com/article/b1mm864qdjxlyl/brazil-advancing-towards-global-transfer-pricing-convergence (accessed 12 January 2021).
113. *See*, for example, J. Romero, S. Tavares and P. Vergueiro, *An Opportunity for Convergence in Transfer Pricing and Beyond*, ITR available at https://www.internationaltaxreview.com/article/b1ky64sf4yxy8g/an-opportunity-for-convergence-in-transfer-pricing-and-beyond (accessed 10 January 2021).

First, as the world moved into a new way of doing things, i.e., virtually, a lot of investment in necessary/relevant resources had to be made, and taxpayers and tax administrations in most countries had to look for ways to continue their operations in order to meet their various objectives despite the harsh times. From a transfer pricing perspective, the complexities often involved in the transfer pricing analysis are exacerbated, especially for taxpayers in jurisdictions where tax administrations still rely heavily on tax audits to prove the viability of a transfer pricing outcome presented by the taxpayer. How can safe harbours help in this situation? As resources are stretched out on both ends, stakeholders could agree to develop temporary simplification measures to be applied during the pandemic period. Although the economic conditions at the moment might not be ideal for setting up safe harbours, mutually agreed upon results can go a long way in easing the burden for taxpayers and tax administrations.

For already existing safe harbours, an option would be to allow taxpayers to momentarily opt in or opt out of the safe harbour or to adjust the arm's length ranges currently applied under the safe harbour with proper oversight, e.g., allowing flexible conditions for opting in or out.[114] This could be achieved through considering and applying any comparability adjustments[115] to take account of the varying economic conditions, especially when foreign comparables data is used.

All in all, the international tax arena is on an important trajectory towards the standardized application of rules for prescribed transactions (in the context of the digitalization of the economy). There is a glimmer of hope not just that the pandemic will end soon but that there will be more prospects and appetite for transfer pricing simplification post the digitalization debate, which would be a great relief for tax administrations and taxpayers.

114. *See also* S. Prasanna and G. Capristano Cardoso, Developing a Transfer Pricing Policy Framework for the Current Economic Crisis and Beyond, 27 Intl. Transfer Pricing J. 5 (2020), Journal Articles & Papers IBFD.

115. *See*, for example, A. Orlandi, R. Iervolino and M.C. Latino, Methodologies for Applying Transfer Pricing Adjustments to Comparable Companies Following the COVID-19 Economic Downturn, 27 Intl. Transfer Pricing J. 6 (2020), Journal Articles & Papers IBFD.

Index

C

D

E